JEFFERSON HUNT
Leader of the largest party of '49ers to set out
from Salt Lake City to Southern California

JOURNALS OF
FORTY-NINERS
Salt Lake to Los Angeles

With diaries and contemporary records
of Sheldon Young, James S. Brown,
Jacob Y. Stover, Charles C. Rich,
Addison Pratt, Howard Egan,
Henry W. Bigler, and others

edited with historical comment by

LeRoy R. Hafen
Professor of History, Brigham Young University

and

Ann W. Hafen

UNIVERSITY OF NEBRASKA PRESS
LINCOLN AND LONDON

∞

First Bison Books printing: 1998
Most recent printing indicated by the last digit below:
10   9   8   7   6   5   4   3   2   1

Library of Congress Cataloging-in-Publication Data
Journals of Forty-niners: Salt Lake to Los Angeles: with diaries and contemporary records of Sheldon Young, James S. Brown, Jacob Y. Stover, Charles C.
Rich, Addison Pratt, Howard Egan, Henry W. Bigler, and others / edited with
historical comment by LeRoy R. Hafen and Ann W. Hafen.
p.   cm.
Originally published: Glendale, Calif.: A. H. Clark Co., 1954
Includes bibliographical references and index.
ISBN 0-8032-7316-9 (pbk.: alk. paper)
1. West (U.S.)—History—1848–1860—Sources.   2. West (U.S.)—Description and travel.   3. Pioneers—West (U.S.)—Diaries.   4. Mormons—West
(U.S.)—Diaries.   5. Overland journeys to the Pacific—History—Sources.
6. California—Gold discoveries—Sources.   I. Hafen LeRoy Reuben,
1893–   .   II. Hafen, Ann W. (Ann Woodbury), 1893–1970.
F593.J676   1998
978'.02—dc21
98-23337   CIP

Reprinted from the original 1954 edition by the Arthur H. Clark Company,
Glendale CA.

To
LESLIE E. BLISS
Librarian, Henry E. Huntington Library

Contents

Illustrations

Acknowledgments

Copies of diaries and other documents reproduced in this volume have been made available through the kindness of the following institutions: Henry E. Huntington Library, Church Historian's Office of the Mormon Church, Brigham Young University Library, Yale University Library, Bancroft Library, Utah State Historical Society, California State Library, and the Daughters of the Utah Pioneers.

Dr. John W. Caughey, Mrs. Ramona Farrer Cottam, Mr. Doyle L. Green, and Dr. Vasco M. Tanner have graciously supplied copies of important documents.

We have been assisted by the following friends in identifying places along the route: Mr. William R. Palmer, of Cedar City, Utah; the late Dix Van Dyke, of Daggett, California; Mr. Lamont Huntsman, of Enterprise, Utah; Mrs. Juanita Brooks, of St. George, Utah; and Mr. Charles Kelly, of Fruita, Utah.

Work on this volume, as well as on the preceding one in this *Series,* was materially aided by a Huntington-Rockefeller Grant.

JOURNALS OF FORTY-NINERS

Salt Lake to Los Angeles

Historical Background and Summary

The route of the gold-seeking Forty-niners from Salt Lake to Los Angeles approximates the modern highway U.S. 91. This trail has had a long and interesting history. Its southern half was identical with the western end of the Old Spanish Trail that extended from Santa Fé to Los Angeles;[1] its northern half was utilized primarily by the Mormons.

Although the Forty-niners, whose diaries are reproduced in this volume, were the first to take wagon caravans over this route, the Old Spanish Trail portion had long been used in the pack horse commerce between New Mexico and California.

The pioneer explorations of this western region had been undertaken in 1776 as a part of the general plan to open a pathway between New Mexico and California, with a view toward re-enforcing the new, struggling California missions by sending aid from the old and well-established settlements of New Mexico.

Father Garcés, famous explorer of the desert trace from the Gila River to southern California, was the first white man to discover and follow the course of the Mojave River, that lifesaving stream which made possible the Old Spanish Trail and the Salt Lake-to-Los Angeles route across the desert.[2]

---

[1] L. R. Hafen and A. W. Hafen, *The Old Spanish Trail, Santa Fé to Los Angeles* (Glendale, California, The Arthur H. Clark Company, 1954).

[2] Elliott Coues, *On the Trail of a Spanish Pioneer, the Diary and Itinerary of Francisco Garcés* (2 vols., New York, Francis Harper, 1900).

From the Yuma villages at the mouth of the Gila, Garcés in 1776 traveled up the Colorado River to the Mojave villages near the southern tip of present Nevada. Then with Indian guides he made his way westward across the desert and reached the sink of the Mojave River. Up the course of this stream to its source in the San Bernardino Mountains, the Father traveled. He then wound down into the Santa Ana River valley and pushed westward to San Gabriel Mission. His trail along the Mojave and thence to San Gabriel was to become the route of the New Mexican caravans of the 1830s and '40s, and of the '49ers of our present study.

Indomitable Garcés did further notable exploring. After going north into the San Joaquin Valley beyond the site of Bakersfield, he followed another route back to the Colorado, going over Tehachapi Pass, across the desert to the Mojave River, and then back to the Mojave villages. His further exploring tour, across northern Arizona to the Hopis, who turned him back, is beyond the scope of our present interest.

Father Escalante, who had lived in Zuni and visited the Hopis, had learned from these Indians about the impassable Grand Canyon and of the peaceable Ute Indians to the north. He concluded that the most feasible path to Monterey, California, was by a route through the Ute country. Accordingly, he and his companions set out on horseback from Santa Fé in July, 1776.[3]

They journeyed northwestward, up the Chama River valley, crossed the San Juan River and its affluents, then climbed the divide to the Dolores River. Reaching dry and rugged terrain in the country of the lower

[3] Herbert E. Bolton, *Pageant in the Wilderness,* . . . (Salt Lake City, Utah State Historical Society, 1950).

Dolores drainage, the party turned eastward to seek an Indian guide. This was the beginning of a long detour that took them eastward to the Uncompahgre Valley, the North Fork of the Gunnison, northward across Grand Mesa and the Colorado River, down Douglas Creek to White River, and northwestward to cross the Green near present Jensen, Utah. Moving westward up the Duchesne and Strawberry valleys, they crossed the Wasatch Mountains to Utah Lake.

Here they reached the region and began blazing the trail which concerns us in this study. From the site of Provo, Escalante and his explorers traveled southward through the sites of Spanish Fork, Payson, Nephi, Levan, and Scipio, pioneering the route subsequently followed to this point by the '49ers and U.S. 91 today.

From Scipio the Spanish party turned westward to the edge of the desert and then went southward along a route that roughly parallels U.S. 91 but about twenty-five miles west of that highway. At Iron Springs, about ten miles west of present Cedar City, Escalante crossed the route of the later '49ers. The padres had by this time (October) regretfully given up their plan to reach California and were heading back to New Mexico.

Their further route concerns us little. They went southward to cross the Virgin River, dreary affluent of the Colorado, onto the "Arizona Strip," skirted the Kaibab Plateau, forded the Colorado at the Crossing of the Fathers, visited the Hopi and the Zuni villages, and returned eastward to Santa Fé.

The Spanish plan to tie the missions of California to the settlements of New Mexico failed of realization in 1776. But exactly a half century later the trails of Escalante and Garcés, far-traveling Spanish padres, were linked together by the exploration work of that great American trail blazer, the Protestant New England trapper, Jedediah Smith.[4]

His was a commercial venture, to find new beaver country for his fur trade company. Supported by his rifle and Bible, Jed Smith, the "knight in buckskin," set forth in 1826 with a small company of men and a limited supply of trade goods. Eventually they reached California with its verdant fields, wide ranging herds, and prosperous missions, now so self-sufficient that they had no need for New Mexican supplies.

Several other beaver trappers and fur traders traversed portions of the route our '49ers were to travel. Ewing Young and Kit Carson followed up the Mojave River on their trip to California in 1829. Peter Skene Ogden and his brigade of Hudson's Bay Company trappers were lured from their Columbia River country to the distant Colorado River by the fur-trapping report of young Jed Smith. Ogden's men visited and fought the Mojaves, and then crossed to southern California, apparently going by way of the trail along the Mojave River.[5]

In 1829-30 a New Mexican citizen, Antonio Armijo, inaugurated the commercial traffic between New Mexico and California – the exchange of woolen blankets for California horses and mules. The route of this first expedition was across northern New Mexico and Arizona to ford the Colorado at the Crossing of the Fathers. Armijo struck the Virgin River near the site of Hurricane, Utah, and followed the general course of the stream to its debouchure into the Colorado. After following the larger river to the

[4] Dale L. Morgan, *Jedediah Smith and the opening of the West* (Indianapolis, Bobbs-Merrill Company, 1953).

[5] For a summary of these expeditions *see* Hafen and Hafen, *Old Spanish Trail, op. cit.*

mouth of Las Vegas Wash, he pushed westward across the desert to the Spring Mountains. His party, it appears, pioneered the trail subsequently used from Cottonwood Springs to the Mojave River, by way of Resting Springs, Amargosa River, and Bitter Springs.[6]

Inasmuch as he missed the important Las Vegas Springs and excellent pasture lands, it remained for some subsequent and now unknown person to make the important short cut from Cottonwood Springs, by way of Las Vegas to the Muddy River, thus obviating dependence on the Colorado River, and avoiding the longer route by way of that stream.

The trading party of 1830 led by William Wolfskill and George C. Yount is the first recorded company to make the trip from New Mexico to southern California along the general course of the route that later became famous as the Old Spanish Trail.[7] This trail pursued the Escalante route to the Dolores River, then veered northwestward to cross the Colorado River at present Moab, Utah, and the Green River near present Greenriver town. Through the picturesque badlands to Castle Valley, over the Wasatch Mountains into the Great Basin, ascending Sevier River and crossing a second mountain range, the trail reached Little Salt Lake near present Parowan, Utah. From this landmark to Los Angeles, the Old Spanish Trail and the route of our '49ers followed the same course.

For about eighteen years caravan trade over the Old Spanish Trail was as regular as the seasons. Each fall the packers set out from New Mexico weighted with

---

[6] L. R. Hafen, "Armijo's Journal," *Huntington Library Quarterly,* November, 1947, pp. 87-101.

[7] For the fullest account of this trip and of the trail in general, *see* the first volume of *The Far West and the Rockies Series.*

woolen blankets. Arrived at California, the traders rode up and down the coast bartering their wares for horses and mules. Then in April the New Mexicans assembled their bands in the grassy pastures near modern Colton in preparation for the long drive eastward across the Trail to Santa Fé.

The forbidding desert region, stretching from Cajon Pass in California to the Mountain Meadows at the head of the Santa Clara branch of the Virgin River in Utah, was difficult and dangerous terrain that exacted a heavy toll from the droves of horses and mules. Soon the longer *jornadas* between watering places were littered with the bones of animals that perished from dearth of water and grass.

In addition to the regular and legitimate traders along the Trail, troublesome bands of horse thieves found adventure and profit in raiding the great herds in the unfenced pastures of California, and driving their stolen stock eastward over the Spanish Trail to market. Reckless Mountain Men from the Rockies, renegade New Mexicans, and susceptible Indians joined forces to make their surprise attacks and dash away for Cajon Pass, to push their loot beyond capture by the Californios. The stolen stock that survived the hard drive over deserts and mountains found a ready market in New Mexico, at the fur trappers' rendezvous in the mountains, or in the settlements on the Missouri frontier.[8]

Another variety of commerce across the Old Spanish Trail was the disreputable slave traffic in Indian women and children. This old and recognized species of trade in the Spanish colonies dated back to the

---

[8] Chapters on "Horse Thieves" and "Slave Catchers" in Hafen and Hafen, *op. cit.*

encomienda system instituted by the earliest Spaniards in the West Indies and in Mexico. The bringing in of Indian children from the frontier tribes to the settlements, and holding them there, was looked upon as a practicable method of civilizing and Christianizing these wild natives. Through early training these children became competent servants in the house, or herdsmen with the flocks. Upon reaching maturity they ordinarily married, became free citizens, and were absorbed in the community.

A continuous reservoir of Indian children to supply the New Mexico market was found in the country along the trail to California. The strong Ute tribes regularly raided their weaker neighbors to procure children for bartering to the Spanish traders. The destitute, hungry Diggers of the Nevada desert frequently sold their own offspring to procure horses for food and guns for killing game. Sometimes the Mexican slave catchers found it easier and cheaper to raid Indian camps and to capture children themselves, rather than to procure them by trade. Indian slaves brought from fifty dollars to two hundred dollars apiece in the New Mexico market.

The various kinds of traffic above described had caused the Old Spanish Trail to become an established well-worn route long before the Mormons came to settle the Great Basin in 1847.

John C. Fremont, returning from his longest exploring tour – to Oregon and California in 1843-44 – traveled the Old Spanish Trail from near Cajon Pass to the Little Salt Lake. Here where the Trail turned east to cross the Wasatch Mountains Fremont left it, to continue northward along the west base of the mountain range to Utah Lake. There he crossed the mountains eastward by way of Spanish Fork Canyon, and continued back to the States.[9]

His course from the Mojave River to the east side of Utah Lake was the route our '49ers were to follow five years later. Fremont was the first to chart this trail, "deviously traced from one water hole to another," and to publish a good description and map of the route.

Miles Goodyear, a Connecticut youth who had come to the mountains with the Whitman-Spalding party in 1836, had withdrawn from the Oregon-bound group and by 1845 had developed, near the site of Ogden, an outpost that was the first white establishment in Utah. From this post he trailed down to Los Angeles in the fall of 1846 with some packs of buckskins and elk skins. His route presumably was along Fremont's trail of 1844 and, beyond the site of Parowan, was the well known Old Spanish Trail. Arrived at Los Angeles, Goodyear sold his skins to John C. Fremont, to clothe the latter's near-destitute troops.[10]

After making his way to northern California, and having purchased a band of horses enroute, Goodyear traveled east by way of the Humboldt River, expecting to sell his animals to west-bound emigrants on the Oregon Trail. In July, 1847, he met Brigham Young and the pioneer band of Mormons shortly before they entered Salt Lake Valley.

While the main body of Mormons were slowly pushing on westward, after having been driven from their homes in Nauvoo, Illinois, companies of infantry had been recruited from the migrating Saints for serv-

---

9 J. C. Fremont, *Report of the Exploring Expedition to the Rocky Mountains, . . .* (Washington, Gales and Seaton, 1845).

10 For the fullest account of Goodyear's career, *see* Charles Kelly and Maurice L. Howe, *Miles Goodyear, First Citizen of Utah* (Salt Lake City, privately printed, 1937). Records of sales of the skins to Fremont are given on pages 58-59.

ice in the Mexican War. This Mormon Battalion tramped the Santa Fé Trail to New Mexico, and then broke a new trail for wagons across New Mexico and Arizona, to reach southern California in January, 1847.[11]

When the one-year term of service of the Mormon Battalion expired, part of the men re-enlisted for a period of six months, but most of the men gave up soldiering to return to their families, who were somewhere along the western trails. Those men who left the service in '47 made their way to northern California, where Sam Brannan and his shipload of Mormons who had come around the Horn were settled.[12] Some of the Battalion boys found employment, remained the winter in the Sacramento River region, and dug the first gold at Sutter's saw mill on the American River in January, 1848.

The main body of Mormon ex-soldiers journeyed eastward along the Humboldt River route to meet their west-migrating families, and co-religionists. Arrived at the Great Salt Lake in October, 1847,[13] they found the pioneer companies of Mormons located in the Salt Lake Valley and building the capital of their new Zion.

Sam Brannan, enthusiastic about the resources and possibilities of settlement in California, had journeyed eastward in the spring of 1847 and had met the west-

11 Daniel Tyler, *A Concise History of the Mormon Battalion in the Mexican War, 1846-1847* ([Salt Lake City] 1881). A number of diaries of members of the Mormon Battalion are published in the *Utah Historical Quarterly*, IV (January-October, 1931).

12 Reva Scott, *Samuel Brannan and the Golden Fleece* (New York, Macmillan Company, 1944) ; J. A. B. Scherer, *The First Forty-niner* (New York, Minton, Balch and Company, 1925).

13 Journal History [A very valuable, chronologically arranged manuscript compilation in the Mormon Church Historian's office, Salt Lake City], October 16, 1847.

bound pioneer band of Mormons in the Green River Valley. He tried to induce Brigham Young to push on to the sunny green land on the Pacific shore, but the Mormon leader was more interested in isolation from persecutors and competitors, than in a region too rich and inviting; he chose to settle his people in the valleys of the Rocky Mountains. Brannan returned to California disappointed and embittered.

Faced with the problems of establishing homes and supporting themselves in a semi-desert region, the Mormons needed help and re-enforcements. The Battalion men, with fresh memories of the fruits and grains of California and the great herds of cattle and horses on boundless pastures, suggested this Pacific Coast land as a source of supply.

Accordingly the Mormon leaders at Salt Lake City organized a party to go over the southern route to California where they should obtain cattle, seed grain, and fruit cuttings. Jefferson Hunt, lately captain of Company A of the Mormon Battalion, appears to have been the principal person advocating the trip to California. But neither he, nor any member of the party, had traveled the desert southern route between Salt Lake City and Los Angeles. Miles Goodyear, who had taken a pack horse train over the route the year before, described the trail to the Mormons. Apparently they anticipated little difficulty in following it and reaching their destination.

The Mormon authorities at Salt Lake City appointed Asahel L. Lathrop, Orrin P. Rockwell, and Elijah K. Fuller to head the company being sent to southern California. "An Epistle of the Presidency, and High Council of this Stake of Zion to the Saints in California," was carried along. It advised the Mormons then in military service in California not to re-enlist, but to come to Salt Lake City and to bring along cows, seed grain, and "every kind of valuable root, grape cuttings, and every kind of fruit seed." [14]

The California-bound Mormon company comprised nineteen men, including Jefferson Hunt and his grown sons, John and Gilbert. They set out on horseback on November 18, 1847. John Hunt later recalled:

We took provisions for 30 days which we estimated would be ample time to reach our destination. But we found the directions very hard to follow, and lost the trail so often and spent so much time hunting it again, that we finally ran out of provisions before we had reached the vicinity of Las Vegas. We then did what I think no other party of "Mormon" emigrants ever had to do – we killed and ate our horses. Three horses in all were consumed. Two of them belonged to John Y. Greene and the other to Wm. B. Cornogg. The first we killed at Mountain Spring, just beyond Las Vegas; the next was dispatched at Amergose springs, and the final one near the Mojave river. Our equipment consisted of 20 pack animals, and a saddle horse each, with plenty of arms with which to defend ourselves, and the slight provisions already mentioned.

When we reached a point where Barstow station (on the Salt Lake route) is now located we camped, while two of our strongest men – Shaw and Cornogg – rode ahead to get provisions. They sent a Mexican to us with beef and fresh mounts, and we moved on again, arriving at Chino ranch [15] after 45 days on the trail. . .

We were exhausted when we reached the Chino ranch, but Col. Williams was very generous in his treatment of us. He furnished us wild cows which we milked after strapping them down, and plenty of flour from which to make our bread. We remained there five or six weeks, resting up and preparing for the return trip. Finally, on February 15, 1848, we started out, with about 200 cows, for which we gave him $6 each, and a few

[14] Journal History, Nov. 16, 1847.
[15] Rancho del Chino, the large establishment of Isaac Williams. The headquarters house was about three miles southwest of the present town of Chino, California.

pack animals and mares, also about 40 bulls. He told us he would give us all the bulls we wanted to drive off. They all died but one from thirst while about 100 cows also perished. Occasionally the Indians would sneak up close enough to kill one of them, but otherwise they did not bother us. We got back to Salt Lake in May, 1848.[16]

While the Mormon company was recuperating at Isaac Williams' Chino Rancho, Miles Goodyear, who had sold his Fort Buenaventura near the site of Ogden to the Mormons, arrived in southern California over the same trail. Miles's younger brother Andrew, after telling of the Mormon party's troubles, writes: "We came through with a much smaller party, plenty of provisions, and without the loss of a single animal, Miles being so well acquainted with traveling among Indians." [17]

Behind the Lathrop company on its return to Salt Lake City traveled a party of the Mormon Battalion soldiers whose re-enlistment period in the army had expired. These men, organized under Captain H. G. Boyle, employed Porter Rockwell as guide, and set out from San Diego on March 21, 1848. In addition to their pack animals and loose stock, they took along a wagon, loaded with fruit cuttings and grain. This wagon, which must have been one of those the Mormon Battalion had brought across Arizona in 1846, is recognized as the first wagon to cut a track between Los Angeles and Salt Lake City.[18]

Miles Goodyear also made another trip – his third,

---

[16] Journal History, Nov. 18, 1847. In the entry of May 15, 1848, Lathrop reports that he purchased two hundred cows at $6.00 each, and lost forty on the Mojave Desert. Note the time consumed on the return trip.

[17] Kelly and Howe, *op. cit.,* p. 96.

[18] Journal History, June 5, 1848; "Autobiography and Diary of Henry G. Boyle," MS. in possession of his son, W. H. Boyle, at Provo, Utah; and Daniel Tyler, *op. cit.,* p. 331.

at least, and final journey – over the trail between Los Angeles and Salt Lake City in the spring of 1848. The large band of horses, which he drove before him, he took on to the Missouri River, anticipating a ready sale in the brisk market induced by the war with Mexico. But the market had collapsed with the end of the war. However the gold discovery in California and the rush to the new Eldorado gave promise of good prices for horseflesh in the mines. So Goodyear revamped his plans, drove his horses back over the plains and mountains, and along the Humboldt route to the California mines. There he sold his stock at good prices, having completed a total drive of some four thousand miles, one of the longest and most remarkable horse drives in history.

We come now to a consideration of the immediate background of the '49er treks, and shall thereafter present a summary of the various trips over the route in 1849.

News of the gold discovery at Sutter's mill in January, 1848, was carried to the world and the great rush to Eldorado was to come the next year. The wave of overland gold seekers set out from the Missouri and Mississippi rivers with the appearance of the first grass of spring in 1849. The favored route was the Oregon Trail along the Platte, and the Humboldt river course across the northern Nevada desert.

Some groups, because of a late start or as a result of difficulties enroute, reached Salt Lake City in late July and August, beyond the season for a safe journey across northern Nevada on the short, direct route to the gold mines. The recent tragedy of the Donner party, caught in the snows of the high Sierra Nevadas, was still fresh in men's minds, to temper enthusiasm with caution.

Certain parties that started west from Salt Lake City in late July found water and grass so scant that they returned to the city.[19] These and the later arrivals from the East were faced with the problem of either staying in the Mormon capital until the following spring, or else taking the longer but safer "Southern Route" to Los Angeles and thence up the Pacific coast to the mines.

Inquiring argonauts were advised by the Mormons to take the route to Los Angeles. Captain Jefferson Hunt, they testified, had traversed the trail twice, and would be a safe and capable guide. He agreed to lead a caravan for ten dollars per wagon. He advised the emigrants to wait until fall for their trip over the hot desert; and in the meantime to recruit their animals in suitable pastures of the Utah Lake region. A large number of emigrants followed his advice. Some moved to the appointed rendezvous in late July; others arrived in August or September.

The first company to reach Los Angeles over the trail from Salt Lake City in the fall of 1849 was a party of packers. Available information about these men and their trip is scant. They passed the Hunt wagon train at Chicken Creek, Utah, on October 8; and the Record Book of Rancho del Chino notes their arrival on October 27-29, 1849. These packers made fast time, enjoyed good health, but lost about thirty animals from the scarcity of water and grass. (The available records concerning this party will be reproduced below, in Part I.)

Of the gold seekers assembled in the pastures near Utah Lake preparatory to the journey to Los Angeles, some were unable or unwilling to pay the ten dollar

[19] Entry of July 28, Sheldon Young diary; (*see* part III: A).

HENRY W. BIGLER; WILLIAM J. JOHNSON; AZARIAH SMITH; JAMES S. BROWN

Four members of the Mormon Battalion who were at Sutter's Mill when gold was discovered on January 24, 1848. Bigler's diary fixes the date. Photograph taken at the Fiftieth Anniversary Celebration of the Gold Discovery. Published in this volume are descriptions of the 1849 trip from the diary of Bigler, and the account of Brown.

fee to Hunt for guide service. These dissenters, with wagons, formed what we shall call the Gruwell-Derr Company. They employed a Mexican guide and set out ahead of the main wagon train. No journal of their trip has come to light. One member of the company says there were twenty-three wagons in the train.[20] Evidently the party endured great hardships. When their food was nearly exhausted a group of six men pushed ahead from Mountain Springs to the California settlements on foot, and returned with supplies. The Jefferson Hunt party caught up with the main body of this advance train on the Mojave River, found the members in a destitute condition, and contributed food for the starving women and children. (Documents on the Gruwell-Derr Company will be presented below, in Part II.)

Reconciled to waiting for cool weather, the main body of gold seekers spent August and September recruiting their stock and making arrangements for the further journey. Some fretted at the delay while others – as related in the Stover Narrative reproduced below in Part VI – enjoyed an interesting social life among the Mormons.

Although the various parties were scattered over considerable territory, the central gathering place was on Hobble Creek which runs through the site of Springville, five miles south of Provo, Utah. From this point the main party set forth on October 2. (Accounts of this wagon train trip are given below in Part III.) The caravan lay over next day, organized the company, and chose officers. The camp was on what

---

[20] Peter Derr (*see* part II: A). Addison Pratt, who was not in the party, says there were fifty wagons in the train. For his entry of October 15, and the last sentence in his diary, *see* part III: B.

they called Election Creek, now Peteetneet Creek, that
flows through the present town of Payson. Rules and
regulations for governing the party were adopted.
These were read and explained by Lewis Granger, one-
time minister, and later a hotel keeper at Los Angeles.
Provision was made for a colonel, an adjutant, and
captains for seven companies. Each of the companies
in turn was to take the lead of the caravan one day,
then fall to the rear. A Mr. Baxter of Michigan was
elected colonel; Dr. McCormick of Iowa City was
chosen adjutant; Jefferson Hunt was commander and
guide.[21] The individual companies soon had nicknames,
such as: San Joaquin (Sand Walking), Bug Smashers,
Buckskins, Wolverines, Hawkeyes, and Jay Hawkers.[22]

The main company moved forward from Election
Creek on October 4, but traveled slowly – eight miles
the first day and ten the second – giving opportunity
for those behind to catch up. Hunt went back to Provo
to hurry up some Mormons who wanted to travel with
the train. Some of these were going as missionaries to
the Hawaiian Islands, others were on their way to
California to mine.

Addison Pratt's wagon, which left Salt Lake City
on the 2nd, camped with some other emigrants at the
site of Payson on the 6th, and caught up with the
principal company two days later at Salt Creek, which

21 W. L. Manly, *Death Valley in '49* (New York, Wallace Hebbard, 1929),
pp. 104-105; a story written from San Bernardino, probably by Sidney P.
Waite, on May 1, 1883, published in the *San Francisco Chronicle* and copied
in the *St. Louis Republican* of May 14, 1883 (found in vol. 1 of the Jayhawker
Scrapbooks, Henry E. Huntington library); and "Sheldon Young's Log,"
reprinted below.

22 *See* Bigler's diary, under date of October 20 (part v: A); Margaret
Long, *The Shadow of the Arrow* (Caldwell, Idaho, Caxton Printers, 1941),
p. 258: "Story of Asa Haynes as dictated to Nancy H. Wiley, his daughter"
(copy in Henry E. Huntington library); and John G. Ellenbecker, *The Jayhawkers of Death Valley* (Marysville, Kansas, privately printed, 1938), p. 12.

runs through the site of Nephi. Pratt says there were then about one hundred wagons in the train.

At the Sevier River, on October 12, Apostle C. C. Rich, James S. Brown, and F. M. Pomeroy caught up with Hunt and added their wagon to the train. The last of the Mormon contingents left Salt Lake City October 11 and 12 and assembled at Fort Utah (Provo) on the 14th. Here they were joined by Captain O. K. Smith and a company of non-Mormon (Gentile) packers. The Mormons, about twenty in number, were mostly packers, but they had two wagons along. This Mormon company elected J. M. Flake as captain.[23] The non-Mormon party, under Smith's leadership, also numbered twenty. The two parties traveled together, or near each other, until they caught up with the Hunt wagon train on Beaver Creek (near the present city of Beaver, Utah).

The main wagon train had reached this point by easy, regular stages and without encountering any serious difficulties. The progress and incidents of the trip are recorded in Sheldon Young's Log and especially in the adequate diary of Addison Pratt (both reproduced below in Part III).

Upon reaching Beaver Creek on October 18, the Hunt party saw the Gruwell-Derr wagon train climbing the mountain to the south.[24] Captain Hunt's company remained on the creek two days, refreshing their stock on the grass of the valley, while a party continued down the creek to see if the canyon below was passable for wagons.

Here Captain Hunt told the officers of the wagon train that he had heard of a short cut down the river

---

[23] Entry of October 14 in the diary of H. W. Bigler, and of October 15 in William Farrer's diary, (*see* part V: A, C).

[24] Entry of October 18, Addison Pratt's diary; (*see* part III: B).

southwest, and then across a plain, to intersect the Old Spanish Trail near Antelope Spring. Admitting that he had never been over the route, he said that if the company wanted to try it he would go along, provided he be relieved of all responsibility as to success of the venture.[25] The plan was discussed and the company voted to try the cutoff.

Accordingly, on October 21, the train moved down the creek twelve miles and camped. The next day they left the creek and after traveling another twelve miles made a dry camp, driving the stock back to the creek for water. The next day there was much discussion as to what course to follow. About forty wagons turned back to Beaver Creek to take the known route. The others remained at the dry camp awaiting the return of Hunt, who was out ahead scouting a route.

After having pushed into the desert some forty miles without finding water, Hunt returned to camp on the 24th almost dead from thirst.[26] The remaining wagons now drove back to the creek, and the next day continued up the stream to where the known trail left it. The company had lost seven days on Beaver Creek and in the futile attempt to travel a short cut. Captain Hunt, who had suggested the route, without recommending or guaranteeing it, was nevertheless blamed for the failure and loss of time. The company began to be filled with dissension, and threats were hurled at Hunt.

In the meantime, on the 23rd, the Flake and Smith

25 Good expositions of the problem and decision are given in the Farrer and the Bigler diaries, October 23 entries; (see Part v).

25 James S. Brown, *Life of a Pioneer, being the autobiography of James S. Brown* (Salt Lake City, Geo. Q. Cannon and Sons, 1900), p. 134. "Sometime in the night Captain Hunt came into camp, so near choked from lack of water that his tongue was swollen till it protruded from his mouth; his eyes were so sunken in his head that he could scarcely be recognized. His horse, too, for the need of water, was blind, and staggered as he was urged on. Their stay had been thirty-six hours, on the sands, without water."

companies had caught up with the long wagon train at Beaver Creek. Captain Smith came in with a purported map and description of a wonderful short cut route to Walker's Pass in the Sierra Nevadas. It was hundreds of miles shorter than the Old Spanish Trail route, by way of Los Angeles, and was supplied with ample grass and frequent watering places, so he said. The map and the information were said to have come from Barney Ward, early trapper and Mountain Man, who was reported to have traveled the route three times.[27] Apostle Rich visited Captain Smith on the 23rd and was well impressed with the possibilities of the short cut.[28]

Just where Smith saw Barney Ward is not clear. Neither Henry Bigler nor William Farrer of the Captain Flake Company, that traveled with or near Captain Smith's party, tells of seeing Ward.[29]

The new route prospect was so alluring that a large

---

[27] Elijah Barney Ward was born in Virginia about 1820 and came to the Rocky Mountains at the age of fifteen. He lived among the trappers and Indians until the Mormons came in 1847. After joining the Mormons he served as Indian interpreter, trader, and guide. In December, 1849, he described the geography of the southern Utah country to the P. P. Pratt Exploring Expedition.

In the *Deseret News* of September 7 and subsequent issues, 1850, Ward advertised to pilot emigrants over the southern route from Salt Lake City to California. Other matters interfered and he did not go with the D. W. Cheesman party of 1850 (*Annual Publications, Historical Society of Southern California*, XIV, 283). On June 9, 1851, Ward acted as interpreter at a conference between Brigham Young and Chief Wakara.

Ward was married to an Indian woman. Their children married white men. He and James Anderson were killed and scalped on April 11, 1865, during Utah's Black Hawk War. Andrew Jenson, in his *Latter-Day Saint Biographical Encyclopedia* (Salt Lake City, Jenson Historical Company, 1920), III, 552-54, gives a sketch of Ward and tells of his children.

[28] See the entry of October 23 in the Farrer diary (*see* part v: c).

[29] It is possible that Capt. Smith saw Ward on October 19 or 20, when Smith was traveling in the Fillmore region and while he was ahead of Bigler and Farrer. Ward was encountered in the Sevier Valley by the P. P. Pratt Exploring Expedition in December, 1849. Smith may have met Ward earlier, in Salt Lake City or elsewhere.

number were inclined to try the short cut, which branched from the known trail a few miles northeast of Mountain Meadows, on the route ahead.

From Beaver Creek the Hunt wagon train now moved southward along the known route. They made a dry camp among the cedars the first night and the next day reached the first creek in Little Salt Lake Valley.

On October 28, Apostle Rich, H. W. Bigler, and a few other Mormons who had given up their wagons for pack animals, left Hunt's wagon train, joined Captain Flake's company of packers, and pushed ahead. Later that day they caught up with Captain Smith's company of packers, who had crossed over from Beaver Creek by a shorter route and had come along the north side of Little Salt Lake, while the Flake party had taken the regular trail on the south of the lake. (See Farrer's entry of October 28, published below in Part V.) The two companies of packers now traveled together. They went west from the site of Enoch to Iron Springs, and then followed the Old Spanish Trail northwestward around Iron Mountain.

On the evening of October 30, Apostle Rich, ranking ecclesiastical authority, called his Mormon party together and urged them to act in unison. A vote was taken, which resulted in a decision to take the so-called "Walker Cutoff" when they reached the divergence of the routes. Rich suggested that Flake continue as captain. As Bigler records, the vote "was unanimous that Bro. Flake be our Captain and that Bro. Rich council him." In view of the strong Mormon inclination to obey church leaders, it is clear that for important decisions Rich would be the real leader. We shall hereafter refer to this group of Mormon packers as the Flake-Rich company.

This party and the Captain Smith company of packers turned from the Old Spanish Trail on November 1, a few miles southwest of the site of Newcastle and traveled westward, passed what is now Enterprise, and moved up Shoal creek.

In the meantime, the Hunt wagon train, disorganized and broken into several parties since the debacle at Beaver Creek, followed the regular trail through Little Salt Lake valley, and around Iron Mountain, skirting the Escalante desert. There was much discussion of Captain Smith's proposed short cut that was supposed to save about five hundred miles of travel and bring the gold seekers to the mines of northern California in twenty days.

Captain Hunt was determined to continue on the known and comparatively safe Old Spanish Trail. The attitude of certain members of the company toward him confirmed his decision. Addision Pratt recorded in his diary of October 29, near Little Salt Lake:

> Here our camp split again and a part left us. Our Colonel, Baxter was his name, left with them. Here Bro. Hunt came to me and told me that his life was at stake as there was a party that intended to kill him if their cattle died in crossing the deserts and he thought was but one way to escape and that was to have the company voluntarily take the intended cutoff and leave a few wagons of us to go where we were of a mind to. He wished me and all the brethren to ask the Lord for his delivery. We told him we would.[30]

As the main body of the wagon train neared the forking of the routes, a general meeting was held on November 3 at the site of Newcastle to decide upon the course to take. J. W. Brier, a Methodist minister "who liked to give his opinion on every subject," was the chief exhorter. He "took the opportunity to fire

---

[30] Addison Pratt diary (*see* part III: B).

the minds of the people with a zeal for the cutoff and closed by saying . . . 'sink or swim, live or die, he should take the cutoff, go it boots.' " [31] Others made similar speeches.

Then Captain Hunt was called for. His speech did not win the votes, but it was remembered, and was often pondered thereafter, especially by those who took the Death Valley route. Hunt said he had never been over the proposed route and he knew no one who had. He doubted its feasibility, said the packers might make it, but he did not think the wagons could. He had contracted to guide them over the Old Spanish Trail and if only one wagon chose to take that Trail he was bound to accompany it. As Stover recalled it, Hunt concluded: "If you want to follow Captain Smith, I can't help it, but I believe you will get into the jaws of hell; but I hope you will have good luck." [32]

When they came to the parting of ways on November 4, about one hundred wagons – all in the train except seven – turned to the cutoff route. After the division, each company stopped to bid the other adieu. Some of the men had bored holes in trees, filled these with powder, and "firing them, exploded the trees in symbol of the break-up of the company." [33]

While Hunt and his seven wagons crawled southward toward the rim of the Great Basin and nearer to Santa Clara Creek, the hundred wagons followed the trail of the Captain Smith and Flake-Rich companies westward up Shoal Creek.

On the third day the main wagon train was brought to a halt on the brink of the canyon of Beaver Dam Wash, in the high timbered plateau near the present

[31] Pratt's diary entry of November 3.
[32] Stover's narrative (see part VI: A).
[33] James S. Brown, op. cit., p. 136.

FOUR JOURNALISTS OF THE TRIP OF 1849
Upper: Charles C. Rich and George Q. Cannon
Lower: Addison Pratt and William Farrer

Utah-Nevada state line. The packer companies ahead had found a trail by which they had descended into the canyon, but the wagons could not follow. While the train encamped near "Mount Misery," scouting parties sought a possible wagon route.

After some vain searching, enthusiasm for the cutoff began to die, and there was talk of taking the back track. Mr. Rynierson, according to Lewis Manly, spoke to the crowd:

> My family is near and dear to me. I can see by the growth of the timber that we are in a very elevated place. This is now the seventh of November, it being the fourth at the time of our turning off on this trail. We are evidently in a country where snow is liable to fall at any time in the winter season, and if we were to remain here and be caught in a severe storm we should all probably perish. I, for one, feel in duty bound to seek a safer way than this. I shall hitch up my oxen and return at once to the old trail. Boys (to his teamsters) get the cattle and we'll return.[34]

As Rynierson drove out of camp a large number of other wagons fell in behind him. Others, upon returning from futile attempts to find a road, hitched up and took the back track also. Some, who had horse and mule teams, concluded to abandon their wagons, pack their horses, and follow the Captain Smith trail down Beaver Dam Wash. This they did, as the Stover account relates (Part VI).

When some of the searchers for a route returned to camp and reported finding a practicable course to the north, the remaining group, comprising about twenty-seven wagons, decided to go forward. This was the company of daring – or foolhardy – individuals whose ordeals and route and subsequent publicity have made them famous as the Death Valley Party. Their story,

[34] Quoted in Manly, *op. cit.*, p. 110.

widely and frequently told, is purposely excluded from
the present study. We have chosen instead to present
new materials on the other – and wiser – individuals
who escaped the horrors of Death Valley.

Of these, there were several parties, on two routes.

First, was the seven-wagon remnant of Captain
Hunt's train. This small party continued with the
Captain on the Old Spanish Trail and in due time
reached southern California. The story of this journey
is well told in the Addison Pratt diary and in James
Brown's account, in Part III.

Second, was the main body of the original wagon
train that started on the cutoff, but turned back with
Rynierson from Mount Misery. It returned to the Old
Spanish Trail and followed the path of Hunt's wagons
to California. Although this was the largest party, no
diary of the trip has been found. A. C. Erkson's brief
story, reprinted as section B, in Part IV, gives some of
the incidents of the trek.

Of the trip of the lead company of packers, especially
the Mormon contingent, there are a number of excellent journals and reports. The diaries of Henry W.
Bigler, C. C. Rich, and William Farrer, and the reminiscent reports by George Q. Cannon and J. H. Rollins
are published in Part V.

The story of the second company of packers, made
up at the wagon train stalled near Mount Misery, is
told in Jacob Y. Stover's good reminiscent account,
republished as Part VI. This company finally caught
up with Captain O. K. Smith, and after he turned back,
the Stover party continued on.

The route of these packer companies, which will be
identified in detail in the diaries cited, was down
Beaver Dam Wash to a point near Magotsa, westward

and northwestward to Meadow Valley Wash; and westward to Coyote Spring. From here the Flake-Rich party turned southeast to reach again Captain Hunt's wagons encamped at the Trail crossing of the Muddy, near present Glendale.

After Captain Smith and some of his men turned back to the Old Spanish Trail (to be picked up by the Pomeroy train and taken on to California) Stover's party continued on west and southwest and finally reached the track of Hunt's wagons.

Two more wagon trains made the trip from Salt Lake City to Los Angeles in the fall of 1849, following the route of the Captain Hunt train.

The first of these was the Pomeroy Company, composed principally of the wagons of the Pomeroy brothers, freighters from Missouri, and their hired help. They were joined by a few emigrants, as related by Judge Walter Van Dyke. (The accounts are printed in Part VII.) This party, which comprised altogether about fifty wagons,[35] left Salt Lake City November 3. At Iron Springs (west of present Cedar City) they picked up a party of men – apparently a group from Captain O. K. Smith's company – that had made an abortive attempt to get to California on the short cut and had retraced their steps to the Old Spanish Trail.[36]

The Pomeroy Company ran short of provisions. Upon reaching the Muddy branch of the Virgin they met another party of men. These appear to have been the remnant of Captain Smith's party that turned back part way with Smith and then followed the Flake-Rich company tracks down Pahranagat Wash and to

---

[35] *See* David Seeley account (part VII: B).

[36] David Seeley sketch, *op. cit.* Stover says that Smith and a small party headed back over the trail and that they finally were picked up and brought on to California (*see* part VI: A).

the regular trail crossing of the Muddy. Here this
group was joined by some of the Pomeroy company
men and together they pushed ahead of the wagon train
with packs on their backs.[37] Others left the wagon train
at the Amargosa River.[38] The remnant of the wagon
train arrived at Cucamonga Rancho on February 1.
The accounts of the Pomeroy Company journey are
grouped together in Part VII.

The second wagon train that followed Captain
Hunt's in late 1849 was led by Howard Egan. It comprised about forty persons and traveled with three
wagons. This company, which left Salt Lake City on
November 18, 1849, made a fast and successful trip to
California. In fact, it made the journey to Williams'
ranch in fifty days, which was good time, considering
the conditions. Major Egan kept a diary of the trip,
which was published by the Egan family in 1917 as
*Pioneering the West, 1846 to 1878; Major Howard
Egan's Diary,* etc. The journal of the trip to Los Angeles is reprinted in Part VIII.

[37] See Edwin Pettit account and the Goudy Hogan journal (part VII:
A, C).

[38] David Seeley, *op. cit.*

Diaries and Contemporary Records

Part I

Packers: First Over the Trail in 1849

Of the packers who traveled from Salt Lake City and reached California in late October, 1849, the records are scant and confused. Sheldon Young wrote at Chicken Creek, south of the site of Nephi, Utah, on October 8: "A train of packers passed us." (*see* Part III: A.) He supplies no further information.

James Waters, experienced fur trapper and Mountain Man, was apparently the guide to this packer company of gold seekers. Waters had been a trader on the upper Arkansas and had previously traveled this trail to California. In 1845 he brought back from the Pacific Coast packs of abalone shells to trade to the mountain Indians. Later he was to become a very prominent citizen of San Bernardino, California, and to build business houses and an opera house there. His biographer writes:

> In September, 1849,[1] he came to California by the southern route, through the Cajon Pass, to avoid the snows of the Sierra Nevadas, the most direct road then to the new gold discovery on the American River, near Sutter's Mill. He served as guide for a company of 140 New Yorkers on this trip.[2]

[1] He may have started in September, but he reached Rancho del Chino on October 29, as the Chino records testify. *See* below.

[2] Biographical sketch of James W. Waters in John Brown and James Boyd *History of San Bernardino and Riverside Counties* (Chicago, Lewis Publishing Company, 1922) II, 676.

The registration book at Isaac Williams' Rancho del Chino records the arrival in 1849 of many companies by way of the Gila route across Arizona.[3] On pages 28 and 29 important information is given on arrivals from Salt Lake, as follows:

[page 28]   Left here on the 27th inst.
 Daniel Kitchings – Texas
 William Lamb – Do
Hon. I. M. Hoge of Washington County Arks: arrived on the 27th
 Oct 1849. Capt of a company of 130 men via the Great Salt Lake [4]
Sept. [Oct.] 27. James Logan of Clarksville Arks
      David Logan arrived on the 26. 1849
      Thomas G. Hackney
      Jacob Rogers
Sept [Oct.] 28 Jno F N [W?] Jones Hannibal Mo.
      Samuel Cross   " "
      Dr. H Merideth   " "
      Chs Merideth   " "
      D S Tisdale   " "
      A Woods   " "
      Jos M Davis   " "
      Wm Davis   " "
      R Robinson   " "
      Henry Sarvis   " "
      Wm H C Nash   " "
      Wm C Coffman   " "
      Jno McKee   " "
      Jno Henry McKee   " "
      E H Townsend   " "
      Wm Marsh   " "
By way of Santa Fe N M and Salt Lake [5] all well and calculate to

---

[3] This interesting and valuable record book is now possessed by the Henry E. Huntington Library at San Marino, California. Transcribed and edited by Lindley Bynum, it was published in the *Historical Society of Southern California Annual Publications* (Los Angeles, 1934), pp. 1-55.

[4] Here is the first mention in the Chino records of an arrival from Salt Lake City.

[5] The route of these sixteen men from Santa Fé to Salt Lake is not indicated. They could have gone north, along the foot of the front range of the

Better. we will leave here on the 5th Inst. for the gold regions
we are now in good health

[page 29]   L J C Duncan   Ga.

D Seymour Beache of Litchfield Ct arrived Oct 27th, 1849
Carbine 1141 left here 29th Oct. . 1849 bound for the Sacramento
via Los Angeles with but little prospect of getting any where

C. MITCHELL

R. R. Givens arrived here Oct. 28th. *broke*

October 29 / 49

Jams Waters arvd from the Grate Salt Lake with a party 1.14
men all arrd to the Cheano in good helth with loss of abot 30
Muls for the wate of water and grass [6]

Perry B. Marple, native of Virginia, and late from Missouri arived
here, Oct. 29 1849, en route to the Gold mines of the West   Let
fortune favor those who undergo all the hardships of the enterprise, & hope will attend him the residue of the expedition.

Rockies and intersected the Oregon Trail; or they may have gone through
Abiquiú and followed the Old Spanish Trail most of the way to Salt Lake.

In the "Record Book of Rancho del Chino," p. 3, we read: "The Company
consisting of Hamilton Jackson Geo & Chas Churchill left New York
February 5, 1849 traveling via Ohio Mississippi & Arkansas rivers to Fort
Smith, from thence over the Great American Desert to Santa fe! on our
road we met but one party of Comanches they were friendly having large
numbers of horses & mules, at this time we had ninety seven men under
command of Capt I. A. N. Ebbetts, arrived in Santa fe May 28 left Santa fe
May 31 and traveled to Abicue from thence to the Rio Chamas this river
being so rapid we could not cross it, and it was deemed advisible to return
and take the Gila route, at this time our Company numbered one hundred
and fourteen men under command of Capt Day — June 9 turned back and
arrived in Abacue June 11. we then made up a Company of ninety seven
men under Command of Capt Miller and hired Francisco a Mexican guide
to conduct us to the Pacific coast we traveled down the Rio Grande to
Kearneys pass — and in five days from the time we left the Rio Grande we
struck the Rio Gila. we traveled on the Gila to the Pimas Village. left it
then for one day then struck it again and traveled to the Rio Colerado. the
river was very high — crossed it Aug. 7. loosing one mule by drowning the
Indians were friendly towards us at this point our company was disbanded
and we traveled to Col. Williams ranche with only six men —"

Capt. Day, Hay, and Hoge may be the same person. Of the 114 men under
Capt. Day, 97 re-organized under Capt. Miller and took the Gila route.
The other 17 may be the Hannibal party, members of the Capt. Hayes
Company, of whom John F. W. Jones writes; p. 29.

[6] The 114 men that James Waters reports, added to the 16 from Hannibal,
listed above, would make the 130 first reported.

The members of Capt. Hayes Company from Hannibal Missouri
have enjoyed fine health the entire trip [7] The company lost but a
small quanity of stock considering the number of dry stretches in
we had to encounter — we had one Jornada of forty miles one of
seventy five without any water that was fit to use and several
small Jornados without wood Water grass and dam little ground.[8]

JNO. F. W. JONES Hannibal Marion County missouri
Capt Bonlin, Roberts & others, come on in will wait for you in
the promise Land [end of page 29].

---

[7] This is probably meant to read: "those members of Capt. Hayes (or
Hoge's) Company that are from Hannibal, Missouri, have enjoyed fine
health the entire trip." Jones is writing for the Hannibal party, which he
heads.

[8] The reproduction of the "Record Book of the Rancho del Chino" printed
in the *Historical Society of Southern California Annual Publications* (Los
Angeles, 1934), p. 33, gives a very inaccurate rendition of this paragraph.

Part II

The Gruwell-Derr Wagon Train

The first wagon train to leave the Utah Lake region for southern California in the fall of 1849 set out a week or two ahead of the bigger and better known train led by Jefferson Hunt. That first train employed as guide a Mexican who was familiar with the pack horse route to Los Angeles.

We call this first company the Gruwell-Derr train because our only specific accounts of the trip are given by Gruwell and Derr. These brief reminiscent reports are far from satisfactory, but are the best available. References to the company found in the journals of other diarists are noted in Parts III and V.

A: PETER DERR EXPERIENCES

[This report is a Bancroft library manuscript entitled, "Account of Experiences of Peter Derr of Humboldt County, California, who came Through on the First Train South from Salt Lake to California, 1849." This short but historically important document was obtained by one of H. H. Bancroft's interviewers, probably in the 1880s.]

The first train that came through to California by the southern trail from Salt Lake was made up at Kurdasville [?], Missouri River. It numbered 49 wagons, 300 men bearing arms and numerous women and children, cattle, etc. They started June 3d, 1849, but did not reach Los Angeles till the January following. When they reached Salt Lake the Mormons told them the grass was all burned off on the direct route, so after a stay of 6 weeks at Utah Lake, 23 wagons started southwest, on what was then only a mule trail. In the mean time a Mormon by the name of Hunt had made up a train of 107 wagons, they each paying him $10, to pilot them to Southern California. The train of 23 wagons was composed of families with but little money who could not afford to pay the pilot fee.

They cut their way south some 300 miles when they struck the trail from Santa Fé.[1] Those never having been over a mountain trail can have no idea of the difficulties to be overcome to pass wagons over them. Often they would have to leave the trail for miles and cut their way through brush and trees in the canyons, not being able to follow over the steep and narrow mountain side. The rest of the 675 miles trail was equally difficult. There were three "roadometers" in the train so they knew the distance traveled.

About 300 miles from Los Angeles it became evident that the supply of provisions would not hold out, and the train was soon put on half rations. A party of 6 consisting of Peter Derr, two Greuell brothers, two other white men and a Spaniard,[2] started ahead on foot for provisions. The distance was greater than anticipated and the suffering endured by these men was most horrible. They were 22 days from the train before reaching Chocomonga where they first found food. Their provisions were all gone the 10th day out. There seemed to be no game of any kind on this desert. The 9th day they found a colt nearly dead from starvation, which they tried to eat, but it gave them the diarrhea very badly. At the Mohave River they tried

[1] This would be at Little Salt Lake, where the Old Spanish Trail emerged from the mountains near the site of present Paragonah.

[2] The "Spaniard" was doubtless the guide the company hired. The names of the other two men are not known.

to catch fish in blankets but succeeded in only catching a few minnows. Some two days later Derr shot a
wolf which was all they had the rest of the 11 days.
Every portion including entrails and skin was eaten.
They tried to shoot some crows but were too weak to
aim. Once a Cal. lion came close to them, but Greuell
failed to kill it with a double barrell shotgun. For the
last 7 days they had absolutely nothing. Some of the
party were determined to kill the Spaniard to eat, not
concenting to Derr's claim that he had a right to a
chance with the rest. Greuell would have killed him
but for being prevented by Derr.[3]

Finally they reached Chocomonga where they found
a negro who had been with Fremont, and knew how to
treat them, giving them but a little at a time, thus saving
their lives. They got a lot of provisions at Williams
Ranch and reached the train in four days.[4] It was only
by proper treatment that some were prevented killing
themselves from overeating. The train led by the
Mormon Hunt – came up the same night. He had tried
a "cut-off" and had to return after 14 days to Derr's
route.[5] Strangely enough, but one death occurred, and
that at Los Angeles, of an elderly lady.

B: J. D. GRUWELL'S ACCOUNT

[J. D. Gruwell dictated to S. B. Moore on October 18, 1887, this
account of his 1849 trip. The original manuscript is in the Bancroft
Library, University of California at Berkeley. J. D. Gruwell appears
to have been one of the older sons of Jacob Gruwell, or of his brother.
According to J. Y. Stover (*see* VI: A) Jacob Gruwell was a Methodist preacher from Montrose, Iowa, who preached while crossing the

[3] This, along with Addison Pratt's reflections on Gruwell, gives him a
somewhat unsavory reputation.

[4] Pratt met them returning on Dec. 9 (*see* part III: B).

[5] Hunt's party had lost seven days on the attempted cutoff from Beaver
Creek.

plains. Addison Pratt says, in the December 6 entry of his diary below, that one of the Gruwell brothers had ten children and the other eleven.[6]]

Came from Iowa to Calif. in '49 across the plains in ox teams, 7 Mo Enroute – with 64 wagons – All went well till we reached Salt Lake – It being late in the season we concluded to winter at Utah Fort but learning that the Mormons were about to attack us we broke camp[7] and with a Mexican guide took the south route for Los Angeles which was the pioneer train over that route being 5 days at times going 3 Miles. At Santa Clara Canyon the Indians ran off 9 head Cattle and shot one full of arrows – We surprised one of the braves who had his bow bent to fire on us by shooting him on the spot, which threw the enemy into disorder and so we escaped further trouble[8] – Soon after leaving this place we ran short of provisions and my brother and myself started in pursuit of ra-

[6] Data on the older family are supplied in the biographical sketch of Melvin L. Gruwell, found in *Pen Pictures from the Garden of the World, or Santa Clara County, California* (Chicago, 1888), pp. 266-67. Melvin was born in Indiana in 1826, youngest son of John and Ruth Gruwell. There were nine in the family, five boys and four girls.

"In 1849 the eldest brothers, Asa, Robert, and Jacob, came with their families overland to this State [California], and all spent the winter in Los Angeles. Asa settled in Stanislaus County, leaving it to come to this county in 1861. Robert went to the mines at Rough and Ready, and after remaining there less than two years became a pioneer of Santa Clara Valley. Jacob first made Stockton his home, but settled in this county in 1851."

The account goes on to say that Jacob was a minister of the Southern Methodist Church and still lived in San Jose in 1888. Robert and Asa were then dead. The father, John, the younger sons, Melvin and Laban H., and two sisters followed the older brothers to California, coming overland in 1852. A biographical sketch of L. H. Gruwell is found in the *History of Napa and Lake Counties, California* (San Francisco, Slocum, Bowen and Company, 1881), p. 237 of the Lake County part. He was born in Quincy, Illinois, November 22, 1836.

[7] Pratt tells of Mormon difficulties with the Gruwells; entries of Dec. 9 and 21 (Part III: B).

[8] They left on the spot a note explaining the difficulty and giving warning to the Hunt train. Pratt tells of finding this note.

tions – Instead of reaching the settlements in 3 days we were 13 days and for 3 days and nights had nothing to eat [9] – We returned to the Camp with beef Cattle and provisions being over a month enroute – On our return we proceeded on our journey and reached camp without further trouble – We wintered at Los Angeles and then proceeded north and met a part of our Caravan 300 miles from the settlements they having taken the Northern route – We went direct to Eldorado County and engaged in mining where I made plenty of money and for 18 months pursued that occupation.

In '51 I purchased Land in Santa Clara Co, and commenced farming. – In '52 [?] I got married and the following year sold out and went to Lake Co. to engage in the Stock business – & remained there till '70 when I moved to present neighborhood and rented lands and was the pioneer farmer of this section, putting in the first crop that was ever raised. In '72 I purchased the farm on which I am living and since then have been engaged in farming –

In coming into Cal. I came as a poor boy [10] and what fortune I have at the present was made by hard labor and industrious habits – being perfectly temperate all my life.

C: Notes of Benjamin Hayes

[Mr. Hayes, who later became a prominent citizen of southern California, came to the Pacific coast by the Gila River route, arriving at Rancho del Chino on January 30, 1850. On that day he records:]

First came to a collection of Indian huts, of the workmen of Williams. Off to the right a mill, con-

---

[9] These figures are at variance with those given above by Derr.

[10] This statement and the one above telling of his marriage in 1852 would indicate that this man was a son of one of the Gruwell brothers with the big families.

spicuous amid the verdure. The large dwelling of
Williams off to the left, then two or three waggons of
emigrants. A peep into a waggon as I pass shews a
little work-basket. Looking to one side, there is a rosy-
cheeked child, and a father, with a brow of care,
sitting by the fire.

"Just in?"

"Yes."

"By Salt Lake?"

"Yes."

And then a brief but vivid sketch of suffering.

Riding up to a large house, found we could have
lodgings, supper, etc. Sociable set of men, all emigrants
or American traders. All in a bustle. Tales of privation.
Good supper. Flour $1 the *almud* at the mill. Children
around "saying their lessons," American ladies stirring
about, a novel scene for us, we are again *near home.*
Adjoining the house is a large field of wheat, as fine as
any in the world. Five families staying at this house;
all came by Salt Lake. Among the topics of conversation is the neighboring mountain range northward,
where, it is reported, gold has been found; two
companies have been sent there prospecting. It is said
many families are still behind on the Salt Lake road,
comparatively destitute. A real fear prevails in regard
to them.

This is the first attempt of waggons to come through
by the Salt Lake route . . .[11]

I have received many interesting details of the Salt
Lake Route, from Mr. Grewell (who keeps our

[11] *Pioneer Notes from the Diaries of Judge Benjamin Hayes, 1849-1875*
(Los Angeles, privately printed, 1929), p. 67.

[12] Apparently, Gruwell quickly went into the hotel business. This paragraph
and the following one are quoted from the original Hayes "Notes" in the
Bancroft library. The text varies slightly from that in the published version
cited above.

hotel),[12] Mr. Louis Granger,[13] Mr. Stickney, Mr.
Shearer and have recorded them from their respective
diaries.[14]

We did not go over to seek the acquaintance of Col.
Williams. His house is now full of strangers, whom he
is entertaining. He has sent out to the Mohave Desert,
and relieved many. His hand is open to everybody. . .

[Feb. 4th.] Mr. Nagles represented wheat to be
worth from $3 to $5 per bushel, at Salt Lake City;
flour, $8 to $10 per 100 lbs.; corn, $1 per bushel; beef,
8 to 10 cents per lb. Then, on that route, would come
a story of starvation, abandonment of valuable property, suffering of women and children in long marches
over deserts or in snow; in a word, as one described it
to me, "the losses and suffering of the emigrants have
scarcely ever been equalled in the history of any
expedition on this continent." All happily forgotten
when, on the 31st of December, 1849, he emerged out
of the Cajon Pass, and "encamped on a field of oats
and clover surrounded by a meadow covered with
grass; vines hanging full of half-dried grapes; many
thousands of fat cattle, and everything presenting the
appearance of *May.*"

The influx of so many emigrants simultaneously
rendered the price of labor cheap; some were working
for Col. I. Williams, of Chino, for their boarding,
others at Los Angeles for $1 per day.[15]

---

[13] This is the Granger who helped organize the Hunt train. *See* Manly,
op. cit., p. 105.

[14] We are unable to find in Haye's "Notes" the diary quotations referred
to here.

[15] *Pioneer Notes, op. cit.,* p. 73.

Part III

The Jefferson Hunt Wagon Train

By far the largest party to set out from Salt Lake City for southern California in 1849 was the one led by Jefferson Hunt.

As Captain of Company A of the Mormon Battalion, Hunt had marched along the Santa Fé Trail from the Missouri River to New Mexico and across Arizona to California. After termination of his military service in California he returned to Salt Lake City, traveling the Humboldt River route. In the fall of 1847 he went with the Mormon party to southern California and returned to Utah with stock and seed grain. Having made a round trip over this southern route, and being an experienced western traveler, he was qualified to lead the gold seekers to California.

Jefferson Hunt was born in Bracken County, Kentucky, on January 20, 1803. He accepted the Mormon religion in 1834 and experienced the difficulties of the sect in Missouri and Illinois. After his experiences in the Mexican War and in leading the '49ers to California, Hunt lived in Provo until he joined the company that settled San Bernardino, California. He represented San Bernardino County in the California legislature. Hunt returned with the Mormons to Utah as a result of the Johnston Army episode, and settled at Huntsville (named for him) in Ogden Valley. He died at Oxford, Idaho, in 1879.

As indicated above, in our Historical Background and Summary, Hunt agreed to guide the California emigrants of 1849 for ten dollars per wagon. When all were assembled the caravan included 107 wagons. The number of men and of stock are not accurately reported, but there were over four hundred persons in the train and about one thousand head of horses, mules, and oxen.

The story of the trip in detail is recounted below. Sheldon Young tells of activity prior to the beginning of the trek and reports daily happenings until they reach Beaver Creek. Addison Pratt gives an excellent diary of the entire journey. James S. Brown and Sidney P. Waite's reminiscent accounts give additional information.

A: SHELDON YOUNG'S LOG

[Sheldon Young joined the gold rush in the spring of 1849. He left Joliet, Illinois on March 18, followed the Platte River route and the Mormon Trail, and arrived at Salt Lake City on July 22, 1849. He kept a diary of his entire trip from Illinois to his arrival at Rancho San Francisquito, California, on February 5, 1850.

Although some pages of his journal are missing and others are illegible, his is the most complete and valuable day by day account kept by any member of the party that took the Death Valley route.

Young's diary is not so detailed and satisfactory as some of the others published in this volume, yet it is the best source available for the beginning of the journey southwest from Salt Lake City. The portion of the diary that pertains to the Salt Lake to Los Angeles route ends abruptly on October 23, in the desert a little beyond Beaver River.

Sheldon Young was born in Connecticut on July 23, 1815, and died in Moberly, Missouri, August 18, 1892. His obituary, in the *Moberly Weekly Monitor* of August 25, 1892, gives little biographical data, except to say that he was an old sailor, that his wife died in 1887, that he lived alone but near a stepson during his last years, and that his son from Galesburg, Illinois, attended the funeral.

"Sheldon Young's Log, 1849, Joliet, Illinois to Rancho San Francisquito, California," was obtained by John B. Colton, chief promoter of "The Jayhawkers of 1849" organization, from Sheldon Young's son, Lewis C., in March, 1897. It is now in possession of the Henry E. Huntington Library, by whose kind permission the portion pertaining to our present study is published here.]

[JULY] 25th Packed our load again and left the city [Salt Lake City] on the South Route. Went ten miles and camped on the Cottonwood.[1] Lost one yoke of oxen.

26th Had very good roads. Fell in with a number of wagons bound for the Utah.[2] The Utah is the starting point for the South route. Went fifteen miles to Willow Creek.[3] Had good grass and good water.

27th Went sixteen miles and had a very bad hill to climb.[4] The rest of the road no water for sixteen miles to the American Fork.[5] This stream is full of trout. Five miles from Willow Spring is the boiling spring. The water is very hot, – scalding hot.

28th This day lay in camp. Gritzener [6] went back to the city for oxen. Had some repairing going on. News has arrived from California. Distressing times on the road.[7] A great many were returning to the

[1] This would be Big Cottonwood Creek. Little Cottonwood enters the Jordan River about a mile south of the mouth of Big Cottonwood.

[2] The Utah settlement and Fort Utah, on Provo River, were started in the spring of 1849; now the city of Provo. It was the southernmost Mormon settlement in 1849.

[3] Site of present Draper.

[4] The road went over the mountain ridge dividing the Salt Lake and the Utah valleys. The modern highway now goes around the point of the mountain instead of over the ridge.

[5] The town of American Fork now stands on this stream. The mileage here is sixteen miles, not thirty-two.

[6] This is probably Frederick Gretzinger, of Oscaloosa, Iowa, listed by J. B. Colton in the "Jayhawker Papers" (H. E. Huntington Library) as a member of the Jayhawker party that later went through Death Valley.

[7] This would be on the road west of Salt Lake City, toward the Humboldt River.

Mormon settlement. A great many had lost their teams and were taking it afoot. Some were intending taking the South route.[8]

29th   Had good roads and went twelve miles to the Fort[9] and camped. A very pleasant country. Plenty of grass and water.

30th   (Lay in Camp from July 30 to Oct. 1 '49.)[10] Went to Hobble Creek,[11] the place of starting. An abundance of grass and good water. Weather continues warm and no rain. The intention being to go by the Santa Fe Trail Route,[12] it being too late to go the Northern Route, we were obliged to lay in camp two months waiting for the weather to get cool enough on the Santa Fe Trail Route and did not start until Oct. 1st.

OCT. 1st, 1849.   This day lay in camp. Had a meeting for organizing. Meeting adjourned to move on to Spanish Creek,[13] seven miles from Hobble Creek. Went back to meet

2nd   Went seven miles to Spanish Fork, a stream two rods wide and two feet deep. Went six miles to a small stream and camped.[14] Feed rather dry. Company got together ready for a move.

3rd   Lay in camp all day. Chose our officers. Our officers consisted of one Colonel, one assistant and seven

---

[8] To Los Angeles.

[9] Fort Utah, present Provo.

[10] This sentence is written in, in ink.

[11] Hobble Creek, which runs through present Springville, had been so named by O. P. Huntington when he lost a pair of hobbles on that stream.

[12] He means the Old Spanish Trail route, to Los Angeles.

[13] Spanish Fork Creek, down which the Spanish party of Father Escalante came in 1776. The town of Spanish Fork is now located on the stream. The distance from Hobble Creek is about five miles. Young's mileages are frequently too large.

[14] They called this Election Creek, from the activity here the next day. (See Pratt's diary part III: B, October 6 date). This was later called Peeteetneet Creek, which runs through Payson.

captains of seventy-five wagons. Our company is divided into seven divisions to guard the seven days a week. Snow on the mountains. Chilly winds in the Valley.

4th Left camp at ten o'clock and went eight miles. Camped on a small stream of pure cold water.[15] Very good grass. Captain Hunt, our guide, is in our company. Everything going on right.

5th Went ten miles. Had good roads. Came to a small stream of water and camped. Plenty of grass and willows for fuel. This day left the Utah Valley.[16]

6th This day went fourteen miles and camped on a small stream of good water.[17] Plenty of grass. Had a good road, but rather dusty. No game seen. Pleasant day. Mountains not very high and no snow on them. Plenty of wolves, but no other game.

7th Lay in camp this day. Had preaching waiting for some wagons back. Nothing worthy of notice occurred in camp this day.

8th This day had a very dusty road. The most of the road was descending. Went fifteen miles and camped on a beautiful bottom.[18] A train of packers [19] passed us. Had a pleasant day.

[15] This was doubtless the Creek on which Santaquin is now located.

[16] He has crossed the divide into Juab Valley and is probably encamped on Willow Creek.

[17] This camp apparently was on Salt Creek, near the site of Nephi. Here they lay over the next day, waiting for wagons in the rear. Pratt's wagon caught up with the main camp at Salt Creek on the 8th. Young's mileage estimates in this region are high. He makes it sixty-nine miles from Spanish Fork to the Sevier River; Pratt's rodometer measures it fifty-five miles; the modern state highway map gives it as sixty miles.

[18] This was on Chicken Creek, southwest of Levan. His distance is exaggerated; he makes it thirty-one miles from Salt Creek to the Sevier River; Pratt measures it twenty-four miles; and the modern highway gives it as twenty-six miles.

[19] This was the company of packers discussed in our introduction and in part I above.

9th   Had some rough roads. Went sixteen miles and came to the Sevier [20] (River) and camped. Plenty of Snake Indians about the camp to trade. An old flint-lock gun will fetch a good pony. Pleasant day. Had a shower of rain last night.

10th   Forded the Seviere [sic] and went three miles. It was slow fording and could not get to the next camping place in season, so laid over. We have now one hundred wagons and four hundred men.[21] The Seviere is a stream six rods wide, three feet deep, not very rapid, muddy water, sandy bottom.

11th   Lay in camp on account of two sick men, not being able to travel.

12th   This day went 23¾ miles. Had some rough roads and some pleasant valleys. There was plenty of hares [22] killed today. Found good camping at a large spring.[23] Our train numbers are increased to 106 wagons.[24]

13th   Had good roads, plenty of grass, wood and water, – is cool and chilly. The mountains on each side of us is covered with snow. This day it is snowing all day on the mountains. We are now in a very large valley. There is a quantity of wild flax. Went ten miles.[25]

14th   Lay in camp all day. Discovered the ruins of an ancient city. There was earthenware and glass. It was five miles in extent.[26]

---

20 The old road reached the Sevier River a little north of where U.S. highway 91 now strikes it.

21 C. C. Rich, under October 12 date, says the train consisted of "about one hundred wagons."

22 Commonly called jack rabbits.

23 Cedar Creek, site of Holden. They have passed through Round Valley (Scipio) and over a divide to the large valley northwest of the Pavant Range.

24 The size of the train varied somewhat, as rear wagons caught up, or others dropped behind.

25 Camped on Chalk Creek, site of Fillmore (capital of Utah, 1851-56).

15th   Went 12 miles. Rained in the evening. Beau-ful roads and plenty of grass and water. Eight miles from camp came to quite a stream of water [Meadow Creek] from that to camp, plenty of grass. This is the most pleasant valley that we have passed through.[27]

16th   Had a pleasant day. Found plenty of earthen-ware. Had very good roads considering the country. Passed over two mountains and passed through a small valley between the two mountains. Went twenty-one miles and arrived in Little Salt Lake Valley[28] and camped at a spring. Grass very good.

17th   This day went six miles, crossed a stream of good water, – good camping, then went over a moun-tain, very rough road and crooked. Went twenty-three miles and camped on a small creek. Not much grass but plenty of sage and willows, – Sage Creek.[29]

18th   This day went six miles and came into a beau-tiful valley,[30] plenty of grass and water, camped for the rest of the day. Had fine sport killing mountain hare. Some Indians here.

19th   Concluded to lay in camp all day. There is a stream thirty feet wide, eighteen inches deep, Beaver Creek, plenty of willows for fire. We have pleasant days and cool, frosty nights.

20th   This day lay in camp. Sent out some pioneers to look out a new road.[31] We are 210 miles from the city of Great Salt Lake.

[26] Rich, under October 13 date, says they called it Potters Creek, because of the abundance of broken Indian pottery found there. Religious services were held while they rested for the day (Sunday).

[27] The camp was at Corn Creek, a little northwest of the site of Kanosh.

[28] This is an error; they have not yet reached Little Salt Lake Valley. The camp, shown by the Pratt and Rich diaries, was at present Cove Fort.

[29] This was Wild Cat or Indian Creek, both tributaries of Beaver Creek.

[30] Beaver Creek, which they reached near the site of Greenville, about three miles below the present city of Beaver.

[31] They are scouting a short cut to Antelope Spring, as discussed above in the Historical Background and Summary.

21st   This day followed down the Beaver. Had a hard road, – went twelve miles.[32] Plenty of hare here but poor camping place. Plenty of trout in this stream.

22nd   This day had good roads. Went twelve miles and camped without any water and not much grass.[33]

23rd   We lay in camp all day.[34]

B: ADDISON PRATT'S DIARY

[Addison Pratt was born in Winchester, New Hampshire, February 21, 1802. At the age of twenty he went to sea, sailing around the Horn and to Hawaii. He was on the sea for several years, returning home only for short visits. On one of these, in 1828, he met Louisa Barnes, whom he married on April 3, 1831. After a few more trips he gave up the sea and bought a farm in New York state.

He and his wife were converted to Mormonism in 1837. They moved toward Jackson County, Missouri, and finally settled in Nauvoo, Illinois. Called to go on a Mormon mission to the Society Islands, he left his wife and four children and set sail on a whaler in October, 1843. He was one of the first Mormon missionaries to the Samoan Islands.

Returning from his mission in 1847, he arrived at San Francisco in June. He joined the Mormons who had come to California by ship with Samuel Brannan. Pratt went to the gold diggings in May, 1848, but remained only four days, as scouts eager to return to their families, reported a journey over the Sierras possible. He traveled east to Salt Lake City with members of the Mormon Battalion. Enroute he caught fish for the party. "They gave it as a general opinion," he wrote, "that I could catch a mess of fish if I could only find rain water standing in a cow track."

Upon reaching Salt Lake City on September 28, 1848, he found that his family had just arrived there the week before. After spending

---

32 Camp was just below the canyon, at the site of Minersville.

33 This was the limit of their drive into the Escalante Desert, on the supposed short cut. When Hunt failed to find water ahead, the train turned back to Beaver creek and continued on the known trail.

34 Here is a break in the diary; some leaves are missing. The journal is not resumed until November 10, when Young is with the Jayhawkers on the route towards Death Valley, and hence beyond the scope of this study.

but a year with his wife and children he was again "called," along with some companions, by the Church leaders to go on a second mission to the Pacific Islands. They were to join the Jefferson Hunt train, travel with it to California, and then continue at the first opportunity to the islands.

He reached Tahiti in May, 1850. His wife and four daughters joined him there six months later. The French government drove the Mormons from the islands in 1852. Pratt and his family returned to California. There he later joined the Spiritualists and spent his remaining years in California. He died at Anaheim on October 12, 1872 (biographical data from Andrew Jenson's *Latter-Day Saint Biographical Encyclopedia*, III, 698-99).

Addison Pratt left a biographical sketch and diaries covering many years of his eventful life. These were presented to the Mormon Church by Pratt's granddaughter, Nettie Hunt Rencher, of Snowflake, Arizona. (Pratt's daughter Lois married Jefferson Hunt's son John.) Extracts from these (but not including the 1849 trip) were run serially in the *Improvement Era*, 1949-50, by Mr. Doyle L. Green. Mr. Green generously provided us with a copy, from Pratt's Journal No. 8, of the diary which we publish herewith.

Parts of the diary were previously copied into the Journal History, kept in the Mormon Church Historical Library in Salt Lake City. Portions of this copy were printed in Margaret Long's *The Shadow of the Arrow* (Caldwell, Idaho, 1941,) 140-45, 149-53; but large parts were omitted without indications of the deletions. Much of the value of the journal was thus lost. It is a pleasure to be able to present the diary here in full.]

Brothers Rich, Brown, Blackwell [35] and myself joined company, procured a wagon and three yoke of oxen, as I had been obliged to eat up the most of the cattle I took from California and my funds were low.

[35] C. C. Rich was going on a Mormon mission to California. His diary of the trip is printed in part V:B.

James S. Brown was to go on a mission to the Islands. He had been working at Sutter's Mill in January, 1848, when the historic gold discovery was made there. His biography, *Life of a Pioneer*, is cited above. The pages devoted to this 1849 trip with the Hunt wagon train are reprinted in part III: C.

Hiram H. Blackwell was a missionary being sent to Hawaii.

Bro. Tompkins made me a present of a yoke of oxen to help me through.

THE 2nd OF OCTOBER our wagon being loaded, it was sat at the Council House, which is on the temple block [Salt Lake City], to take our departure as we had a rodameter [36] on our wagon for measuring the distance from place to place. Our oxen were all well shod. Mine were shod by Bro. Lawson. My wife and daughters had accompanied me to this place and were standing there. . . . [incident about a man having tobacco who had promised to quit smoking] We were now ready for a start and my family had come to the conclusion by this time that rather than have me stay there and hear the different reports about my going and staying that I had better be gone at once and they gave me up quite reconciled. Bros. Rich, Brown and Pumroy [37] had horses and as conference was so near[38] they concluded to stop until it was over. Blackwell and myself pushed ahead as fast as possible as the emigrant company had already started and Capt. Hunt was trying to hold them back till we came up. As there were many hindrances, we did not cross the bridge at the East fork of City creek till sunset. (The creek forks at the mouth of the canyon one branch runs on the west and the other on the east side of the city.) We traveled ten miles that night and stopped at Bro. John Brown's on Cottonwood Creek. Here is a large settle-

---

[36] The Mormons had invented such an instrument to measure the distance on the trip of the pioneer band to Salt Lake Valley in 1847. Whether this was the same instrument or another we have not determined.

[37] Francis Martin Pomeroy later went with the Flake-Rich company of packers (see below). A biographical sketch of Pomeroy is given in the *Utah Genealogical and Historical Magazine,* IV, 22-24. He was in the Brigham Young Pioneer Band that went to Salt Lake in 1847. In after years he pioneered at Mesa, Arizona.

[38] The semi-annual conference of the Mormon Church is held each year in early October.

ment of brethren mostly from Mississippi.[39] As one of
our cattle belonging to Bro. Brown had not been
worked for more than a year he was very fat and tend-
erfooted and when we arrived here he was so lame he
could go no further. The next morning Blackwell went
back and told Mr. Brown who came up and traded him
for another. This hindered us two days. When my wife
heard of it she came up on horseback.

The Spring before there had been a fort built in
Utah Valley [Utah Fort, Provo] [40] and about fifty
families had commenced a settlement there and Capt.
Hunt among them. My eldest daughter Ellen had
gone up there with a party to visit and expected us
along in a day or two when she would see me start off
with the emigrants but we had been hindered till they
were on their return. I met them here. In their absence
they had met with an accident and capsized their
carriage. She had received a severe blow upon her
cheek bone and her face was very much colored by it.

After everything was arranged here we moved forward on the 4th at noon, accompanied by my wife and
Bro. Brown. We camped that night on Willow Creek
[Draper] 20 miles from the Council House. Some of
the gold diggers came up and camped with us.

5th   Took leave of my wife and Br. Brown drove
ahead and found a very hard hill to ascend which is a
divide between Utah and Salt Lake Valleys. Here I
expected to see Blackwell throw away his tobacco

---

39 These Mississippi Saints, having come west in 1846, ahead of Brigham
Young's "Pioneer Band," had wintered at Pueblo, Colorado, 1846-47, and
the next spring came on to Utah. John Brown was leader of this group.
See his *Autobiography of a Pioneer, John Brown, 1820-1896* (Salt Lake City,
privately printed, 1941).

40 Places that have been identified in the preceding diary of Sheldon
Young, will not be mentioned again in the footnotes, but modern location
will occasionally be inserted in brackets in the text.

according to his promise but he did not. Proceeding down the divide we came in sight of Utah Lake. This is a beautiful sheet of water some forty miles long and lies in a sort of triangle. It is surrounded by a large valley covered with a heavy growth of grass. About noon we crossed the American river [American Fork] and at night crossed the Provo river, on this stands the Utah Fort. Here we found Capt Hunt who had left his company and came back to hurry us very kindly. This fort is 46 miles from the Council House.

6th   Started ahead with Bro. Hunt but he being on horse soon left us, and at noon crossed Hobble Creek [Springville] and towards evening crossed Spanish Creek [Spanish Fork], and at night overtook and camped with a part of the company on Election Creek [Payson]. The main part of the company had gone ahead had organized and elected their officers on this creek and gave it this name.

7th   Started early in the morning and left the rest in camp. All the streams that I have mentioned since crossing the divide have a swift current and discharge the waters into Utah River [Lake] and will all afford excellent mill seats [sites] and in the summer are full of trout and suckers but the first night we stayed at Bro. Browns there was a snow storm that drove all the fish into Utah Lake. There are 3 gristmills and 4 sawmills in Salt Lake Valley. There is perpetual snow in sight of the city which causes cold nights. We had frosts on my garden every month I stayed there.

At noon stopped to bate our cattle near some of those deep wells when one of our oxen fell in and would have drowned had we not taken another yoke of cattle and drawn him out.[41] At night overtook another portion

---

[41] Probably at or near Spring Lake.

of the company on Willow Creek [42] and camped with them, traveled today 17 miles.

8th   Traveled 8 miles and overtook the main body of the camp about 100 wagons on Salt Creek [Nephi]. Near here is a mountain of salt.

9th   Started in a body this morning with Capt. Hunt as our head pilot. The body was organized with a Colonel, Adjutant and a Captain to every 10 wagons. Traveled today 24 miles and camped on the Sevier River.

10th   Traveled 2 miles. Crossed the river and went into camp on account of some sickness. Stayed in camp one day while on this river. Some Indians [43] came and sold the camp some horses for rifles. While in camp here I had some opportunity of exploring around the country which is a barren waste covered with sage brush save the river bottoms which are covered with grass, on the hills were a few dwarfish cedars. This is the largest stream between California and Salt Lake City. It discharges its waters into a dead lake of the same name and has the appearance of affording plenty of fish at certain seasons of the year. I saw some signs of beaver on its banks.[44] While here, Bro. Rich and Brown and Pumroy overtook us.[45] I received letters from home by them stating that my family were all well. They brought with them three horses and a mule. Now all but the teamster had an animal to ride. This made it easier for us.

12th   We continued our journey past through what we called Rabbit Hollow [Scipio Valley], up to this

---

[42] In Juab Valley, a little north of Mona.

[43] These were Utes. Famous Chief Wakara dominated this territory.

[44] The Sevier River country had been trapped for beaver ever since Jedediah Smith's visit to it in 1826.

[45] They had remained in Salt Lake City for the Conference and then had hurried along on horseback.

time I had shot no wild animals as the emigration was
ahead of us and they drove everything off the road.
The hares were so plentiful here that the ground would
well compare with a sheep pasture and notwithstanding the signs were so great there were none of these
animals in sight. As the valley was covered with grass
except the farther side, there was plenty of sage brush
and when we entered that the hares commenced in
every direction and about 200 gunners were soon on
the alert and rifles were popping and balls whizzing
in every direction. Bro. Rich and myself stationed
ourselves to one side and soon shot five. We then had
a mountain to ascend and descend and it took us till
late in the evening to reach a camping place as water
was scarce. We camped on Cedar Creek [Holden].
Here was plenty of dry cedar wood. Dressed and
cooked the game which made a feast for all hands.
We had by this time increased our mess. I had no
acquaintance among the gold diggers in particular
but Blackwell found a cousin named Mastin among
a company of wagons from Mississippi, and as ours
had to be put in a company, we chose that one. Town[46]
was the captains name, in our company. We found them
to be a kind hearted obliging company of men to travel
with and we very often messed with them, especially
with Mastins wagon and one other named Martin.[47]

13th   Traveled but six miles today and camped on
a fine stream [Chalk creek, Fillmore], a tributary of
the Sevier. This morning as the camp started off the
hunters surrounded a large sagebrush where a large

[46] Captain Town, or Towne, also of the Death Valley party. See Long,
op. cit., pp. 125, 126, 168, 204.

[47] This may have been Jim Martin of Mississippi, subsequent leader of
one of the Death Valley parties. See Margaret Long, The Shadow of the
Arrow, pp. 122, 123, 171, 180, 183, 258, 273. There was also a John D.
Martin from Texas, in the Death Valley list of Dr. Long. op. cit., p. 293.

number of hare had hid themselves. The dogs soon started them when the rifle balls began to fly in every direction so plentiful that I was afraid to go among them so passed on. The company killed about one hundred hares, besides some sage hens. This stream would sustain a small settlement. The bottoms are covered with dwarf cedars. On the headwaters of this stream are a tribe of Indians called Parraances.[48] We spent the 14th here as it was Sunday. This gave me some time to stroll around and over this plain in every direction are specimen of broken pottery exhibiting much ingenuity in its carving and coloring, showing that the makers possessed much mechanical genius.

15th Traveled 12 miles and camped on Willow Flats [near Kanosh] here are low praries covered with immense quantities of grass. Hares continue to be plentiful. I kill some every day till our mess is getting tired of them. There was a company of 50 wagons broke off from Capt. Hunt at Utah Valley and went ahead under the convoy of a vagrant Spaniard [49] and they reported to have found immense quantities of silver ore near this place, tho it was unobserved by us.

16th Passed over some beautiful rich bottoms covered with green grass which is uncommon at this season of the year on this route. Passed over a high divide into a beautiful round valley [Cove Fort]. I shot the largest hare in this valley I have ever seen. 23 miles today.

17th A hard days travel. The roads very dusty distance 22 miles and camped in the night on Sage Creek [Wild Cat or Indian Creek], a muddy stream

---

48 Pahvans, according to the Journal History rendering of the diary.

49 The Gruwell-Derr party. Peter Derr (*see* part II) says there were 23 wagons in their train. The identity of the Spanish or Mexican guide has not been determined.

and but little grass. This is a tributary of Beaver Creek, as it had high banks on each side and the cattle were troubled in getting a drink.

18th Traveled five miles and camped on Beaver Creek [about three miles below present Beaver]. This is a fine stream. Has wide bottoms on each side covered with good grass. Stayed here two days. The camp had now all come up, about 125 wagons and about 1,000 head of cattle. Among the gold diggers was Bro. Emmet and his daughter, Lucindy, a girl of about 17 years. I think this creek would support a settlement of some thousand. The creek had the appearance of affording an abundance of trout in the summer but there were very few in it at this time. I caught one of about 2 lbs. weight. There were a lot of hares and sage hens in the brush on each side. This creek discharges its waters in to Sevier Lake [50] and a range of mountains separates us from the little Salt Lake. As we came onto this creek we saw some of the wagons that had gone ahead of us high up the mountains.[51] To avoid the mountain some pioneers were sent out to search a path through a canyon on this creek into a valley below. They returned and reported it to be passable. When it was concluded to try to find a pass through a dry plain there was below the canyon and on the South side of the creek, that was supposed to strike the Spanish trail that came through the little Salt Lake valley leading from Santa Fe to Pueblo de los Angeles.[52] This route has been traveled by pack companies

[50] Beaver Creek turns north and flows toward Sevier Lake, but loses its waters in the desert. The Beaver Mountains separate the stream from the lake.

[51] This was doubtless the Gruwell-Derr train, following the regular trail toward Little Salt Lake Valley.

[52] The Old Spanish Trail came from the upper Sevier River, crossed the mountains, and entered Little Salt Lake Valley near the site of Paragonah.

ever since lower California was first settled [53] and it is strewed all the way with horse bones that have died of fatigue, thirst, abuse, starvation and some killed by the Indians.

21st Started down the [Beaver] creek. The hunters ranged along the road through the sagebrush. I shot five hares to my share and gave them, two to my friend Lorton and three to some French and Germans that were short of provisions and they were very thankfully received. Passed through the canyon and camped 12 miles from where we started on the creek. Here was an old beaver dam with some trout in the pond.[54]

22nd Went 12 miles and camped without water as the road was very dusty, the weather warm, and the cattle began to suffer with thirst. Many wagons had not taken water with them for their own use and when they began to suffer and their cattle also, a great dissatisfaction prevailed and many of them tried to blame Capt. Hunt who was not in the least the instigator of the move. The wagons stopped here and the cattle were driven back to the creek where they found a Capt. Smith with a company of packers and had maps and charts that described a cut off called Walkers pass that was a much nearer route than the one we were going and no dry deserts to pass through, but grass and water all the way.[55] Many of our company were panic stricken with the idea of going that way so left us without consulting the officers in the least. A general commotion was visible or rather a rebellion. Slurs

[53] The attempt to open this trail was made in 1776, soon after Upper California was settled. But it did not become a regularly traveled route until 1830. See Hafen and Hafen, *Old Spanish Trail* (Glendale, California, 1954).

[54] The camp would be at present Minersville.

[55] Captain O. K. Smith's company had just caught up with the wagon train. Smith's information and the supposed short cut to the California mines are discussed above, in the Historical Summary.

were frequently thrown out about the Mormons and some even went so far as to threaten Capt. Hunt's life if they did not get through safely and the greatest unreasonableness was shown by them.[56]

Bro. Hunt began to feel that his case was very uncertain among them as they expressed themselves determined to blame him for every mishap even when it was a matter that did not concern him at all. In company with Capt. Smith was a party of brethren from Salt Lake City [57] on their way to the mines and they invited Bros. Rich and Pomroy to accompany them which they readily agreed to, but were not to leave us till we had passed little Salt Lake. As some of the companies had already left us the balance thought it best to turn back and go over the mountain to Little Salt Lake.

24th Turned back and camped again on Beaver River. Here we found the brethren and a Brother Phelps handed me a letter from my family. They were all well.

25th Went up to the head of the canyon and camped. Here the rocks form sort of a dam across the creek and the water above is deep and the water runs slow. It was the company's day to watch the cattle that I belonged [to] and I was busy but those that had time to fish caught some beautiful trout. Some of them weighed about five pounds.

26th Left Beaver creek and traveled up the mountain and camped without water for the cattle.[58] Plenty

[56] Hunt's part in the abortive attempt to find a short cut from Beaver Creek to Antelope Springs is also described in the introductory Summary.

[57] This was the Captain Flake company of Mormons, whose journey is detailed in diaries published below (*see* part v).

[58] Rich's diary says they traveled eight miles on the 26th, and twenty-one on the 27th. The first camp would be near the summit of the pass.

of firewood and dry cedars but not much grass for the cattle.

27th Drove 27 miles and camped on the first creek in the Little Salt Lake Valley.[59] This is a large valley and affords lots of grass but there is not enough water to accommodate a large settlement. The lake is about 12 miles long and the water appears to be more impregnated with salaratus than salt. There are plenty of wild geese and ducks about it and in the bottom is plenty of hares and sage hens. The mountains on the east side are very high and well timbered with cedar and pine. Some Indians came to us and appeared quite friendly.

28th Traveled 6 miles and camped on 2nd Creek.[60] Here Bros. Rich and Pomroy left us. Bro. Rich talked with Bro. Blackwell as he had seen a great many things in his conduct that did not please him. He had not yet come up to his covenant about tobacco as he had so many times agreed to do tho I had often reminded him of it. But he told Bro. Rich at this place that he had given up his tobacco and should use no more of it.

29th Camped on 3rd Creek [61] and stayed 2 days. Here our camp split again and a part left us. Our Colonel, Baxter was his name, left with them. Here Bro. Hunt came to me and told me that his life was at stake as there was a party that intended to kill him if their cattle died in crossing the deserts and he thought there was but one way to escape and that was to have the company voluntarily take the intended cut off and

---

[59] The twenty-seven miles was the distance from Beaver Creek to the first creek. *See* the Mormon Way-Bill table in the Appendix. In that list the stream is called North Kanyon Creek, probably Buckhorn Spring of today.

[60] Little Creek and Red Creek (by Paragonah) join before flowing into Little Salt Lake.

[61] Center Creek, that runs through present Parowan.

leave a few wagons of us to go where we were of a mind to. He wished me and all the brethren to ask the Lord for his delivery. We told him we would.

31st Traveled 13 miles and camped on a stream called the "Little Muddy." [62] This runs into the desert and sinks. There is cottonwood timber on this creek and signs of deer but we did not see any.

1st Nov Went to cedar springs and camped.[63] In the night we had quite a snow storm but it melted off by daylight. Near the spring is a great deal of iron ore.

2nd Traveled 11 miles and camped at a spring [64] on the mountain side. The spring oozes out of the ground and makes a large stream which, after running a few rods, sinks back into the ground.

3rd Traveled 11 miles and camped on Piute Creek.[65] Some Indians came to us and appeared friendly. Gave them some clothing. Here I caught Bro. Blackwell smoking. I determined to say nothing more about it but leave him in California. As we expected to come to the divide tomorrow, a meeting of all hands was called and a general feeling on the subject of taking the cut off was called for. We had in company several preachers of different churches and among them was one Brior [J. W. Brier]. He was a Methodist. He was a fellow that liked to give his opinion on every subject and this was a time of importance with him. When the crowd came together he was called on to make the first speech. He accepted and took the oppor-

---

62 Coal Creek. They crossed it about six miles north of Cedar City.

63 Iron Springs of today.

64 Antelope Spring, shown on the St. George sheet, U.S.G.S. quadrangle map. It is near the northern point of Iron Mountain. The entry of November 2nd is omitted from the typed copy of the diary supplied to us; so we reproduce the day's record as given in Dr. Long's book, *op. cit.*, p. 142.

65 This is now called Pinto Creek, probably a misinterpretation of the spelling of Piute. The creek runs through present Newcastle.

tunity to fire the minds of the people with a zeal for the cut off and closed by saying that the road across the deserts they know to be a bad one but they did not know what the road on the cut off was but hoped it was a good one and go it he should sink or swim, live or die, he should take the cut off "go it boots." Then others were called out and made similar speeches. Then Capt. Hunt was loudly called for. When he came out and asked what they wanted of him they told him to tell something about the cut off. He told them he had never been the cut off, nor had never seen anybody that had been it, therefore, he could tell nothing about it. They then took a vote to see how many would go the cut off. Nearly all of them voted in favour of it to the great satisfaction of Capt. Hunt. He came to me a little before the meeting and now said he, "It is a time of vast importance to me, and let us put up our united prayers to the Lord for my delivery," and when the meeting was over he expressed great satisfaction at their decision and hoped they would hold to it.

4th SUNDAY. Started ahead about noon. Came to the divide or the rim of the interior basin of California.[66] This includes nearly 1800 miles of unexplored country. It extends westward from this mountain we are now on, to the Sierra Nevada range and all the rivers and lakes within its borders either sink in the sand or are exhausted by evaporation. None of them go to the ocean. The mountain we are now crossing is called the Wasatch and extends to the great Salt Lake and how far from here I know not. Here the road forks [67] and the cut off takes along the side of this

[66] J. C. Fremont was the first to describe the geography of this interior region and to name it the Great Basin. Pratt is not yet at the rim of the Basin.

[67] The forks of the routes were about seven miles southwest of Newcastle, according to the St. George Sheet, U.S.G.S.

range. But the old Spanish trail crosses south. Here the wagons began to file off on the cut off till they left but 7 to go the old trail. We were now just in the edge of the Piute country and they are said to be a warlike race. After we had divided into two companies, each company stopped to bid the other adieu and as we began to give each other the parting hand, Bro. Hunt put on a very long face as if he were about to shed tears. I could not but smile at his sad looks when our wagons started off and left him with a party that still urged him but he told them that his contract was to pilot them across the desert and as long as there was one wagon that wished to go that way he was obliged to go with them, and notwithstanding some had threatened his life, I could see in many of them a strong attachment for him. Not long after he came on and over took us I laughed at him a little for his crocodile tears. "Ah," said he, "It was policy for me to affect something before them for many of them have treated me very kindly and I would to God I could get them out of the trouble they are now going into. They cannot get through with their wagons that way and I hardly think Bro. Rich with the horsemen can, but they stand by far the best chance, but I told Bro. Rich if he found mountains that they could not pass to be sure to slide back into this trail quick as possible and come on and overtake us. "This," continued he," is the happiest day of my life. I cannot recollect the time when I made so lucky an escape from death before as I have in getting rid of this company.[68] There is a certain set of mobocratic spirits among them that were determined to take my life before we should get through the deserts. Now we will travel on fast as possible and get out of

---

[68] Pratt gives a new and important interpretation of Captain Hunt's position and attitude.

their way for they will soon be coming on after us when their cattle begin to die for there is neither grass nor water that way." Traveled about 9 miles and camped on a small stream of cold water that goes a little way in the basin and sinks.[69] At night snow fell about 3 inches deep.

5th   Followed up the river to its source which is a number of large springs in a beautiful valley covered with a dense growth of good grass. Before noon the snow had all disappeared except on the mountain tops. Passed on to the head of the rim [70] camped without water for our cattle, we had enough in kegs for our own use. Distance today 12 miles. Here are plenty of scrub oaks that bear an abundance of very nice acorns. Dwarf cedars are scattered about this region.

6th   Began to descend the rim of the great basin toward the great valley of the Colorado River that discharges its waters at the head of the Gulf of California. Traveled 11 miles over a rough country and camped on a stream called the Santa Clara,[71] a tributary of the Virgin River. Here I saw the first California quail that I have seen east of the Sierra Nevada. These are a beautiful spritely bird whose flesh is well flavored. Here are found corn fields, the first signs of cultivation I have seen by the Indians and from various signs we saw they are very plentiful in this region.[72]

[69] Meadow Creek, that flows from the north end of Mountain Meadows.

[70] Famous Mountain Meadows straddles the rim of the Great Basin. The lush meadow grass extending for about eight miles, made this a favorite resting place for the early trader caravans on the Old Spanish Trail. Here in September, 1857, was to occur the terrible Mountain Meadows Massacre of 157 men and women; see Juanita Brooks, *The Mountain Meadows Massacre* (Stanford, California, Stanford University Press, 1950).

[71] The road descended the Santa Clara's Magotsa fork, which heads in the Mountain Meadows.

[72] There were several Indian farms scattered along Santa Clara Creek. The Shivwits still have a small reservation there.

7th   Continued down the stream. Saw inscribed on a tree by the company that was ahead of us that they had shot an Indian for stealing some of their oxen and warned us to be on the look out for them for they expected we should be attacked by them.[73] A few minutes later we saw plenty of fresh tracks in the sand made by a party that had crossed the road a little ahead of us and as the trees and grass and shrubs were thick on each side of the road we expected an attack and prepared for it but we passed along unmolested. At noon we left Santa Clara proceeding up the mountains. We camped at Sulphur Springs.[74] Distance today, 9 miles.

9th   Left Sulphur springs about 10 o'clock in the morning and continued an ascending road till we got among the mountain peaks.[75] Here our road led through a serpentine canyon which looked to me as if nature had left it on purpose for a road. It is a romantic looking place with perpendicular precipices on either side, when we came out into a sort of slope or valley with mountain grass. This grows in bunches and notwithstanding it is yellow and dry it bears large seeds that are nearly equal to oats for cattle and horses. This is seven miles from Sulphur Springs and on the divide between Santa Clara and Virgin River.[76] Here we camped without water. This is a very barren country. Wolves [coyotes] seemed to be the only animals.

10th   Began to descend a very rough canyon. The rocks are flinty and sharp at its mouth. We could see

[73] For Derr's account of the incident, *see* part II: A.

[74] The Mormon Way-bill and later travelers called it Camp Spring. It is located one and a half miles from the point where the road left the Santa Clara.

[75] The road re-enters the route of U.S. highway 91 and is to follow it rather closely as far as Las Vegas, Nevada.

[76] They are crossing Beaver Dam Mountains, on a route used since Jed Smith's second trip to California, that of 1827.

the line of the Virgin 10 miles off, winding its way through a high dry desert dotted here and there with bunches of grease brush.[77] This is something like a shrub that underbrushes much of the woodland in the state of Indiana, and is called spice brush. It derived its name from a greasy substance that fries out of it while it is burning. There is a solitary looking vegetable of the prickly pear order, called prickly pine,[78] scattered all over these deserts, growing from 3 to 30 feet high, some grew in a columnar shape, and these we would often mistake for Indians, others would branch out and on the extremity of each is a bunch of leaves or spines, each having a very sharp point. I think I haven't seen any place between Salt Lake and the Virgin that exhibits such strong signs of gold as the mouth of this canyon, but as we were out of water and our horses had not drunk since the day before we had not time to prospect for it.[79] Those of us who have horses to ride made our way as fast to the Virgin as possible. On our right we could see the dry bed of a stream [80] coursing toward the Virgin. It was nearly in the direction that we were going. A mile or two before us lay the Virgin. We stopped where there was a grove of cottonwood and willow. Some large springs were some fifty yards from the river. They formed quite a stream that ran down through a deep mud flat and near

[77] Creosote, an evergreen, with leaves that appear varnished. This shrub is first encountered here, but is dominant throughout the desert country extending to Cajon Pass.

[78] The joshua tree, also common on the higher elevations through the desert.

[79] At a later date a spring was found one and one-half miles off the road to the north. In our youth this spring was resorted to on our numerous wagon trips over this route. No gold has been found in this region, but the Apex Copper Mine, a few miles to the east, was worked for some years after 1900.

[80] Beaver Dam Wash, the upper course of which the Smith and Flake-Rich companies of packers were threading.

the river. Bro. Hunt showed me where there was a
beaver dam across it when he was there before but the
heavy rains last winter raised the dam and the beavers
had left it.[81] I saw a number of stumps of cottonwood
trees that had been cut down by the beavers. They were
from 8 to 12 inches in diameter. Their manner is to
take a calf like a wood chopper and cut in on both sides
with a slant, pull out the chips with their teeth and
leave a very handsome stump. They work around the
tree, leaving it highest at the heart. The bed of the
river Virgin is some twenty rods wide and perpendicular banks on each side, in some places a hundred feet
high, composed of pebble stone rocks and among these
rocks lived a multitude of little timid rabbits called
conies [cottontails] and I believe they keep the best
lookout for enemies of any wild animal I ever tried to
shoot.

The stream of the Virgin at this season of the year
is low and winds its way along a sandy bed some 10
rods wide, and on either side are bottoms covered with
saltpeter grass [salt grass] and affords tolerable feed
for the cattle. I could find no fish but very small ones
in this stream though I think there must be plenty in
it in the spring of the year. We had to drive our cattle
across the river at this place to get feed as there had
been camps that had eaten the grass off on this side.

[The entries of November 11 to 14 are missing from the copy
supplied us by Mr. Green, so we insert the entries for the four days
as copied in the Journal History of October 8, 1849.]

SUNDAY, NOV. 11   We crossed the dry bed of the
stream above the springs and traveled down the river

81 This place is called Beaver Dams, currently a resort nestled beneath
the cottonwood trees beside the fresh spring water.

on the desert which is high and dry, covered with hard gravel. After traveling about 5 miles, we descended a steep slope into the river bottom;[82] traveled about six miles further and camped.[83]

MONDAY, NOV. 12   We traveled down the river 14 miles and forded it six times.[84]

TUESDAY, NOV. 13   In the morning we were visited by men belonging to the [Gruwell-Derr] company traveling ahead of us; they were hunting cattle which had been stolen by the Indians. When they left us, going ahead, we followed them, and before noon we met a cow with an Indian's arrow sticking in her thigh. We extracted the arrow, but the flint with which it was pointed still remained in the flesh, and so we made an incision with a knife large enough to admit the finger and took it out. We then took the animal along with us. When we approached, we saw an Indian driving the cow, but as he espied us, he dodged behind the willows, which grew thick on either side of the road. At first, the poor cow was so badly frightened that we could not get near her; but when she saw that we were white men, she became perfectly gentle and stood still while we cut out the arrow. We traveled 8 miles, when we went into camp as some of the cattle were getting worn out; one cow gave entirely out, and several of our animals are becoming very weak and thin, and yet the most of the journey is yet before us.

WEDNESDAY, NOV. 14   We continued our journey

---

[82] U.S. 91 follows the same course about five miles over the elevated flat bench on the north side of the Virgin. The descent to the river used to be on a steep grade down "Big Bend Hill"; the present highway has cut a straighter and easier grade.

[83] They were near the Arizona-Nevada state line, and about three miles above the site of the town of Mesquite.

[84] They are about five miles below the site of Bunkerville. The quicksand in the river always made the crossings difficult and dangerous.

down the river and before noon we came to a canyon
through which the road leads away from the Virgin.
As there was neither grass nor water between this point
and the next stream called the Muddy, we stopped and
turned our animals out to graze. We were visited by a
severe squall of rain and wind, and Brother James S.
Brown and I, who guarded the cattle on that day,
sought shelter in a cave. In continuing our journey up
the canyon, we overtook Mr. Dallas, the owner of the
cow we had found. He also owned seven wagons who
had gone on ahead to the Muddy; he hailed from
Galena and was on his way to the California gold mines
with men and means and his family. The road in the
canyon was very sandy, which made the pulling very
hard on our weak cattle. In the evening we came to a
steep hill [85] which we had to ascend in order to reach
the bench land above. This hill is about two hundred
yards long and rises with a circular sweep near the top
it is rocky and nearly perpendicular. We drove as far
up as our teams were able to pull the wagons, when we
blocked the wheels of each wagon and put ten or
twelve yoke of oxen on the forward vehicle, and thus
we got up with much difficulty; it was so steep near
the top that an ox could barely stand without pulling
at all. Mr. Dallas told us that he had chains enough
with his teams on the Muddy to reach down the hill
from the top and hook onto the wagons below, in which
case the cattle pulling on the top of the hill could
draw them up. But we knew that our cattle could not
stand it long without grass and water. By the use of
a coil of 2-inch rope found in one of the wagons and
all of our lighter chains, we managed to pull all our

---

[85] Virgin Hill, very difficult to negotiate. The modern highway climbs
by a gradual ascent near the same place. The road left the river near the
location of the highway bridge at Riverside.

wagons up. Mr. Dallas told us that a wagon belonging
to a doctor in the company ahead had gotten nearly
to the top when a chain broke and the wagon, with
almost lightning speed, ran to the bottom of the hill
where it was smashed to pieces, and the things with
which it was loaded destroyed. It had taken Dallas
and his men two days to get up the hill; but we were
all up by 3 o'clock in the morning. We camped on top
of the hill till daylight, nine miles from the Virgin.

NOVEMBER 15, 1849   At daylight, we hitched up
our teams and drove ahead three miles, where we
unexpectedly found some bunch grass, here we stopped
an hour and hunted our cattle, the cows that belonged
to Mr. Dallas, and the one belonging to Mr. Sowder-
wager were left in the canyon, as they were so feeble
that they could not get them up the hill. The rain that
fell the day before had moistened the grass so that the
cattle ate very readily without water, after they had
eaten we started over the fourteen mile desert that lies
between the head of the canyon and the Far muddy
creek, and arrived there a little after noon,[86] this desert
is hard gravel and good traveling, here we found
Dallas'es wagons, and about a dozen others of that
company that followed the Spanyards [87] we also found
among them a yoke of oxen that they had taken in Salt
Lake Valley, from Chancy West, they had been
quarreling about the cattle and by that means we soon
found out the whole matter. We stayed here the next
day. This creek is fed by warm springs [88] and the water
is warm and pleasant to bath in this time of year, I
found some fish in the creek much resembling a well

---

[86] They reached the Muddy about three miles below present Glendale and
the highway bridge.

[87] The Gruwell-Derr wagon train.

[88] The large springs, source of Muddy Creek, are about eight miles
northwest of Glendale.

known fish in the rivers of New England, called carp.
They bite readily at a hook, the largest of them weighing near a pound. As I saw lumps on some of their
sides, I cut them open and found them sacks, containing
a sort of wireworm.

17th   Moved up the creek three miles and went into
camp again, as we had a fifty mile desert to cross when
we left here, we thought it best to recruit our teams as
there is plenty of grass here; on the morning of the
18th I was out in pursuit of some ducks that frequented
a pool there was in some grass, as I was creeping
through the grass I espied Bro. Rich and Brown, on
the side of the pool, they discovered me at the same
time, and Bro. Rich called out, at the top of his voice
"good morning Bro. Pratt" at the sound of the voice
the ducks arose out of the water and flew toward me
and as I returned the salute and said, "good morning
Bro. Rich" I at the same time discharged my fowling
piece at the ducks, where two fell from the flock, and
Bro. Rich often laughed at me afterwards about the
oddity of the occurrence. Bro. Rich had just before
arrived in camp with his company of packers from the
mountains and reported great distress among the
wagons that had taken the cut off.[89]

He tried to have Captain Smith return with him,
but he was determined to find a road through to California, or die in the attempt.

We are all very much rejoiced to see Bro. Rich and
his company of "Mormon Boys," they have had very
hard times in the mountains, had lost some of their
animals and expended nearly all of the provisions, and
as he and Bro. Hunt had the authority from the Church

[89] The experiences of these packers who attempted the short cut to the
mines are given in the diaries of H. W. Bigler, C. C. Rich, William Farrer,
and the reminiscent account of George Q. Cannon; (*see* part v).

to transact all business for the church, and the people of Salt Lake valley, that come within their reach, and they laid their authority before those men that had the cattle, at first they were quite unwilling to give them up afterwards consented to do so, and they sold the cattle to Dallas for provisions to fit out Bro. Rich's company to cross the deserts into California. Some Indians came to us while on this creek, and appeared quite friendly, said they belonged to the Panvances and were at war with the Piutes which are the owners of this country here, many of them could talk Spanish, and when they found that several men in our company could speak it, they avoided conversation with us as much as possible, when we concluded they were mission Indians. Some of them that had run away from California, and were now on their way there to steal horses. As Bro. Rich and company came down the creek, they told us that there was fine fields of wheat, corn and beans, above us that belonged to the Indians they irrigated their lands from this stream, and their field had the appearance of bearing very heavy crops.[90]

As we had such a long desert to cross it was thought best to travel in the night so that our cattle would not suffer so much thirst as they would in the daytime. Consequently we had everything arranged and on the 20th at noon we left the creek and started up a canyon [California Wash] that led us out into the desert, on one side of this is a sort of barrier prepared by the Indians, and from this they attacked a pack company, that was the first that passed here this fall.[91] The first part of our road was sandy, after that it was good, at two o'clock in the morning we had traveled twenty-two

[90] Descendants of these Indians are still farming in the same place, on the Moapa Indian reservation.

[91] This apparently was the company of packers discussed in part I.

miles, a little off of the road, at this place we unexpectedly found a little grass and water,[92] the last rains
we found would facilitate our crossing deserts very
much.

21st   At ten o'clock in the morning we started ahead
again, and at ten in the evening the wagons reached
Vegas Creek, this rises from some large springs and
runs down through a large valley, covered with immense quantities of good grass.[93] This would support
a great number of cattle, and the soil appears to be
very rich. As I went ahead with the horsemen we
reached there about sunset, and before coming on to
the edge of the grass we passed over a wide mud flat
covered with meskeet trees, the largest I had seen.

We had seen no horses for several days, and as our
provisions were getting low, it was our object to get
all the wild game we could, and as we were stringing
in a line, I heard someone ahead cry out "A hare." I
looked ahead and saw a hare at the top of his speed
coming nearly in a parallel line with the road, those
on ahead shot as he passed, but he escaped unhurt
until he came on a line with me, when I gave him a
shot that keeled him over. We went into a camp and
soon had him roasted, and as Bro. Rich, Hunt, and
myself were picking his bones, "This," said Bro.
Hunt," is a sort of God send, for the wagons will not
be up with us until midnight and we could get nothing
to eat until they came," but they did arrive about ten
o'clock, when we got supper. This place is about 450
miles from the Council house at Salt Lake City.[94]

92 About midway between Crystal and Dry Lake.

93 *Las Vegas* (Spanish for meadow) was an important way station in the
desert. The large meadow was fed by a creek that rose from springs to the
west. The Mormons started an Indian mission and colony here in 1855. Part
of their fort (now a museum) stands in the modern city of Las Vegas.

94 The distance by modern highway is now 448 miles.

22nd   Traveled six miles and camped on the head of the Vegas. Here we began to see the sacrifices of property made by those that were on ahead of us, they [Gruwell-Derr Company] had camped here, and lightened their wagons of clothing and feather beds, there were piles of goose feathers and down lying in heaps, as if it had got to be troublesome times with them. The head of this stream is a curiosity, we found the water running in tolerable streams, from several of those wells [springs] that I have heretofore described, and were filled with[in] six or eight feet of the surface with quicksand and this was kept in perpetual motion,[95] caused by the sand settling back into the channel and stopping the water until it had gathered force enough to burst its way through the sand, and as the water did not come to the surface at the same point, at such time, it kept the sand continually rolling and shifting from side to side in grand commotion. In one of them there were some lumps of hard load about the size of turtles and as they were lighter than the sand they were kept diving about in it until we thought they had life and could not be satisfied until we got one out.

23rd   Traveled over dry hard desert, and the road a little ascending, and the ground covered with stones from the size of gravel to that of a man's head, they were covered with sharp points and corners, are very hard black and shining and I think are what are called pyrites. This is the worst days travel we have had for our cattle's feet, those that are barefooted cripple very much. Traveled fifteen miles and come into the dry bed of a stream, that had some cottonwood trees on it,

[95] These springs are all boxed over and utilized — along with drilled wells — for the culinary supply of Las Vegas. In one of the headhouses a person may still see the sand continually boiling up in this spring.

followed it up until we came to a spring,[96] but the grass around it had been eaten up, by those who had preceded us, here we found the head and horns of a large mountain sheep, that had been killed by them. This is a mountainous romantic looking place.

24th   Went ahead three miles and found plenty of grass and water, here we camped and as Bro. Emmet had a blacksmith bellows and some tools along we went about shoeing the barefooted cattle, the grass at this place is dry and yellow, but our cattle filled themselves.

25th   Passed through a canion, and on the right hand there are high mountains of solid rock,[97] there is one, that as near as my memory serves me, looks about the size and shape of the rock of giberalter.[98] Traveled ten miles and camped at Cedar springs,[99] this is right among the Cedar hills and pretty high land, there are some small springs that come out of the hills, and rather poor water, it runs a little way and sinks. Grass is scarce here, we saw some large kilns, where the Indians burn their pottery wares, as these hills are clayey, and from the number and size of their kilns [100] I expect the business is carried on at times with some energy.

---

96 Cottonwood Springs, at present Blue Diamond village. This little town, which houses workers of the nearby gypsum mine and plaster mill, utilizes the water of the springs. The road has come west from Las Vegas on a route considerably north of U.S. highway 91. The '49ers' road did not reach U.S. highway 91 again until it came to the Mojave River.

97 This is the sharp escarpment of the Charleston Mountains, and is very impressive with its height, mass, and variegated colors. See the Las Vegas quadrangle, U.S.G.S. The large ranch at the mountain base is the old Wilson ranch.

98 Pratt, as noted above, had sailed the seas for a number of years. The massive rock he refers to is probably the unusual one just west of the Wilson ranch.

99 Mountain Springs, just over the divide on the west side. We used a jeep to get to this location in 1951, but a new road on this route is projected.

100 We were informed by a 76-year-old Indian at Wilson's ranch in 1951 that these pits were used by the Indians, not as pottery kilns, but for roast-

26th Began to descend the mountains, and before noon got into a large open desert [Pahrump valley], as the road is good and a little descending with all and the weather cool we traveled at a good rate. I went ahead with the horsemen with Bro. Brown's horse, the animals had got so poor that we had to walk most of the way. Bro. Brown's horse got his back so badly galled at Beaver Creek that he had not been fit to ride much since, and I had lead him the most of the way while Bro. James [Brown] and Hyrum [Blackwell] drove the team, his back is now well. Toward evening we came to a dry bed of a creek with one or two large willow trees on it and some water standing in holes,[101] we startled some hares here and I shot one. We left the wagon track here and kept to the right and in the night found what seemed to be the bed of a wide water run, it had hay or bunch grass in it, some of the bunches were as large as a hay cock, we found water in holes the wagons kept the track and camped without water. As I was depending with Captain Hunt on the pack boys for supper the hare seemed to be another "godsend." The next morning we overtook the wagons just as they were yoking up had traveled twenty-seven miles, as they had some water in kegs they gave the cattle a little.

27th As we started off we espied with a glass a lake off to the right about ten miles [102] but did not spend time to go to it. After we left the camp ground,

ing mescal cactus. He said the Indians would dig out a hole, put heated rocks into it, and place the mescal cactus in to roast. Next time they would throw out all the rocks used before (which had lost their power to retain heat) and thus in time the pit would be surrounded by a high ring of burned out rocks.

[101] Stump Springs, in Pahrump Valley. There is considerable recent agricultural development — depending on wells and pumped water — farther north in the valley.

[102] This was probably the Dry Lake at the old Manse ranch.

I saw a half dozen head of horses and cattle that had
been left by those that were ahead of us, some were
dead and others were nearly so, one horse we drove
along, at noon we came to a spur of a mountain that
we had to cross. The road over it was stony and steep,[103]
as we were some way ahead of the wagons, we went
to cleaning stones out of the road, and by the time
they came up we had it so well cleaned that they went
over without doubling teams, traveled until 8 o'clock
and camped at some springs called Archalette,[104] distance today 22 miles. Stayed here two days, a great
abundance of grass here, we cut some to carry over the
next desert. A year or two since [1844] some Spaniards
were camped on this spot with a drove of horses and
were attacked by a band of Indians, and were nearly
all massacred. Bro. Rich and his company of packers
left us here and went ahead, the last day that we were
here the most of the wagons that we left on Far muddy
come up with us. There are some hares, conies, and
quails about this spring. Saw a quantity of clothing
thrown away here, had seen before we got here, some
wagons that had been left by those ahead of us, and
also a note left for Dallas stating that they were short
of provisions and were in great distress, were living
on the cattle that gave out.

30th   Traveled 7 miles and come to Salaratus
Creek [105] or Vegas, before descending into the bed of
it we could see off to the right a large flat, part of it

---

103 Emigrant Pass, five miles east of Resting Springs. They are following
the Old Spanish Trail as marked on Avawatz Mountains Quadrangle,
U.S.G.S.

104 Resting Springs. The large flow of water comes out of a tule-filled
area on the side of a rusty-red hill. Fremont called the springs Archilette,
for a man of that name, killed here by the Indians just before Fremont's
arrival on April 29, 1844. See Fremont's *Report of the Exploring Expedition,*
p. 264.

105 Amargosa River, that flows south, and then north toward Death Valley.

was covered with grass and a part of it was white as snow with Salaratus,[106] that was the head of the creek the bed of which is some 300 feet below the deserts around it and some 50 rods wide, we had to descend into it on a short and crooked ridge which was a divide between two rivers that discharged water into it in wet weather. The lower end was steep and it was with much difficulty we descended without upsetting our wagons. We traveled down the stream about five miles and camped on a fresh water stream that come into it.[107] This stream [Amargosa River] is a grand curiosity, there is quite a stream about knee deep and so strongly impregnated with alkali that it is about the color of madeir wine and is said to kill cattle when they drink it, in many places grass is plenty and good, the banks or walls on each side appear to be composition of clay lime and salaratus and in many places presents the appearance of dilapidated walls of ancient castles and other works of art and among these lives an abundance of conies and in the brush a plenty of quails.[108]

DECEMBER 1st Left the Vegas after following it down about 6 miles here the high banks run out and we passed over a sandy desert to Salt Springs.[109] As we drew near the spring we left the wagon track and followed Capt. Hunt up a narrow canion leading our

---

[106] This white alkali area is near the hot springs, two miles above the town of Tecopa.

[107] This is the creek that runs by China Ranch, where Ah Fou had a ranch in the 1890's. Data from O. J. Fiske of San Bernardino, who knew the Chinaman.

[108] They are following the Amargosa River through Tecopa Canyon. The now-abandoned road bed of the Tonopah and Tidewater Railroad threads the canyon.

[109] Salt Springs are to the east of the modern U.S. highway 127, leading from Baker north to Death Valley, and just south of where the highway crosses wide, flat Amargosa Valley and its small river. We visited the Salt Springs in 1951 and tasted the unpalatable water.

horses, when I espied some grain, and spoke of it as something uncommon in this region, when we come to move off it, and spoke of it again, and observed that if we could find quartz among it we might perhaps find gold, as I was the only one among us that had been in the gold mines, was why I took more notice of it at first than the rest, we then all four of us commenced looking, who were besides Capt. Hunt and myself, Mr. Rowan and a son of Mr. Forgs, we had not gone far before Mr. Rowan says "Here is gold," on looking I saw that he had found some in a stratum of quartz about four inches wide running through a ledge of granite. It was a collection of small particles the largest about the size of a pea.[110] We found one or two other specimans but the spring that was close by was so salt that we could not drink it and we had to go ahead to the camping place to get water which we found standing in holes, left by the last rains. We also found running water but it was very salt, we found some grass and reeds which we cut and fed the tops to the animals.

2nd   About noon we left here and traveled all night passed several wagons that had been left, the next day about noon came to Mud Lake.[111] This is a dry bed of a lake some two miles across, it is composed of dry clay on a water level and in winter it is covered with water we found some muddy water standing in holes, and some dry bunch grass, we stayed here until the 4th and thought the water hurt our cattle as they began to give out fast after we left here we had passed dead horses and cattle for several days, but it began to be our turn to leave them. They were the cattle that come from the States those that only come from Salt Lake

110 The Amargosa Gold Mine was developed here next year (1850).
111 Shown as Red Pass Lake on Avawatz Mountains Quadrangle, U.S.G.S.

were in good heart. From Salt springs to Mud Lake
30 miles.

4th Left Mud Lake and traveled to Bitter spring [112]
distance ten miles. Here were several cattle some dead
and some alive, we drove one ox along a few miles,
but had to leave him again as he was too weak to travel,
as this water was bad and no grass here we left about
sundown there is a gradual ascent from here to a rise
about 6 miles from the ridge, the Sierra Nevada range
is in sight. It began to rain a little before we left the
bitter spring and soon after it began to snow and the
wind blew cold our team was ahead and it had been the
most of the time since we left the cut off, as it was much
the smartest in the company, one of my oxen began to
fail and laid down in the yoke two or three times, when
we unyoked him he soon laid down again and refused
to get up, when I gave orders to have him shot. Blackwell, who was driving team, threw down the whip and
exclaimed "I am discouraged, we shall never get to the
top of the hill in this world." I laughed at him a bold
fellow to be sent on a mission to a foreign land to get
discouraged at the death of an ox; that I didn't intend
to get discouraged if I saw them all dead, but pick up
what I could carry and go ahead. Bro. Pomeroy joined
with me and laughed too, when he picked up the whip
and drove on, the wind blew cold and night was dark
and the snow fell so fast that we were almost unable to
follow the wagon track. I was ahead looking for the
track when Blackwell cried out in a howling pitiful
voice, "Oh! that I was in a good warm house, in a good
warm room with a fire in it with a table and candle
lighted on it and a book to read, how happy I should

[112] Still called Bitter Springs, shown on the Avawatz Mountain Quadrangle.

be." "Oh! said I, that would be a fool to this place if you was always stowed away in such a soft corner, you could never triumph in the song of coming up through great tribulations and washing your robes and making them white in the blood of the lamb." Bro Brown had taken my revolver and gone back to shoot the ox, to bring up the yoke, and drive the loose one. Bro. Blackwell was driving the team, Bro. Pomeroy was driving three horses, I was leading one horse and hunting the road. The other wagons were a long way behind, they got their wheels clogged in the snow and had gone into camp. Bro. Hunt had told us if we could push ahead to a place of safety to do it and then come back and help them to get up if there was any of them to help, in this way we pushed along until we came to the head of a canion and the road led down it. It was down with a steep slant and a good road, the canion was deep and sheltered from the wind and the cattle were encouraged at going down hill and they went ahead at good speed and we soon got down to where it was so warm the snow melted as it struck the ground. Here we stoped and released the team from the wagon. Bro. Brown soon came up with the Yoke which was made of black walnut, we split it up and made a fire of it and some hot coffee, which seemed the only restorative in chilly times, got a snack of something to eat with it and then all crawled into the wagon for a nap.

5th   At day break Capt. Hunt came up nearly chilled. We turned out made fire and got him some hot coffee and he revived again, said the snow had fallen 18 inches deep on the wagons and they were in a bad fix the snow had melted and run down by the wagons until our cattle had plenty to drink but there was nothing for them to eat. Blackwell turned out and look around saw that the snow had melted away around us and the prospect was that the sun would soon be out warm and clear he gave two or three savage whoops of triumphal joy when I turned to him and said "if you had given those whoops last night just before we had reached the top of the hill it would have sounded to me far more manly than it does now." But he made no reply. We soon hitched up and went ahead in search of feed for the cattle as all the grass that we had cut was gone. As we were ready to start off Mr. Swan came up driving a pony he had picked up on the road, he was much chilled we gave him some hot coffee and bread and he revived. We left him to gather sticks and keep a fire until the other wagons came up. Capt. Hunt went on with us after we came out of the canion we came into a desert that was crusted over with gravel and in dry weather it was hard and smooth but the rain and snow had softened it until we sank into it half leg deep. This made heavy work for our jaded cattle after we crossed this flat we came onto a sort of bench covered with sagebrush and among it some bunch grass. Here we went into camp distance 6 miles. About 3 o'clock P.M. we saw all the wagons coming. Capt. Hunt went back to meet them, they had left some of their cattle in the snow and Mr. Lawderwaper had gone back after them. He returned the next day without them, they had got to weak to drive.

6th Started for the Mohave River. Passed some wagons that had been left and soon after overtook an old Dutchman who was dragging a chest, said his company was on the Mahovey, that his team gave out that he had been back to those wagons we passed after the chest. Reached the Mahavey about 4 o'clock,[113] found about a dozen wagons camped there. They were in distress some of them had been out of bredstuff for 6 weeks. They were living on their cattle that gave out. There was an old man by the name of Forsket he was said to be a celebrated bogusmaker and had been in partnership with three different men that had been hanged for it, but he had escaped. There were 2 wagons, one had a woman and 10 children in and the other woman and 11 children in, they were the families of two brothers one or both of them are methodist preachers their names are Gruell.[114] They are from Iowa and while there they were known to be in the mob party that burned some barns and stacks of grain that belonged to some of the Brethren and while they were in the Utah valley old Forsket told them that the old men were in persuit of them to take their lives and the two men fled as Soloman says the wicked do.[115] We found plenty of grass here and a plenty of wild grapes and water standing in holes but none in the bed of the river, staid here and rested one day. I shot two hares, it is 12 miles from the last camp to this place, it was a pitiful sight to see these poor haggard women and children. Bro Rich had given them a little flour and we gave them a little bread, we were nearly out.

113 There were two principal places where the Old Spanish Trail and the Salt Lake Road reached the Mojave, at the site of Cady (southeast of Harvard Siding) and at a point eight miles east of Daggett. The *Mormon Way-bill* (in Appendix), compiled by Joseph Cain who was in the Flake-Rich Company, gives the mileage from Bitter Springs to the Mojave as 30¾ miles, and from this point to the last crossing of the river (near Oro Grande) as 51½ miles. These distances would indicate that these '49ers came to the river at a point eight miles below Daggett.

114 *See* the Gruwell narrative; part II: B.

115 This was the period of bitter religious controversy, prejudice, and persecution. Gruwell says that they were in danger, hence one reason for their start ahead of the Hunt train.

8th Traveled up the Mahave, I left the road and followed up the dry bed of the river in hopes of finding deer, but there was no water in it they had all left the neighborhood the bed of this river looks as if it conducted a formidable stream in the spring of the year [116] and as it takes its rise in the Sierra Nevada, there can be no doubt of it. Traveled eleven miles and camped here we found running water in the Mahovey here were some wild ducks and I saw some racoon tracks, the first that I had seen since leaving the American fork above Sutter's fort, plenty of cottonwood.

9th Traveled 5 miles and camped as the river took a broad bend to the right we had to leave it here [117] and it was fifteen miles to the next water. Whilst here the two Grewells came to their families, they left Salt Lake valley in a fright had taken the northern route to upper California, had gone down the coast to Pueblo de Los Angeles then up the Calhoun pass to us, and I presume were not a little chagrined at meeting Bro. Henry Rollins who was with Bro. Rich and was their supposed enemy. Said they had suffered very much on the northern rout, told of seeing 500 head of dead cattle in sight of each other, water was so scarce they drank cattles blood.[118] About twenty footmen came up to us while here and part of the company who had taken the cut off said they had left the wagons in great distress, thought some would starve.[119]

[116] Only on the rare occasion when a flood occurs is the wide gravel bed covered with water.

[117] At the site of present Barstow.

[118] This statement is strange. The Gruwells had not been on the Northern, or Humboldt, route but had accompanied their families on this Southern route until out of provisions and had then gone ahead to California to obtain supplies. Whether they gave the Pratt party this misinformation to avoid possible reprisals, or whether Pratt misunderstood, it is difficult to determine.

[119] This may be the Stover party, whose experiences are told in part VI.

10th   Started across the great bend and came to the river again at night,[120] the weather at night is very cold on this river, it freezes several inches. Traveled 15 miles today.

11th   Bro. Pomeroy left us today and went ahead with his three horses, traveled five miles and camped with those we had overtaken, no running water here but in holes, and the ice on them is six inches thick, met here Mr. Davis who had come from Williamses ranch with provisions to sell to those that were in distress.[121] some fat fresh beef tasted good to us, and I presume it tasted better to those that had been living on cattle that were so poor they couldn't stand alone. The water in the Mahovey sinks and rises several times. I traveled through the bottom in persuit of deer, but found now the bottoms are a mile or two wide here and is intermixed with willows and grass until it affords some of the finest range I ever saw, but the deers had been all routed by those that had gone ahead of us, we saw a note left for us by Bro. Rich that his company camped here two days and hunted. They killed 5 deers they were in the snow storm here that we had at the head of the canion I have mentioned.

12th   I traveled ahead on horseback with Messrs. Hunt and Rowan, I shot a hare, on the road. We overtook Bro. Pomeroy who told us he camped on the other side of the river the night before and saw a number of deer, but killed none. We had now come to where there was quite a large stream running we pitched our camp

---

[120] A little above the site of Hodge.

[121] Apparently, he came in response to the appeal taken to California by the advance Gruwell-Derr Company delegation. Isaac Williams sent out these supplies from his Chino Rancho. *See* his statement regarding aid to the distressed, in the "Chino Records." A resolution of thanks was introduced in the California legislature in 1850, but was blocked. A century later it was passed.

on the side of it, and Bro. Rowan and myself crossed
the river in persuit of deer. Before we started Bro.
Hunt told me I had better leave my double barreled
fowling piece and take his little rifle, he said it was well
loaded. I did so, when we crossed the river on old logs,
as Rowan was an old deer hunter I told him to order
the place of the hunt, who said it would be to hunt to
windward to keep the deer from smelling us, and to
keep a gunshot apart. I obeyed order, when we proceeded. We were soon out of sight of each other when
I saw a deer standing in an open space in a thicket of
willows as it was a short shot, I drew sight and fired,
and the deer dropped in its tracks. Mr. Rowan had
heard the shooting and hollowed to me to see if I had
seen deer. I answered in the affirmative. When he came
to me and we perseived the others but found they had
gone to leeward and we gave up the chase, took our
deer and returned to camp. This was considered a prize
among us in these scarce times for provisions. Traveled
8 miles today.[122]

13th As the wagons were starting off I crossed the
river to hunt. I had proceeded two or three miles when
I found myself in the fork of the river and finding
the stream fast rising, I found it prudent to get back
again as soon as possible. I turned back to cross the
river when I found my way greatly obstructed by a
dense thicket of brush closely interwoven by grapevines
and hanging until they were blue with grapes, with
much trouble I forced my way through when I came to
an end of them, and as the weather had moderated
much, the ice had got so rotten it would not bear me,
only in places and knowing I had a good days travel
ahead of me, after I should regain the shore I pulled
off my shoes and stockings and went onto the ice bare-

[122] Camp near present Helendale.

footed which I found to be rather cold and breaking through at every third or fourth step, and often scraping my shins against the ice, and the water under it about 18 inches deep. This lasted for about a dozen rods when I came to another thicket of brush and grapevines which I supposed to be the opposite shore but on getting through them I came to a dense mass of tules, about ten feet high when they stood up, but they were bent down about half way and formed a complete mat. As these were impenitrable I took my gun in one hand and a stick in the other, I got upon them and by crawling upon my hands and knees with the help of the stick and gun I could crawl along at a very slow rate, if I attempted to stand I immediately sank down among them and so there was no other alternative, but I found it a tiresome job. When I got across I was well exhausted and as I came into another thicket of grapes I stoped and ate some of them and I was much revived and after crossing one or two more thickets I came to the main channel of the river and had to pull off my pants to wade it and then got back onto the road again. As wolves are fond of grapes there are plenty of them on this river I often shot at them but as I used shot in my fowling piece I killed none dead, but often saw traces of blood. I followed the road and when I came to the river to my great surprise I found the wagons camped on the other side of it. Had I have known that they had the river to cross, it would have saved me all that trouble. Here is where we leave the river [123] for the head of the Cahoon pass, and the water is all in one channel and the stream is clear and pure running over a sand bottom. Distance today nine miles, as it is a long drive to the next grass it was thought advisable to lay

---

[123] Near the site of Oro Grande, where the Old Spanish Trail left the Mojave River.

by here a day and most of us went up the river to look
for gold as it is reported there had been some found
there, but found none, saw a large buck deer but did
not get a shot at it, saw much sign of hares.

15th   Left the Mahovey river and as we drew near
the pass could see a notch in the Sierra Nevada range
that there was nothing beyond it higher than the ground
we stood on and the clouds beyond it looked as though
we were coming to a jumping off place. As we were
on a high dry desert dotted here and there with grease
brush, we camped within three miles of the pass among
dwarf cedars as we found some bunch grass in a hollow.
In the night there came up about twenty men more
from those that had taken the cut off.[124] The first that
came from them did not like to tell much about their
proceedings but there was an Irishman among these
that was overjoyed to see Captain Hunt and told him
that they were in great trouble and said that when they
found so many mountains that they could get no farther
they began blaming one another for leading them that
way and saying if they had have followed Capt. Hunt
they would have been safe, he said they would have
sooner that he had have been there to have shown them
the way to go than to have seen the face of God. And
by such expressions as he made use of we found that
Captain Hunt would have been looked upon as their
Savior not withstanding some of them were so bitter
against him when we were among them, I could not
pity them much as I knew their hatred was unfounded.

16th   It began to snow about daylight and by the
time our teams were ready to start the ground was
covered with snow and it was still falling fast. We
started ahead and soon come to the head of the Cahoon

124 This may have been the Stover party, or a group that had pushed
ahead from the wagon train that went on the cutoff as far as Mount Misery.

pass,[125] and after passing over some rough ground, we came to a divide which is a sharp ridge between two rivers that led into the pass, and the road led down there, it is a crooked and steep place to descend and with much difficulty we descended to the bottom of it without upsetting our wagons. The snow was still falling fast and we were much troubled to find the road, we now had come into the dry bed of the Creek and the descent had been so rapid that the atmosphere was moderated until there was no snow in the Creek bottom and it was raining here. The deserts, or dry plain from which we had descended is 3000 ft above the level of the ocean. We followed down the bed of the stream a few miles and came to a spring where we camped. This stream has cut its way through mountains until the perpendicular banks in some places are near a hundred feet high. We found but little feed here but it was raining hard and we had to stop. The water now began to run down the creek, and just below us there was a very rocky pass to go through and we had a road to work through before we could pass. The water rose so high in the creek that we were obliged to stay there two days in which time we explored the mountains about, found some very rough and broken country. There are some sign of Deer here, but the emigrants before us had frightened them all away. Grease brush grows very rank and plenty and on dist Mts. we can see plenty of pine and fir and I think there is gold among the hills as there is plenty granite and quartz.

19th The wagons started down the canyon while Capt. Hunt and myself took the horses and some worn out cattle over a spur of mountains into the great

---

[125] The elevation of Cajon Pass is 4301 feet. There have been several routes down from the desert.

Cahoon pass, which is a wide bed of a stream which is now nearly dry but in the spring of the year, from its appearance, must be a large stream.[126] The canion that the wagons were in went around the spur into it below. We drove our cattle down to the junction, where we left them in charge of Mr. Forbes's son and then we followed the canyon up to the wagons the river was now running with a swift current. While at the last camping place, the Grewells and those wagons we saw on the Mahovey came up with us, and we were all jamed together in the narrow pass and all had to be helped but our own wagon, it helped itself up and down the rocks but the rest had to be lifted and pried to get them up and down. After all was through this roughest place we found between Salt Lake and California, our wagons went down a few miles and camped 13 miles from the head of the canion.

20th   Went down a tolerable road (except a plenty of water in some places as we had to occasionally keep in the bed of the creek) to the mouth of the Cahoon pass, distance 10 miles.[127] Here we found plenty of grass, wild oats were just coming up and birds were singing as in spring, the hills here are covered with shrub oak, that afford an abundance of acorns and these invite the grisly bears, out of the mountains, as we saw frequent excavations made by them and several skulls of monstrous size.

21st   Left the Cahoon pass and traveled down a beautiful valley about 10 miles wide and some 60 miles long, traveled ten miles and came to cocommingo

126 They apparently went over the spur from Glen Helen Ranch to Sycamore Flats and the mouth of Lytle Creek Canyon. *See* San Bernardino Quadrangle, U.S.G.S.

127 This was well out in the open valley, as it was but ten miles (see next day's entry) from the Cucamonga Rancho.

ranch [128] or farm, it is on the right hand side as we proceeded down. Immense herds of cattle and horses could be seen in every direction feeding upon the young grass that was starting up in consequence of the recent rains. The buildings of this ranch are on a high hill that overlooks the valley and affords a beautiful prospect.[129] We stayed here over night, bought some fresh beef, corn, wheat, and a little wine made on the ranch. They had a vineyard and beside grapevines there were figs, pears, apple, apricot and peach trees. The Steward of the ranch was a negro from the United States and was acquainted with Bro. Hunt as he was a waiting man in the army for some of the U.S. officers, the balance of them were Spanyards. Those Grewells were here and got drunk enough to be quarrelsome and breathed out a great deal of malice against the Mormons and the Spanyards that were there wanted us to whip them, said they did not like to hear us spoken against as a people, that they were acquainted with the Mormon battalion when they were in California and they were good men, but we told them that those men were a drunken pack and were not worth minding. We inquired about Bro. Rich and his company and were told that they were at Williams ranch or Ranch del China waiting for us, had all arrived safely.

22nd Started for there, which is on the opposite side of the valley and ten miles distance, the buildings on the ranch are in sight. We arrived there a little

---

[128] The Cucamonga Rancho was granted to Tiburcio Tapia by Governor Alvarado in 1839. After Tapia's death in 1845 the rancho passed to his daughter María Merced, who married Victor Prudhomme, a French resident of Los Angeles. Prudhomme owned the property in 1849. *See* G. W. and H. P. Beattie, *Heritage of the Valley; San Bernardino's First Century* (Pasadena, California, San Pasqual Press, 1939), pp. 138-69, for a history of the rancho.

[129] The ranch buildings were on the Red Hill northeast of Upland and west of present Cucamonga.

after noon, found Bro. Rich and about thirty brethren
from Salt Lake, all glad to see us. This ranch com-
prises a tract of land some ten miles wide and thirty
long and Williams the owner of it was formerly an
American hunter and obtained a grant for this land
while it was under the government of Mexico, and he
has now a large herd of cattle on it he says 35,000
head.[130] The hills and plains are covered with them but
I hardly think he has so many. Bro. Rich and Company
were at work for him repairing a Mill race and were
to have grinding done for their work, as he had no
bolt, we had to sift the meal, it was pretty coarse, but
we had found by sad experience to have none was still
coarser, and it was by hard scrabbling to get this, for
emigrants, from various directions were pouring in
here, and all were out of provisions and a great many
were coming by way of Santa Fe, on what is now called
Cooks route, it is the route that the Mormon battalion
traveled. Its surprising to see the crazy anxiety of
the people after gold. Mr. Williams has a large vineyard and many fruit trees in it. The rainy season had
now set in and it was thought best to stay here a while
until it should subside a little. Bro. Riches Co. had
hired a room in one of Mr. Williams houses and we
lived in our wagon near by. As Christmas was near at
hand it was proposed that we should have a company
dinner. A party was sent out after wild game, as geese
brant and ducks are plentiful at this time of the year,
and we were in persuit of them. I being one of the
party I got one brant and two ducks the rest got none

---

130 Isaac Williams came to the Rocky Mountains in 1830 with the Colonel
Bean party from Arkansas. He went to California with Ewing Young's
party in 1832 and remained there. After marriage to a daughter of A. M.
Lugo he was given part of the large land grant, and later acquired the
remainder. His ranch house was about three miles southwest of the present
town of Chino.

but as fish is plenty and cheap we have that answer
for what was lacking. We had plum duf made by Bro.
Pomeroy and the dinner went off well. I found it an
unpleasant job to hunt among those half wild cattle.
It is impossible to go amis of them, as every hill and
valley is full of them and when they see a stranger or
hear the report of the gun they will all run to the spot
with head and tails up as if ready for the combat and
it is not uncommon that they will attack a lone person
and they often made me change my course contrary
to my own wish to keep clear of them. It kept all hands
busy to keep the cattle and horses where we could find
them, some of them strayed in spite of our best efforts,
some of them we found again and others we never
found.

While here the most of those men that took the cutoff
came up and also another company from Salt Lake
among them were Brothers Egan,[131] Bills, Huvy and
some Messrs. Pomery [132] merchants from St. Louis,
they were bound to the gold mines with merchandise,
and when they got to Salt Lake, their teams had failed
and they stoped there and opened a store, they had
sold out most of their goods and had hired some men
at Salt Lake to drive their teams to California, the
wagons were heavy and they were overtaken by the
snow, and because their cattle died they were obliged
to leave most of the wagons in the desert. As we were
about ready to leave Williams'es there was a young
man came up that I had become acquainted with at
Salt Lake by the name of Lorton, he is from New
York and is a painter by trade, as he boarded at Bro.
Holmes'es while there he was frequently in at my house
and the subject of salvation was frequently brought up

131 For Egan's party, *see* part VIII.
132 This party is discussed in part VII.

but he thought but little about it as he was a volitile turn of mind. But when I met him last he was quite [different].

[We continue with the version in the Journal History.]

Said he, "We got to be religious while we were in the mountains. When we thought we would all starve to death, we used to pray and ask the Lord to help us out; and he did. I believe I know now how the 'Mormons' get revelations, and I think General Rich was led by revelation. When we got out of water and some of our men were insane with thirst, we prayed to the Lord to lead us to water. Two of us then dreamed the same dream in which we saw that there was water in a certain canyon about a mile and a quarter off. Each one in turn told his dream in the morning, and both went and found water. We had seen the place so plainly in the dream that when we found it; it seemed as if we had been there before. Another person in our company dreamed that he saw an Indian stand on the top of a mountain and cry to us aloud, saying, 'Thus far you can come, but no farther, and now, if you don't go back, you will all starve.' We came to such a mountain as the man saw in his dream, and though we could discover no Indian, there was no chance for us to go further. We took it for granted that it was salvation to turn back, but starvation to press forward. We had eaten nearly all our horses, and some of our company had drank their blood to quench their thirst. With one voice we all turned back, and in one or two days we struck your wagon trail; none can describe the joy the sight of it gave to us for we had now been two or three days without any thing to eat, and the cry among us was, 'Look out for worn-out cattle left by the wagon ahead.' We ranged along the road like so many hungry wolves, and soon, to our great joy, we saw an ox that had been left, being too poor to stand alone. We cut his throat and soon had him on a sage brush fire, and before it was heated through, we began to eat, and I never partook of anything in my life that tasted so sweet. We soon devoured it and went ahead to look for another ox and thus we continued till we came to the Muddy, where we found some of Mr. Dallas's company. Somebody had gone ahead with a horse to tell them that we were coming, and they prepared supper for us. We sat down and I ate the best supper I ever had in my life. There was another wagon company ahead of us and they sent word that they had supper prepared for us. We hurried on and ate just as hearty again and it tasted just as good; but all did not seem to abate my craving appetite, and I could not account for it." (This is a part of the tale of woe told me by this young man, and I pitied him, for he had lost all he had on the road and needed help. Brother Rich had assisted men in such circumstances till our company had increased to sixty or seventy men and his means were all exhausted. Of the company of fifty wagons which left Utah valley, under convoy of the Spaniard, only two were ahead of us when we arrived at the Cajon pass.

C: James S. Brown's Account

[A member of the Mormon Battalion, James S. Brown had gone to northern California after his discharge from the army. He was one of that little band that was working at Sutter's mill when gold was discovered in January, 1848. After rejoining his people in Utah later that year, he remained in Salt Lake Valley for one year, when he was called along with Addison Pratt and Hiram Blackwell to go on a Mormon mission to the Society Islands of the Pacific. They were to travel with the Jefferson Hunt wagon train to southern California.

His account of this trip, reproduced herewith, is taken from his autobiography, *Life of a Pioneer* (Salt Lake City, 1900), 130-43. Although it is a reminiscent account written years after the events described, it supplements the Pratt story and supplies additional details.]

We then went to preparing for our journey. Apostle C. C. Rich had been called to go through to California, so he and Brother Pratt and I fitted up a team, I having a good wagon and one yoke of oxen; they each furnished a yoke of oxen. In a few days we were ready for the start. We had a rodometer attached to our wagon, to measure the distance.

In the meantime, the emigrants called a meeting before taking their departure. They had employed Captain Jefferson Hunt of company A, Mormon Battalion fame, to be their guide, as he had come through that route with pack animals. He was invited to tell them what they might expect. He described the route to them with the roughest side out, lest they might say that he had misled them by making things more favorable than they really were. In concluding his remarks he said: "From Salt Springs, we cross to a sandy desert, distance seventy-five miles to Bitter Springs, the water so bitter the devil would not drink it; and from thence away hellwards, to California or some other place. Now, gentlemen, if you will stick together and follow me, I will lead you through to California all right; but you will have to make your own road, for there is none save the old Spanish trail from Santa Fé to California, by the Cajon Pass through the Sierra Nevada Mountains."

The emigrant company consisted of about five hundred souls,[133] and one hundred wagons and teams,

---

[133] Sheldon Young, above, said about four hundred persons.

the latter in poor condition. Feeling in high spirits, the company moved out between the 1st and 8th of October. C. C. Rich, Francis Pomeroy and I remained to follow up on horseback, in three or four days. Pratt and Blackwell, taking our team, started with the main body. They got to the Cottonwoods, when one of my oxen became so lame that they could not proceed any farther. Blackwell returned to inform me of the situation, and I went down and traded with John Brown, late Bishop of Pleasant Grove, for another ox, mine having been pricked in shoeing. Then they overtook the main company, and all proceeded together.

On the 8th we followed. I started out alone, to meet with the others at Cottonwood. As I passed the home of Dr. Willard Richards, counselor to President Brigham Young, Dr. Richards came out and met me; he took me by the right knee with his right hand, as I sat on my horse, and said, "Starting out on your mission, I suppose?" I replied, "Yes, sir." "Well, Brother James, I am glad, and sorry; glad to have you go and preach the gospel, and sorry to part with good young men that we need in opening up a new country." At that he gave my knee an extra grip. Stretching his left hand out to the southwest, his chin quivering and his eyes filling with tears, he said, "Brother James, when you are upon yonder distant islands, called to preside over a branch of the Church of Jesus Christ of Latter-day Saints, men will seek your life, and to all human appearance, there will be no possible escape: then look unto God, and His angels shall draw near unto you, and you shall be delivered, to return home to this people. Do not stop to write to Brother Pratt, your president, to Brother Brigham or to me, for you will require the immediate protection of God. Then put your trust in him, and He will deliver you; for I promise you in the name of Israel's God that you shall be delivered from your enemy and return to this people.[134] Goodbye, and God bless you."

Need I tell the reader that my mind was greatly impressed by those prophetic words, their inspired character being established so vividly in my later experience. Prophetic I knew them to be, and impressive they were indeed; and the impression has been deep and lasting.

I then went on to Brother Jacob M. Truman's, on Big Cottonwood Creek, and stayed with him that night. Next morning I passed on to Brother William Bills', where I met with brothers C. C. Rich and F. Pomeroy, and we proceeded on to Provo by the Indian trail, having been joined by Alexander Williams, with whom we stayed.

At Provo we learned that the citizens and Indians had had some trouble, and there was considerable excitement, as there were but few settlers at that place and the Indians were quite numerous. The latter were singing war songs and working up a spirit of war preliminary to making an attack that night or next morning, as was supposed. The people were preparing to receive them as best they could. Guards were posted around the camp, and men put on picket duty, so that any enemy might be discovered readily.

The Indians made no move until after daylight; but just before sunrise they started from their camps in force, to attack us. We advanced to meet them, so as to prevent their assailing us in the small fort, where the women and children were. The savages marched

---

[134] For an account of his experiences in the South Pacific, *see* James S. Brown, *Life of a Pioneer*, chapters 20-35.

up as if to give us open battle. We formed across the road, and each man took his post ready for action. I always have believed that if it had not been for the presence of Apostle C. C. Rich, and his cool, conciliatory action, there would have been bloodshed, for there were some very hot-headed white men, who would have preferred war to peace. Through Brother Rich's influence, the cause of the trouble was looked into, a conciliation effected,[135] and war averted, so that after breakfast we of the missionary party proceeded on to what was called Hobble Creek – now the city of Springville, with a population of over two thousand souls. I remember that we thought the place would be capable of sustaining eight or ten families, or a dairy, believing there was not enough water for more.

From Hobble Creek we passed on from one small stream to another, expressing our opinion as to the capacity of the water supply; and in no instance did we suppose that there was water sufficient for more than fifteen families, judging from what we could see then. Again, the barrenness of the country was such that it did not seem that more than seventy-five or a hundred head of cattle could find feed within reach of water. Now thousands of head of horned stock and horses are sustained at the same places.

We kept on our way until we overtook the wagon train on Sevier River. We came up with the emigrants just as they were ready to move on, but did not find them so full of glee as they were on the start from the city. Still, we rolled on very peaceably until we came to Beaver River, where the country began to look more forbidding. Then the ardor of the emigrants began to weaken.

135 For Rich's version of the incident, *see* part V: B.

At this place the company was joined by a man named Smith [136] with a pack train of about seventeen men; also James Flake, with thirty Latter-day Saints; besides, there were William Farrer, John Dixon, H. W. Bigler, George Q. Cannon,[137] and others, whose names I do not now recall. Smith felt confident that he could find Walker's Pass, in the Sierra Nevada mountains. This supposed pass had been spoken of often, but men had been disappointed as often in finding it, or rather in not finding it. Smith's story excited our whole camp so that there was a general desire to try the new route, and go down through the canyon and out on to the sandy desert. The whole company except a very few favored the idea of leaving the route they had hired a guide for, and they urged Captain Hunt to strike out and look for water. He said, "Gentlemen, I agreed to pilot you through to California on the Old Spanish Route by the Cajon Pass. I am ready to do so, and am not under any obligations to lead you in any other way; and if you insist on my doing so you must be responsible, for I will not be responsible for anything. On this condition, if you insist on changing your route, I will do the best I can to find water, but I do not have any reason to hope for success when I leave the trail."

The company hurrahed for the Walker Pass, and Captain Hunt struck out a day ahead while the company shod and doctored their lame and sick stock for one day. Then we moved out ten miles on to the plain southwest of where Minersville, Utah, now stands, and camped.[138]

---

136 O. K. Smith. The contemporary accounts give other figures as to the size of the two pack trains.

137 For the accounts of Farrer, Bigler, and Cannon, *see* part v.

138 Brown has confused the attempted short cut at Beaver with the Walker Cutoff that Captain Smith advocated.

Sometime in the night Captain Hunt came into camp, so near choked from the lack of water that his tongue was swollen till it protruded from his mouth; his eyes were so sunken in his head that he could scarcely be recognized. His horse, too, for the need of water, was blind, and staggered as he was urged on. Their stay had been thirty-six hours, on the sands, without water. About 2 o'clock next morning our stock stampeded from the guards and ran back to water. Two-thirds of the men went in pursuit, and animals and men did not return to camp till 2 o'clock in the afternoon.

By this time confusion and discontent abounded in camp. A committee was appointed to inquire into the condition of every team, and to ascertain the food supply, with the avowed intention of sending all back who failed to have what were considered the requisites for the journey. I think that one-third of the company, our wagon included, were found wanting when weighed in that committee's balances. But when we were ordered to return, those who gave the command found that they were without authority and no one would heed them. So the discontent was patched up for a time, and we proceeded on to Little Salt Lake Valley, where we struck the old Spanish trail again. Then the company began to split up, some going on after night, and others stopping.

Brother C. C. Rich told me that it had been shown to him that there was going to be trouble, and he felt led to believe that if we would go with the pack train he could at least lead the brethren there back on to the trail and save them. This was in the night, as we slept together in the wagon. He awoke and asked me if I were awake. Finding that I was, he told me what should befall the company. To save the brethren and all who would heed him, he purchased some ponies and went with the packers.[139]

As we passed along the Spanish trail – said to be three hundred and fifty years old [140] – on the great desert, we could follow the route by the bones of dead animals in many places. It is said that many fierce battles have been fought between Mexicans and Indians along this trail. So far as we were concerned, although it was known that the Indians were very hostile, they gave us no trouble.

When we reached what is called the Rim of the Basin, where the waters divide, part running into the Colorado River and on to the Pacific Ocean, and part into the Salt Lake Valley, the company called meetings, and several made speeches, saying there must be a nearer and better route than that on which the Mormon guide was leading them. One Methodist and one Campbellite preacher [141] in the company said that they had started to California, and not hellwards, as the Mormon guide had stated at the outset, quoting what Captain Hunt had said just before starting. Others claimed that they had been on the mountains, and upon looking west had seen something green, which they asserted was an indication of water. Some of them celebrated the proposed separation from us by boring holes in trees then filling these with powder and firing them, exploded the trees in symbol of the break-up of the company.

Next morning all but seven wagons turned off to the right, toward the supposed Walker's Pass. We

---

[139] As matters developed, Rich was instrumental in saving his party.

[140] The Trail was not nearly so old as Brown thought. *See* Hafen and Hafen, *Old Spanish Trail.*

[141] These were probably J. W. Brier and Lewis Granger.

preferred to follow the guide. The company was thoroughly warned by Captain Hunt of the danger of dying from lack of water. In our party there were eleven men, two women and three children.[142] The main company expressed pity for us and tried to persuade us to go with them, but we felt confident that our course was the safest, notwithstanding their superior numbers. They seemed to rejoice at their conclusion, while we regretted it for their sakes. Thus we separated, the emigrant company heading for Walker's Pass, and our small party continuing on the old Spanish trail, or southern route to California.

When the company had separated the weather was very threatening, and it soon began to snow very fast. We pulled on until late in the afternoon, and camped on the mountain. Next day we came to some Indian farms where the savages had raised corn, wheat and squash. We passed on to the Santa Clara, followed it down for three or four days, and found a written notice to those who came that way: "Look out, for we have killed two Indians here." [143] With this warning, we felt that we must keep a vigilant guard all the time. From the Santa Clara we had a very long drive across the mountain and down a long, dry rocky slope until we came to the Rio Virgen. We went along that stream three or four days; where we left it we found a cow with an Indian arrow sticking in her. We next passed over a high plateau to a stream well named the Muddy. There we laid by and doctored and shod our lame cattle.

While we were on the Muddy, Brother C. C. Rich and party came down the stream to us, bringing sad

[142] This is the only place we have found a statement of the number of persons that stayed with Hunt.

[143] The accounts of Gruwell and Pratt say that one Indian was killed.

Amargosa Gold Mine, discovered in 1849 beside the Amargosa River

and heartrending news from the great emigrant company, which had broken into factions and become perfectly demoralized and confused. Some had taken packs on their backs and started on foot, their cattle dying, their wagons abandoned. All were despondent, and unwilling to listen to anybody. I think, from the best information we ever got of them, I would be safe in saying that four-fifths of them met a most horrible fate, being starved or choked to death in or near what was afterwards called Death Valley.[144] In after years the miners of Pahranagat found the irons of the wagons very handy for use in their pursuits.

On the Muddy we burned charcoal and made nails to shoe our cattle, having to throw the animals down and hold them while Apostle C. C. Rich shod them. Brother Rich did his work well, for the shoes never came loose till they wore off.

From the Muddy I accompanied Captain Hunt and Henry Rollins twelve miles and found some small pools of water about two miles to the right of the trail; I went back to turn the packers to it, while Captain Hunt and Henry Rollins went ahead in search of more pools of water and found some. George Q. Cannon and I stayed there as guides for the wagon train, and turned them off to the water. When the train arrived, about 11 o'clock p.m., we had to dip water with cups and water the stock from buckets. Then we pressed on till daylight, made a halt long enough to take breakfast, and pushed on, for there was no feed for our stock.

About 2 p.m. we came to the Los Vegas, where we rested a day, then continued our journey over mountains and across deserts from day to day until we reached a

---

[144] In this he is badly mistaken, as most of the company turned back from Mount Misery and followed the Hunt track to California. A few of those who continued into Death Valley perished.

stream of water about three rods wide. It was so strong with alkali that we dared not allow our cattle to drink of it, but put the lash to them so that they could not get a sup as we crossed it twice.[145] Thence we traveled across a very sandy desert for twelve miles to the Salt Springs, where the train went around the point of the mountain. A. Pratt and I, with three or four others followed on a small trail that passed over a notch of the mountain. While going through a narrow pass, Brother A. Pratt said it looked as if there might be gold there. At that we went to looking in the crevices of the rock, and in a few minutes one of the party found a small scale, and then another. Among the rest, I saw the precious metal projecting from a streak of quartz in the granite rock [Salt Creek mine]. From there we went over about one and a half miles to the Salt Springs, and met with the teams. Several of the party journeyed back to look further for the gold. I took along a cold chisel and hammer, and chipped out some at the place I had found, but as our teams were weakening very fast and there was neither food nor water at that place to sustain our stock, we had to push on across the sandy desert of seventy-five miles, day and night, until we came to the Bitter Springs.

These were the springs that Captain Hunt had told the emigrant company about before they left Salt Lake City, that from thence it was "away hellward to California or some other place." It certainly began to look that way now, when our cattle began to weaken and die all along the trail. The springs would have been as properly named if they had been called Poison Springs, instead of Bitter, for it seemed that from that place our cattle began to weaken every moment, and

145 Amargosa River, that flows toward Death Valley.

many had to be turned loose from the yoke and then shot to get them out of their misery.

We had to shoot one of Brother Pratt's oxen to end its suffering. This act fell to my lot. Oh, how inhuman and cruel it seemed to me, to drive the patient and faithful dumb animal into a barren desert, where there is neither food nor drink, to goad him on until he falls from sheer exhaustion, so that he bears any punishment, to make him rise, that his master sees fit to inflict, without giving a single moan, then to walk around and calmly look him in the face and fire the deadly missile into his brain, then leave his carcass to the loathsome wolves and birds of prey!

In looking back over a period of fifty years since then, the writer cannot call to memory a single act in his life that seemed so cruel and ungrateful as that; and still there was no earthly means to save the poor creature from a more horrible death, which would come if he had been left in that driving snowstorm, when his whole frame shook with cold, there to lie and starve – one of the most miserable deaths that the human mind can conceive of. Of the two evils we chose the least by ending the suffering in a moment, when it would have taken hours if it had not been for this act of mercy, as we call it after taking in the whole situation.

From Bitter Springs our team took the lead to the end of the journey, or to Williams' Ranch, being the first team that ever crossed over the Cajon Pass going west, as I remember.[146] Ascending to the first pass from the Bitter Springs our situation was most gloomy. In mud and snow, with darkness come on, every rod of

---

[146] Two wagons had gone east — the one taken by the Mormon Battalion party in the spring of 1848, and the one sent by Isaac Williams in December, 1849, with food for the starving emigrants.

the road became more steep and difficult. The summit
was two miles ahead and the nearest team half a mile
back. We moved by hitches and starts, and could only
make three or four rods at a time. Two of us pushed
at the wagon while the other drove. Our guide was a
few feet ahead, marking out the road, and saying,
"Crowd up, boys, if possible. Let us wallow on over
the summit, for it is our only salvation to cross and try
to open the road if possible for the weaker teams."

Finally, with a shout of triumph, we reached the
summit in two feet of snow, at 11 o'clock at night. Our
guide told us to go on down and build fires at the first
place where we could find anything for our stock, and
he would go back and cheer the rest on as best he could.

The descent being quite steep, we soon made the
distance of three or four miles to where there was but
six inches of snow, and where we found some feed.
Our matches were all damp, and we were wet as could
be. We split up our spare yoke and struck fire with
flint and steel, crawled into the wagon, and started a
fire in the frying-pan. Then, as there was plenty of
fuel, we made a roaring fire outside, took a bite to eat,
and turned in for a few moments' rest, being satisfied
that the others of the party had halted before they
reached the summit, and as the guide was with them
we thought they would take a rest and come on at
daybreak.

This conjecture proved right, for about 4 o'clock a.m.
Captain Hunt hallooed to us and called for a cup of
coffee. He seemed to be chilled to the bone, so we soon
stirred the fire and got him something to eat. He told
us all the teams would make the riffle, but for us to
have a good fire, for some of the men would be chilled
nearly to death. Then he directed us to go ahead until

we found feed for the stock, and he would remain until the company came up. We advanced about ten miles, and halted for our cattle to feed and rest. In the meantime we discovered the company coming down the slope of the mountain. Our feelings, as well as theirs, were much relieved at the sight, as we beheld each other, and when they had rested their teams they came on to our camping place for another stop, while we moved ahead to the Mojave River. When we reached that stream, I presume that we felt as pleased as a man liberated from a life sentence in a dungeon, for we had reason to feel assured that we would succeed in our journey, as we had only one more hard scramble of thirty miles,[147] and had pleasant weather and plenty of feed and water for our stock, with time to rest in. Some shouted: "Daylight once more; thank God for our deliverance!"

It was while we lay here that some of the company which had parted with us at the Rim of the Basin came up to us with packs on their backs, half-starved. The story of the condition of their comrades was horrifying beyond description. Men, women, and children suffered death alike by thirst and starvation. This painful episode affords one more instance of where the majority had been wrong and the minority right. The new arrivals said that when we parted from them they were sorry for us. But now we were more sorry for them than they had been for us.

We divided our food the second or third time to relieve these starving people, then pursued our course up stream for nine or ten days. There we rested our cattle, did some hunting, and replenished our food supply with wild meat, principally venison, quail and the gray squirrel. We found plenty of wild grapes,

---

[147] It was more than sixty miles to Cajon Pass.

and also discovered that the raccoon lived in that part of the world.

It was about the 17th of December when we crossed the Cajon Pass, in the Sierra Nevada Mountains; from thence we moved via the Cocomonga Ranch to Williams' Ranch, arriving there on December 24th. At Williams' we found C. C. Rich and party; we joined in with them and had a good Christmas dinner. There we traded for new supplies to last us up to the gold mines on the Mariposa and the Stanislaus rivers, in northern California, or the upper country. The writer acted as pilot, interpreter and quartermaster for the company of something like fifty men.

It was about the 27th of January when we left the ranch, from which we traveled to Los Angeles, thence twenty miles to the north, where C. C. Rich and ten or fifteen men left us, and H. Egan took charge of the company as captain.

D: THE SIDNEY P. WAITE SKETCH

[Sidney P. Waite, a boy of twelve, was in the Jefferson Hunt train that left Utah in the fall of 1849. His family apparently continued with Captain Hunt to California, ignoring the lure of the Walker Cutoff.

The brief sketch reprinted herewith is from John Brown, Jr. and James Boyd, *History of San Bernardino and Riverside Counties* (Chicago, 1922), I, 284-85.]

Sidney P. Waite, pioneer, '49er, prospector, hunter, miner, vaquero, and printer, was born June 14, 1837, in Wolf's Den, Kentucky, and moved to the then village of Chicago with his parents, thence to Joliet, where his father erected the first woolen mill in the state of Illinois, having for a partner Joel A. Mattison, afterwards governor of the state. In 1849 the family started for California, outfitting at Council Bluffs. They traveled but slowly and finding it too late in the year to cross the Sierra Nevadas by the northern route, they went into Salt Lake, intending to winter there. Late in August Waite, Sr., with other immigrants who wished to go to California, formed a caravan of 100 wagons, with the intention of going through by the southern route. Capt. Jefferson Hunt was engaged as guide, being paid $1,000, or $10 a wagon. In the middle of September the outfit was organized at Hobble Creek (near where Springville now is) and the journey was commenced, just as small a quantity of provision being taken as would do for the trip. At Mountain Meadow Springs Parson Brier and family, Ira C. Bennett and family, John C. Colton, John Goller, and others left the main party, hoping to get to the mines in California by a shorter route. On the Muddy River a train of pack mules caught up with the caravan. With it was Sheldon Stoddard and there began a strong friendship that lasted until death between Sheldon Stoddard and Sydney P. Waite, over seventy years.[148]

In getting through the Narrows both the upper and lower Narrows in the Cajon Pass, Mr. Waite had to take the wagon apart and pack a wheel at a time down over the boulders and slide the axle trees and heavier portions on sycamore poles down over the precipices and boulders, there being nothing but a horse and mule

---

[148] Waite and Stoddard were pioneers of San Bernardino, California, and lived most of their long lives there. There was some doubt at first whether the Waite family accompanied Captain Hunt to California, or whether it was in the Rynierson train that went two or three days on the Walker Cutoff, and then turned back to the regular trail and followed Hunt's wagons. This statement that the Waites met Sheldon Stoddard and the other packers on Muddy Creek, indicates that the Waites were with Captain Hunt, for it was here that the Flake-Rich party returned to Hunt's train. Bigler's entry of November 21 (*see* part V: A) indicates that Stoddard was with the Mormon packers. (*See* Stoddard sketch, part V: F).

trail, known as the Santa Fe Trail.[149] This is the way some of the pioneers entered the San Bernardino Valley in 1849. Arriving at Agua Mansa [150] December 14, 1849, the famished immigrants applied to Mr. Cristobal Slover [151] for food. He opened his smoke-house, supplied them with bacon and squashes, of which they partook so freely without cooking that nine of the party died and were buried on the east side of the trail on the ridge in Politana between San Bernardino and Agua Mansa.[152]

The Waite family settled at El Molino near San Gabriel Mission, where Father Waite purchased the Los Angeles Star and his son Sydney learned the printer's trade. Mr. Waite, Sr., was the first postmaster of Los Angeles. In 1858 the family moved to San Bernardino, where they lived and died.[153]

[149] The trail from Los Angeles to Santa Fé, or more properly, the Old Spanish Trail.

[150] Agua Mansa was a town founded by a colony of New Mexicans who settled here in 1842. It was located on the Santa Ana River below San Bernardino. *See* Beattie, *Heritage of the Valley,* pp. 96-119.

[151] Cristobal, or Isaac, Slover, married to a Spanish woman, was the one Anglo in the settlement. He had come to the Rocky Mountains with the Jacob Fowler party in 1821, had gone to California with the Pattie party in 1828, and had finally settled at Agua Mansa. A famous and lifelong grizzly bear hunter, he was finally killed in his old age by a grizzly, and was buried at the foot of Slover Mountain, named for him. This mountain, now being blasted down and ground into cement, is located near Colton.

[152] By this time remnants of the Gruwell-Derr party and some that had gone part way on the Death Valley route were intermingled with Hunt's party. We have not found verification of the statement regarding the death of the nine persons.

[153] Sidney P. Waite married the daughter of James P. Beckwourth, famous Mountain Man and frontiersman. We interviewed their daughter at San Bernardino in July, 1951.

Part IV

The Rynierson Company

After the division of the Hunt wagon train on November 4th, all but seven wagons set out on the Walker Cutoff and traveled up Shoal Creek on the trail of the Captain Smith and the Flake-Rich companies of packers. Our best account of this major section of the wagon train to the place of its dispersion near Mount Misery is given in the following extract from William Lewis Manly's *Death Valley in '49* (New York, 1929),[1] pages 109-111.

A: The William L. Manly Report

It was really a serious moment when the front of the train reached the Smith trail. Team after team turned to the right while now and then one would keep straight ahead as was at first intended. Captain Hunt came over to the larger party after the division was made, and wished them all a hearty farewell and a pleasant, happy journey. My friend Bennett, whose fortune I shared, was among the seceders who followed the Smith party. This point where our paths diverged was very near the place afterward made notorious as Mountain Meadows, where the famous massacre took place under the direction of the Mormon generals. Our route from here up to the mountain was a very pleas-

---

[1] This is the most widely known account of the Death Valley journey. The book also gives biographical data on Manly.

ant one, steadily up grade, over rolling hills, with wood, water and grass in plenty. We came at last to what seemed the summit of a great mountain, about three days' journey on the new trail. Juniper trees grew about in bunches, and my experience with this timber taught me that we were on elevated ground.

Immediately in front of us was a canon, impassable for wagons, and down into this the trail descended. Men could go, horses and mules, perhaps, but wagons could no longer follow that trail; so we proposed to camp while explorers were sent out to search a pass across this steep and rocky canon. Wood and bunch grass were plenty, but water was a long way down the trail and hard to be packed up to the camp. Two days passed, and the parties sent out began to come in, all reporting no way to go farther with the wagons. Some said the trail on the west side of the canon could be ascended on foot by both men and mules, but that it would take years to make it fit for wheels.[2]

The enthusiasm about the Smith cutoff had begun to die and now the talk began of going back to follow Hunt. On the third morning a lone traveler, with a small wagon and one yoke of oxen, died. He seemed to be on this journey to seek to regain his health. He was from Kentucky, but I have forgotten his name. Some were very active about his wagon and some thought too much attention was paid to a stranger. He was decently buried by the men of the company.

This very morning a Mr. Rynierson called the attention of the crowd and made some remarks upon the situation. He said: "My family is near and dear to me. I can see by the growth of the timber that we are in a very elevated place. This is now the seventh of No-

---

[2] They were on the high plateau overlooking the canyon of Beaver Dam Wash, affluent of the Virgin River.

vember, it being the fourth at the time of our turning off on this trail. We are evidently in a country where snow is liable to fall at any time in the winter season, and if we were to remain here and be caught in a severe storm we should all probably perish. I, for one, feel in duty bound to seek a safer way than this. I shall hitch up my oxen and return at once to the old trail. Boys (to his teamsters) get the cattle and we'll return." This was decisive, and Mr. Rynierson would tarry no longer. Many others now proceeded to get ready and follow, and as Mr. Rynierson drove out of camp quite a respectable train fell in behind him. As fast as the hunters came in and reported no road available, they also yoked up their oxen and rolled out. Some waited awhile for companions yet in the fields, but all were about ready to move, when a party came in with news that the pass was found and no trouble could be seen ahead. About twenty-seven wagons remained when this news came, and as their proprietors had brought good news they agreed to travel on westward and not go back to the old trail.[3]

B: THE ALEXANDER C. ERKSON ACCOUNT

[Despite the large number in the company that followed Rynierson's lead, turning back to the Old Spanish Trail and following Hunt's track to California, no diary by any of these travelers has been located by us. A statement, given by Alexander C. Erkson to William L. Manly is the general account we reproduce here.][4]

On my way back from Mt. Misery I climbed up on a big rock and inscribed the date – Nov. 10, 1849.

[3] These became the Death Valley parties, whose story is not included in this volume.

[4] W. L. Manly, *Death Valley in '49* (1929 ed.), pp. 493-97. Manly says that this account was dictated to him by Erkson, but that the latter died before he had a chance to review and revise it. This may account for some of the apparent errors in the statement.

In our journey we came to what is called "The Rim of the Basin" and traveled along on that a distance till we came to the Santa Clara River and saw where the Indians had raised corn and melons. We followed on down that stream and found our teams gradually failing. Noting this we decided to overhaul our loads and reject a lot of things not strictly necessary to preserve life. I know I threw out a good many valuable and pretty things by the roadside. I remember six volumes of Rollin's *Ancient History,* nicely bound, with my name on the back, that were piled up and left. We followed along near the Santa Clara River till it emptied into the Virgin River.[5] It was somewhere along here that we first saw some Yucca trees. The boys often set fire to them to see them burn.[6]

The Virgin River was a small stream running on about the course we wanted to travel, and we followed this course for thirty or forty miles. We found plenty of wood and water and mesquite. After a while the river turned off to the left, while we wanted to keep to the right, so we parted company there. We heard of a river beyond, which they called the "Big Muddy" and we went up a little arroyo, then over a divide to some table land that led us down to the Big Muddy. We made our wagons as light as possible, taking off all the boards and stakes we could possibly get along without. William Philipps and others were placed on short allowance. They had an idea that I had more provisions in my wagon than I ought to have, but I told them that it was clothing that we used to sleep on. I divided among them once or twice. When we reached

---

[5] They did not follow the Santa Clara to its mouth, but turned west along the road to cross Beaver Dam Mountains, along the route of present U.S. 91.

[6] The first forest of these joshua trees is encountered on the west side of the pass, at the head of the long slope leading down to the Virgin River.

the Big Muddy we stopped two or three days, for there was plenty of feed. It was a narrow stream that seemed as if it must come from springs. It was narrow between banks, but ran pretty deep;[7] a streak of fog marked its course in the morning. We understood it was not very far from where we left the Virgin River to the Colorado – some said not more than fourteen miles – and that the Colorado turned sharply to the south at that point. Mr. Rhynierson and wife had a child born to them on the Virgin River, and it was named Virginia.[8]

It was a gloomy trip the whole time on [beyond] the Big Muddy. I lost three or four head of cattle, all within a day and a night. Mrs. Erkson walked to lighten the load, and would pick all the bunches of grass she saw and put them on the wagon to feed the oxen when we stopped. I let them pass me and we stopped and fed the cattle and slept ourselves. It was said that we ran great risks from Indians, but we did not see any. I had at this time only two yoke of oxen left.

We overtook the party next morning at nine o'clock, having met some of them who were coming back after us. All were rejoiced that we had come on safely. Here I met Elisha Bennett and told him my story. He said he could sell me a yoke of oxen. He had a yoke in J. A. Philipps' team and was going to take them out. He said nothing in particular as to price. I said that I wanted to see Mr. Philipps and talk with him about the matter, for he had said Bennett should not have the cattle. I went over to see him and spoke to him about

---

[7] The Muddy rises in large springs about eight miles north of present Glendale. The stream, which takes on a milky color derived from fine clay along its bed, still runs in a deep narrow channel at this place.

[8] Doubtless this was the first white child born in southern Nevada.

Bennett's cattle; he told me they had quarreled and I could have them, and so we made a bargain. I gave twenty dollars for the cattle, the last money I had, and as much provisions as he could carry on his back. They were making up a party to reach the settlements at the Williams' ranch, and I made arrangements for them to send back provisions for us. About thirty started that way – young men and men with no families with them.[9]

I got along very well with my new team after that. It was about forty miles from water to water, and I think we camped three times. At one place we found that provisions had been left, with a notice that the material was for us, but the redskins had got the provisions. We struck a spring called ———— , a small spring of water. A child of some one of the party died there and was buried.

We then went more nearly south to find the Mojave River, for we hoped to find water there. It was very scarce with us then. We had one pretty cold day, but generally fine weather; to get along we traveled at night. A party soon struck the Mojave. Here there was some grass, and the mustard was beginning to start up and some elder bushes to put forth leaves. I picked some of the mustard and chewed it to try to get back my natural taste. Here the party divided,[10] a part going to the left to San Bernardino and the remainder of the party to the right to Cucamonga. I was with the latter party and we got there before night.

Rhynierson said to one of the party, "Charlie, you had better hurry on ahead and try to get some meat

---

[9] This may have been one of the groups that caught up with the Hunt wagons, as mentioned in Pratt's diary, (*see* part III: B) under dates Dec. 9 and 15, 1849.

[10] This would be beyond Cajon Pass, instead of on the Mojave River.

before the crowd comes up." Charlie went on ahead
and we drove along at the regular gait, which was not
very fast about these times. We saw nothing of Charlie,
so I went to the house to look for him and found him
dead drunk on wine. He had not said a word to them
about provisions. That wine wrecked us all. All had
a little touch of scurvy, and it seemed to be just what
we craved. I bought a big tumbler of it for two bits
and carried it to my wife. She tasted it at first rather
gingerly, then took a little larger sup of it, and then put
it to her lips and never stopped drinking till the last
drop was gone. I looked a little bit surprised and she
looked at me and innocently asked, "Why, haven't you
had any?" I was afraid she would be the next one to
be dead drunk, but it never affected her in that way at
all. We bought a cow here to kill, and used the meat
either fresh or dried. Then we went on to the Williams,
or Chino, ranch. Colonel Williams was glad to see us
and said we could have everything we wanted. We
wanted to get wheat, for we had lived so long on meat
that we craved such food. He told us about the journey
before us and where we would find places to camp.
Here we found one of the Gruwells.[11] We camped
here a week, meeting many emigrants who came by
way of Santa Fe.[12]

We went on from here to San Gabriel, where we
stayed six weeks to rest and recuperate the cattle. In
the good grass we found here they all became about
as fat as ever in a little while. Here the party all broke
up and no sort of an organization was kept up beyond
here. Some went to Los Angeles, some went on north,

---

[11] *See* above, part II.

[12] By the Capt. Cooke wagon route across Arizona. See the register of
numerous arrivals in the "Record Book of the Rancho del Chino," cited
above.

trading off their cattle for horses, and some went
directly to the coast. We went to the Mission of San
Fernando, where we got some oranges, which were
very good for us. There was a long tedious hill there to
get over. We made up ten wagons. By the time we
reached the San Francisquito ranch [13] I had lost my
cattle. I went down to this ranch and there met Mr.
and Mrs. Arcane getting ready to go to San Pedro. We
came north by way of Tejon Pass and the Kern River,
not far from quite a large lake, and reached the mines
at last. I remember we killed a very fat bear and tried
out the grease; with this grease and some flour and
dried apples Mrs. Erkson made some pretty good pies,
which the miners were glad to get at a dollar, and even
two dollars, apiece.

---

[13] This was the rescue place to which most of the Death Valley emigrants
came.

CHARLES KELLY (RIGHT) AND J. RODERICK KORNS
Pointing to the initials of Henry W. Bigler, cut on November 3, 1849,
in the White Cliffs near the head of Beaver Dam Creek.
Mr. Kelly found this inscription in September, 1938.

Part V

The Flake-Rich Company of Packers

The Mormons who assembled at Provo on October 14 and elected J. M. Flake as captain formed the major portion of the packer company whose story we give in this part. They were subsequently joined by C. C. Rich, H. W. Bigler, and a few others. This company traveled with the O. K. Smith party of packers from Provo until the two companies separated at Division Spring.

The route of the Flake-Rich Company during the eighteen days they spent on the Walker Cutoff and in returning to the Old Spanish Trail has not heretofore been worked out fully. The excellent diaries found and reproduced below enabled us to satisfactorily trace their route.

Also, from the various diaries, we have been able to assemble the names of the following as members of the Flake-Rich Company: J. M. Flake, C. C. Rich, H. W. Bigler, G. Q. Cannon, William Farrer, Peter Fife, James Keeler, Joseph Cain, J. H. Rollins, Thomas Whittle, Darwin Chase, F. M. Pomeroy, Sheldon Stoddard, William Lay, George Bankhead, Joseph Peck, Peter Hoagland, Henry Phelps, and Henry E. Gibson.

A: THE HENRY W. BIGLER JOURNAL

[Henry W. Bigler gained some fame as the diarist who made the first recording of the discovery of gold at Sutter's mill on January 24, 1848. He had served in the Mormon Battalion of the Mexican War, and after release found temporary employment with Sutter. In the fall of 1848 he returned to his people in Utah.

A year later he was "called" to go back to California to mine, as explained in his diary, and he traveled with the Hunt train. After working in the mines for some months he was called on a mission to the Hawaiian Islands.

Henry W. Bigler was born in Harrison county, West Virginia, August 28, 1815. He was with the Mormons at the time of their expulsion from Nauvoo. In his later years he lived in St. George, Utah. We (Ann) remember him as a little bald-headed man who lived in the block behind our home. He died in St. George on November 24, 1900.

The Henry W. Bigler diaries and papers are in the Henry E. Huntington Library at San Marino. Several of the journals have been copied and re-written by Bigler or his children. The diary in Journal Book A has been re-written and amplified at a later date. We have chosen to publish the diary of the 1849 trip from Book B, which appears to be the most satisfactory copy extant. We have endeavored to faithfully reproduce the text, retaining his interesting expressions and spelling. However we have introduced punctuation and capitalization when necessary to make the meaning clear.]

GREAT SALT LAKE CITY.   OCT. 8th, 1849.

MONDAY 8th   Makeing preparations today to go on a mission to California to get Gold for Father John Smith, as he has been kicked & cuft about and finily drove out of the United States because he worshiped God according to the dictates of his own consience and has becum poor, he is Counciled to fit out some person and send them to the Gold mines and he has Called on me to go and is now fiting me out to go with Brother C. C. Rich and others who are sent.[1]

---

[1] Father John Smith was the uncle of Joseph Smith, founder of the Mormon Church. In Bigler's Book A, under date of October 11, 1849, he

Bro. Rich leaves today. It fills me with Sorrow to think of leaveing for I am attached to this place and this people for they are my brethren and my friends, it was with Considerable strugle with my feelings that I Consented to go.

TUESDAY OCT. 9th This day I settled up all my accounts, paid all my debts, Sold my wheat and a fiew bords [boards of lumber] to Bro. Stanes.

WEDNESDAY OCT. 10, 1849 This morning I took some washing to get done at Sister Partridges, after which I went down to the thrashing floor after a little wheat I had thare and some Cooking utensal, my frying pan was gone takeing by some person, stolen I suppose. this rather aggravated me.

THURSDAY 11th last evening Father Smith sent for me he wanted to bless me, he then laid his hands on my head and blest me and also Brother [James] Keeler in the name of the Lord. Brother Keeler is a going for Thomas Calister [2] we will go in the same waggon together; about 2 P.M. we was ready. I told Brother Keeler to call by my house with the waggon and I would be ready. I wrote a note and stuck it on the side of my door for my brother-in-law [John Hess] to take charge of some clothing I had left in a sack; at this moment I experienced what I shall not here attempt to describe. I walked back and forth across my floor and my feelings was spent in a complete shower of tears, every thing I looked upon seamed to

writes: "The bargain between me and Father Smith is this. He to be to all the expense of fitting me out for the gold mines, and after arriving there I am to be saving and prudent and after all the expenses was paid I am to have half the gold." In mining regions of the West this would have been called "grubstaking," but Bigler looked upon the arrangement as a religious "call," that he was obligated to obey.

[2] Bigler says in Book A that Callister was Father Smith's son-in-law, and that Callister fitted out Keeler.

simpethise with me and say go in peace only be faithful
and all will be right. I herd a rattling and looked up
and saw the waggon a coming. I hastened to the
Curtings of the window and wiped away every tear,
and went out to the waggon. I was requested to get in.
I refused. I told Brother Keeler I would walk as I
wanted to call at the tin shop to buy a canteen, I paid
6 bits [75 cents] for one & 2 bits for a quart cup; I
then got in the waggon and we drove to Brother Flakes
on Cottonwood, about 10 miles. Got thare in the night,
all was gone to bed, we mired in the big field. we
had to get in the mud and water with our shoulders
to the wheels; after a long time we got out all wet and
mudy. We called at Brother Chipmans and got some
Butter and 2 large fresh loves of good light wheat
bread for which we paid $2 together with a little tin
pail to carry our butter in.

FRIDAY 12th   This morning we ware detained a
little in getting something made. We found that one of
our horses was sick, supposed to have a tech of the Belly
ache, and to carry out father Smiths Blessings we
bought a mare of Brother Flakes, paid $20 down and
give our note for 100$ with intrest at our Return. At
10 AM we was on the way, went 13 miles and encampt
near the Banks of Jourdan.[3]

SATURDAY 13th   Cloudy. Rained like Sam hill last
night, the top of the mountains was white with snow
that fell in the night, at a bout 8 we was on the march,
went 6 miles and called a halt and Breakfasted, it has
becum clear; a bout 3 PM we arrived at the Utah Settle-

---

[3] The stream that runs from Utah Lake into Great Salt Lake. We shall
not give geographical identifications in footnotes until the party takes the
Walker Cutoff, inasmuch as the places to that diversion point have been
identified above, in connection with the journals of Sheldon Young and
Addison Pratt.

ment.[4] Here we expect to stay a day or to for Company.

SUNDAY 14th Brother [Thomas] Whittle roled in last evening, today a lot of Packers[5] Cum in, this evening we had a meeting and apointed Brother Flake for our Captain until we Cetch up with Bro. Rich.[6]

MONDAY 15th Clear. at 9 we was on the march, when we got about half a mile one of the Captains mules got scared at some indians and threw his pack off which detained us a short time. Came today about 22 miles and encampt for the night, some of the way was vary sandy, hard traveling, Grass & water plenty.

TUESDAY OCT. 16th last night I dreamed I was not going for goal [gold] but was going to the [Hawaiian] Islands on a mission to preach the gospel. Came 20 miles and Campted, the Road was better, had one Runaway scrape. Good Camping.

WE. OCT. 17th Came 25 m. & Campted on the Severe [River]. Good Road except part of the way it was Sandy & dusty. Good Camping.

THURS. 18th Clear, traveled a bout 25 miles, our way was a cross some low mountains & rough, encampt by [Cedar] spring, a beautiful valley lieing west about half a mile from camp. to night I stood guard.

FRI. 19th about 9 we was on the way, the road a little better though vary sandy in places, the Camp got divided or Rather seperated. Capt. Flake is a head with the Camp. Brother Peter Fife says they will not

---

[4] This was present Provo. In Book A, Bigler adds: "Utah settlement is of our own people who came here last spring there are some 30 or 40 families here."

[5] The packers would be the Flake Company. The Capt. O. K. Smith Company of packers joined the Flake Company at Provo, according to the accounts of George Q. Cannon and William Farrer. (*See* part V: D, c).

[6] Charles C. Rich was an Apostle, and so was of higher ecclesiastical rank than any of the other Mormon travelers. His diary is published after Bigler's.

find water.[7] we then made an early encampment for
the night as water was plenty but grass is rather scarse,
made today about 20 mi., tonight I stand my tourn on
gard.

SAT. 20th   this morning I found part of a note left
by Brother Rich dated the 16th inst. Saying all was
well, the particulars was gone, supposed to been
destroyed by some emegrants or a mean Gentile [non-
Mormon]. at 9 oclock we was on our way. the Road
today was vary sandy & loose and as we had the road to
brake, it was covered with sage brush, went about 6 m.
& found Capt. Flake's encampment, they found no
water and are still a head of us. we crost over some
rough mountains. Seen a large flock of Mountain Sheep
or Antelope I rather think. A little before Sunset we
roaled in to Camp with Capt Flake and a Capt. [O. K.]
Smith, a gentile with a crowd of about 20 packers who
are going to Callifornia for gold. today we made about
20 m. Water plenty. Grass rather scarse. Brother
Rollens [J. H. Rollins] was taken sick. Capt. Flake,
Bro. [Joseph] Cain,[8] and myself lade hands on him,[9]
he soon got better.

SUNDAY 21st   Clear and prity, at 9 we was on the
way, went about 5 miles and Crost over a mountain
though not bad; traveled about 20 or 25 miles and Cum
to a Creek but found no grass. we halted and unpacked,
got Supper and watered our animals and packed up
and went a bout 3 m. Found a litle grass and encamped
for the night.

MONDAY 22nd   A little after Sunrise we was on the

---

[7] Fife had been over the route before, apparently with the Battalion boys •
who came up from Los Angeles in the spring of 1848.

[8] Joseph Cain was one of the authors of *Mormon Way-Bill,* part of which
is published in the Appendix.

[9] A ceremony of prayer and blessing performed by elders of the Mormon
Church.

way, traveled about 4 m. and Cum to Beaver Creek. plenty of water & good grass. here we found whare Bro. Rich had Campted nite before last. we found a note directing us to keep down the Creek as the Road Forked at this place. we also learn from the note that the Rode ometer makes it 208 miles from Salt Lake to this place. We continued down the Creek 12 m. past through a Canion into a valley whare we expected to find little Salt Lake. it was now growing late and Capt. Flake Called a vote to know whether we should Camp or Continue and overtake the General (Bro. Rich) as he (Flake) thought the General was not more than 5 m. in advance for we could see the dust arising from the waggons. it was voted to Camp near the River [site of Minersville] as the appearance of the Contry a head indicated that thare was no water for several miles and our road at this spot was leaveing the River down which we had followed. Good Grass & water. made today about 18 miles.

TUESDAY 23d   About 9 o clock we was on our way, went about 3 miles and met the train Cuming back to the River as they had not found any water and grass. their Gide had been out for several miles but found no water. Consequently we turn back to Beaver Creek and Campted. in a fiew minutes Bro. C. C. Rich, James Brown & [F. M.] Pomeroy rode up to our Camp. we was glad to see them. Brother Hunt (or Captain Hunt as we allways Call him) is still out hunting for water.

WE. 24th   At 9 we was on the way to meet the pilot who we expect has found Camping. went a bout 10 miles and [met] Capt Hunt most famished for want of water. he had been out some 40 miles & found no water. the Road is Sandy and vary loose and our 2 animals is most done over, they Cant stand the hard

pulling, their Shoulders is now gaulded and I pity
the poor Horses. the whole train Return back to our
old Camping, Consisting of 113 waggons besides about
50 packers, all bound for Gold. all Gentiles except Bro.
Riches Company. this Company of Gentil Gold digers
had hired Capt Hunt to pilate them through to Callifornia. When the train Came to the forks of the road
at Beaver Creek they held a Council among them
selves to know which road they had better take for
Capt Hunt had told them that thare was a short way.
Considerable of a Cutoff Could be made, but at the
same time he told them he was not acquainted with
the route. But the train had a body of Doctors and
Lawyers, a high council they Called it, and they got it
in their brain that Hunt Could pilate them through.
he told them he knew nothing about the Camping on
the road either, only that he knew a Cut off Could be
made provided they Could find water and grass, but
if they went they must go on their own Responsibility.

THURSDAY 25th Clear. it is thought best that
Brother Keeler and I had better leave our waggon,
and pack the rest of the way through. So we spent the
day in makeing packsaddles until in the afternoon
when we moved up the Creek about 6 m. and Campted
in the Canion. the Conclusion is to Return and go the
other roade by the way of little Salt Lake, and travil
on the old Spanish trail.

FR. 26th this morning the Crowd was buisy until
about the middle of the afternoon. Several articles was
Cashed in the ground. Here we let a man have our
waggon for the sake of the use of it until we arrive in
the mines, whare he will deliver it up to us again.
about the middle afternoon Bro. Keeler and I was all
ready & packed to travil with the pack train. went

about 7 m. and Campted on the top of the mountain without water, plenty of Grass & wood.

SAT. 27th Came today by the Rodeometer 23 m. found water & Grass plenty. Here is little Salt Lake.

SUNDAY 28th this morning Capt. Flake & Bro. Rich told me to take a mare that they had got of a emegrant, that rightly belonged to Brother Alexander Williams of Utah. they vallued the nag to be worth 50 dolars and as the horses I had ware small & young and thin in flesh to stand such a tramp as was before them they advised me to take him and pay Bro. W. $50 when I Returned. Accordingly I took the mare. We then went 10 m. and made a early encampment, plenty of water and Grass. here we went up into the Canion and prospected a little for gold but found none. Little Salt Lake is in sight to the northward and appears to be about 6 or 8 miles long and 1 broad.

MONDAY, OCT. 29th this morning we left Camp, traviled about 14 miles and came to Muddy Creek [Coal Creek]. here is lots of timber along the Creek. after leaving this Creek 9 or 10 miles, Campted at a spring [Iron Spring]. grass tolerable, plenty and lots of good dry sedar for Camp fires. we have now left the waggon train.

TUESDAY, OCT. 30th, 1849 This morning Several indians came in Camp, went 28 m. Campted on lost Creek [site of Newcastle] plenty of water but soon sinks. Grass scarse. this evening after supper Bro. Rich requested the Camp to come together. he told us he wanted that we should have some order and understanding. he wanted Bro. Flake to continue Capt. if the Company was willing. a vote was takeing which was unanimous that Bro. Flake be our Captain and that Bro. Rich council him. Brother Rich wanted we

should be one and observe our prayers. he wanted a
Journal of the Camp kep. voted that Henry Rollens
& Joseph Cain keep the Journal.[10] I understand that
about 14 miles back is a spring [Antelope] in the side
of the mountain but I did not see it, from whare we
started to this place I seen no water. today soon after
leaving Camp Bro. Whittle's Horse runaway and
scattered his pack to the four winds. Soon as he found
himself free from the bagage he stopted and we
gathered up the scattered loading and Repacked and
all was rite once more.

WED. OCT. 31st   Cloudy. Last night it was a greed
on to take a Cut off. after leaveing Camp about 5 miles
it commenced Raining. made about 12 m. and Campted.
Continues Raining. here we expect to leave the Spanish
trail [11] and take the Cutoff and travil a more direct
west without a gide or trail and be in the mines in about
20 days.

THURSDAY, NOVEMBER 1st, 1849   Rained like Sam-
hill all night, got all our bed and bedding wet. I sot
up the most of the night a round a little fire turning
first one side & then the other to it. it was very
disagreeable. partly clear this morning. a bout 10 we
was on the new route, in the afternoon it began to Rain,
in a little while every thread was wet and it was cold
and disagreeable. in a little while it got so mirery that
our horses could hardly get along. at length the Cap.
called a hault by some Rocks which sheltered us first

---

10 This journal has not come to light, but a reminiscent account by J. H.
Rollins was found and is reproduced below. Mr. Cain with A. C. Brower
later published the *Mormon Way-Bill* (Salt Lake City, 1851) which gives
a table of distances on this and other routes.

11 The point of leaving the Spanish Trail was about four miles north of
Hamlin; see St. George Quadrangle, U.S.G.S. This was about eight miles
beyond the site of Newcastle, instead of the twelve miles Bigler estimates.
His mileage estimates here are too high.

rate from the rain. this we called the Rock of Reffuge.[12]
Good feed & plenty of water. we soon gethered wood
and dryed our selves and bed while the cooks was
prepareing supper and I began to feel a little more like
myself

FRIDAY NOV. 2nd   Clear. This morning Snow was
on the mountains. at 9 we left Camp, went up a beautiful little valley [13] about ¼ mile wide, past through
a Canion and over low hills. a long here was a little
snow left that had felln through the night. here we
past over the Rim of the Great Basin. we crost over into
a Canion Running about S.West, made about 25 m.[14]
the Road generally today was rough. we are now
encamped in the Canion on a level spot of grass about
50 acres, wood and water plenty.[15]

SAT. 3d   Laid by until nearly noon for our animals
to rest and eat grass. I cut the 3 first letters of my name
on a Rock & the date.[16] about 11 we left Camp. Con-

[12] The Rock of Refuge is identified by our friend Lamont Huntsman, of
Enterprise, Utah, as being four miles west of Enterprise. He says (in a
letter of July 4, 1952) that stone for four houses in Enterprise was obtained
from this rock formation.

[13] Valley of Shoal Creek, west of present Enterprise.

[14] Fortunately the Farrer diary, printed below, gives much fuller details
for this day's travel.

[15] Headwaters of Beaver Dam Wash.

[16] This site was definitely located by Charles Kelly in September, 1938,
when he found Bigler's initials cut in the volcanic ash wall of the canyon,
one-fourth mile above Bauer's ranch. *See* his account of the discovery in
Desert Magazine, February, 1939.

On August 8, 1951, accompanied by Wiliam R. Palmer of Cedar City, we
followed as near the route of the '49ers as automobile and country roads
would take us. We drove northwest from Cedar City, picked up the old
trail at Iron Springs, followed it around Iron Mountain, and by Antelope
Springs, Newcastle, the forks of the old trails, and to Enterprise. Here we
were joined by an old school friend and present resident of the town,
Lamont Huntsman, who has lived many years in the region. We drove up
Shoal Creek, past the ghost town of Hebron and the Hafen cattle ranches
to the Terry ranch. Following the Clover Valley country road we crossed
the Utah-Nevada state line. About twenty miles from Enterprise we turned

tinued down the Canion a South Course. bad road. made about 12 m and Campted. Grass scarse. Some sign of gold. this morning we expected to Cum to a valley to Camp in. the mountains is high, the Canion narrow in places, dangerous for animals to travil. one place whare we came along to day that one false step would plunged a horse hundreds of feet down the mountain without any possibility of saveing life. Tonight I stand guard and it rains like everything

NOVEMBER, SUNDAY 4th, 1849   Cloudy. Rained in the night. we done first rate by makeing wigwams of willow by planting them in the Ground and lashing the tops together and spreading blankets over them, which turned the rain first rate. at about 10 we left Camp. Continued down the Canion. Rough as you can think. Raining and Snowing like all blazes. at length we found ourselves Blocked up.[17] Capt. Flake and Capt. Smith and Bro. C. C. Rich with some others clem the mountains, which was several thousand feet high, to see if they could see any out let. to think of climing over with our horses was out of the question for the mountains is all most perpendicular, but they could see no outlet for the mountains raised one after a nother as far as they could see. Cap. F. and a fiew others decended the Canion to ascertain if thare was

---

off on a road leading towards Bauer's ranch. Upon reaching the edge of the plateau, Lamont and I walked down the steep canyon road, or trail. Almost at the bottom, we saw "Osborne 1849" incised in a sandstone wall protected by an overhanging shelf of rock.

In the bottom of the canyon a little stream coursed through a dense growth of brush. One-fourth mile above Bauer's ranch (now deserted) is the inscription cut by Bigler on November 3, 1849.

[17] This was at the Narrows, about twelve miles below Bauer's ranch. For interpretation of the locations from here to the point at which the company left Beaver Dam Wash, we depended upon information from an old friend, Jed Terry. He has lived most of his life at Terry's ranch on Beaver Dam Wash, located twenty miles above its junction with the Virgin. He is familiar with the whole area, having coursed it in his cattle drives.

not a possibility to travil down it with our animals by labouring a little. in about 3 hours they returned, Saying it was extremely bad for our animals, being vary rockey and a precipice to assend, but thought by roalling some rocks out of the way we could get along. we had 2 tight steep places and Campt at dark, no grass scarsely at all. we made today about 5 m. It is really surpriseing to see whare horses can go, some of them fell and roalled over with their packs on, Some we helped up the precipice by putting ropes round thier necks and 8 or 10 men at the end to pull and so help them up

MONDAY NOV. 5th   Cleared up in the night, found a dead horse belonging to Brother Cannon. fell in the Creek sometime in the night and drownded. the same horse fell yesterday and roalled over and over down the side of the mountain with his pack on, which no doubt hurt him. Some of the Camp went on top of the mountain this morning and report that they can see a valley about 8 miles ahead. this was good news for we have no feed in this Canion and no man can think how bad the traveling. at ten we was on the march. crost the Creek a great meny times, expecting at every turn to see a valley. in going don this Canion I lost a good spur for Bro. five [Fife], made about 15 m. and Campt in an indian cornfield. the corn was stripted and the standing foder left and was vary good. the road grew better today. a short distance back we past an indian farm,[18] we saw some wheat straw lieing about, beans, sunflowers, and squash vines all in a vary good state of cultivation, ditches for erigation was made, but we find no valley yet as we expected. Some went on top the mountain and say thare is a valley close by.

---

[18] It is remarkable how the Indians had made farms at every available place.

TUESDAY 6th   Clear and nice. at 9 we was on the way. the road grew better. the Canion opens wider. past an indian shanty, they had fled on our approach. here was cowhide not vary long sence, either, sence it was taken off the critters back.[19] we made about 15 m.[20] and Campt in a cottonwood grove near the bank of the stream., the water is getting scarse, sinking in the sand. thare is no valley yet. I think from the looks of the contry we are near the Spanish trail and have not cut off much yet.

WEDNESDAY 7th   Clear. last night I stood guard, this morning Cap. Flake and some others went ahead to see what the Country was like, they returned and say they had been 6 or 8 miles, that the Country becumes more level but broken, no sign of water, that this sinks in a fiew miles below. they said another Cornfield is below about 1 m. We packed up and to the Cornfield [21] intending to lay by and let our animals rest and eat fodder, and not dry fodder neither, for it begins to look more like sumer than winter. the day was spent in shaveing, mending shoes, and Boots, Cleaning guns, &. this morning Brother Keeler and Joseph Peck got to playing and accidently Bro. Keeler received a wound in his foot from the spur of J. P. it sot him all most crazy. This Creek we call farm Creek.

THURSDAY 8th   While breakfasting 6 packers [22] cum

---

[19] The hide must have been obtained from stock employed by travelers on the Old Spanish Trail.

[20] Farrer says twelve miles; and the actual distance was doubtless less, for they are overestimating their mileage throughout this region. Mr. Terry says this camping place was present Motoqua.

[21] Guererro's ranch of today, a mile below Motoqua.

[22] This is a party of packers who left the wagon train at Mount Misery ahead of the Stover party, for the latter did not catch up with Capt. Smith until later. (*see* Stover's account, part VI).

in camp, who had left the waggons some 3 or 4 days ago to overtake us. they say the whole waggon train had left the Spanish trail to follow us. I think they will have to back out and grease and take another rout. I think they will find a bad waggon road in this Canion. at 9 we left Camp. Continued down the Canion 2 or 3 miles, found that the water sinks in the sand. we turned a due west course. after Climbing the bluff we found the Country nearly level, a dry sage plain. the way seamed to be open and by some means the Camp got Seperated. I was in the hind most Company, night Cuming on and we lost the trail of the Company before us. we hallewed and fired guns. at last we herd some person answer. we continued towards the Camp, but finding none we at length saw the flash from 2 guns but herd no report. Br. Whittle took the course by a star and got into camp about 10 oclock, but not a drop of water was thare. the Camp was in a dry bed of a River.[23] we dug in the sand for water but all in vain. a emigrant belonging to Capt. Smiths Cumpany Came in to our Camp, offered to pay any price for a drink of water. thare was none for sail, I had no water and but fiew of the boys that had. the day had been vary warm and I had walked all day, that I was exceedingly thirsty myself, all though I had started with a canteen full this morning I had drank and divided it all out

---

[23] Probably Toquap Wash, that enters the Virgin about one and one-half miles below Bunkerville. An early wagon road, leading from Bunkerville to the mining camps of Delamar and Pioche, went up the gravel bed of the wash some twenty miles to "The Pockets" (holes in sand rock that caught and held rain and flood water), turned east to Tule Spring, and then went north to enter the Meadow Valley Wash at Gann's ranch, a few miles below Elgin. I traveled the road several times as a small boy with my elder brother when he was hauling chickens, eggs, fruit, etc., to the mining camps. I remember that on one or more of these trips we saw the crews working with teams and scrapers, building the railroad down Meadow Valley Wash, Salt Lake to Los Angeles line.

soon after starting. I observed [to] this man that I was so dry myself that if I had a drink I would not take $50 for it. Brother Rich was setting by. Said he, have you no water? no, I replied. after a fiew minutes he cald me to cum thare. I went. he handed me his Canteen saying, drink, you are welcome. his Canteen seamed to be about 2/3 full. I did not expect to get a drink for it was only accidently on my part that I said what I did. I told Br. Rich I would not drink for I was not badly suffering, but he told me to drink, drink, that he himself had not been very thirsty all day. Came today 32 m.

FRIDAY, Nov. 9th 1849 All the Camp got up last night, xcept 1 man, he came in this morning. Mules and horses scattered in every direction. Bro. Rich & Bro. Rollens went on the top of a mountain, reported no prospect of water, we left Camp and traviled up the bed of the Creek, went a bout 3 miles when one of my animals give out. I left hur and put the pack on the one I wride. Bro. Keelers who had the wound in the foot I told him to go ahead with the Camp and if they found water to send and meet me with a Canteen full of water for I should be late in getting into Camp, for the animal I had was nearly give out, for it was with much labour that I could get him along. I was soon left behind without any arms and no one knew I was so far behind. I freequently scratched holes in the sand for water and chewed bullets to make moisture in my mouth. about 3 oclock I seen Bro. Cain cuming. directly I seen him raise his hand and shake it and a tin cup glissnend in his hand, I understood the sign. when we met he handed me a Canteen full of the best water I ever drank. I Clened the Canteen of evry drop. My mouth had began to feel bitter and I began to feel like vomiting, it was not far to Camp. when I got in supper was ready. I eat and drank untill I was satisfied. By this time 2 of the men who had overtaken us yesterday morning Came in on foot leaveing the other 4 behind with their animals – after I had eaten and rested I Returned with 4 other men who had also left horses behind belonging to Capt. S. Company, to fetch in our horses, filling our Canteens full of water. when I came to whare my mare was the men helped me and we poured a Canteen full of water down hur throat, two of the men went on with their Canteens of water to meet the 4 men that was yet behind. it was sometime after dark when I got in with the mare – finily the 2 men returned, not finding the 4 men. they are supposed to be killed by indians. this Creek the Camp call Providence Creek[24] – traveled to day about 10 miles.

SAT. 10th   orders to lay in Camp all day. I and 2,3 others took charge of the animals to herd them on the best pasture. 12 men was sent back with water to look for the 4 men. took with them a spade, should they find them dead, to bury them, in a little while we herd the fireing of guns. Several went to their assistance, expected that an attack with the indians, for 20 or more had been seen following us yesterday and 3 of them had guns, but to our happy disappointment they had met the 4 men and the fireing was a kind of Salute or Cheers. they had found water about 8 miles below our old Camp in a cave on the Creek.

SUNDAY, NOV. 11th, 1849 Sot off this morning about 9. went down the Creek about a mile then struck off to the westward over low mountains all most without number, which made it hard on our animals. in the

---

[24] The creek in Meadow Valley Wash. It appears that they reached the Wash at the site of Gann's ranch, below Elgin.

afternoon 2 of my animals give out. one was the best, as I thought, a horse belonging to Thomas Calester, here I could of Cried! I pitied the poor dum bruits, leave them without a drop of water to perish or for the indians to kill & eat after serving me so faithful to the vary last until they could go no longer. I left them to overtake the Company, got in Camp after dark – this day travil is about 20 miles, and Campted on the Same Creek we left this morning not more than 4 or 5 miles above our old camp. but Capt. Flake thinks we are more than 10.[25] this kind of traveling made us feel rather out of sorts to think we had so meny miles and made so little. Bro. Rich said that this kind of traveling would not do, that his Council had not been taken, if it had we would not been here and that he was not going to travil this way any longer, if we did we would perish in the mountains. that if he could not have his way he would go back to the waggons as soon as he could. we ware [glad] to hear him talk so for it was plain that Capt. F. had not traviled according to the mind of the General, in truth he had not obeyed Council, and that Capt. Smiths opinion had been taken instead of General Riche's. this Reminds me of a dream the General had while on the Spanish trail. He dreamed he found a large old woman in the way. he spoke to hur & asked hur if she would not get out of the way and let him pass. She muttered something and bent a little to one side and he past a round hur and took the Shoot.

Mo. Nov. 12th, 1849   Last night I stood gard. this morning while making preparations to start, I changed my shirt and garment and as they ware in rags I tore them up and Buried them in the Sand. we left Camp

25 Farrer says three or four miles and Rich says eight miles. The camp was probably near Elgin.

about 9 with the intention to travil South.[26] Consequently we traviled back a fiew miles on our back
track. I went to look for the 2 horses I left yesterday
but seen nothing of them. traviled until evening when
we stoped to [let] our horses feed an hour on a good
spot of grass, then packed up and traviled until 10
oclock at night. Capt. F. & S. was ahead looking for
water & camp ground but found none. Campted tonight
without water. Made about 32 miles.

TUESDAY NOVEM 13th, 1849 All hands sat off at
daylight this morning in hopes to find water soon, one
of Capt. S. men laid out all night alone, about 10 it
began to rain. I left the train and went on the top of
som mountains to look for water. I could See no
prospect. by this time it began to rain and I was soon
wet to the hide, in passing over the table lands among
the Rocks I soon quinched my thirst by drinking the
rain water that had gethered in the hollow places in
the rocks. I soon seen the train strike Camp. I made
up to them, water was plenty for both man and beast,
standing in large puddles on the Ground. every man
had filled his Canteen & camp Kittle with water that
had fell and was buisy in getting Something to eat.
thare was no timber, nothing but a kind of large weed
that grows on the desert for fuel and not withstanding
it was raining all the time I never seen anything burn
so well as these weeds, all the Camp is up but one
man belonging to Capt. S. Company, in the evening
it began to Clear up and the Son shone a little. we
campted in a gully dug away in the bank and got dry
ground to lay on. I had went to a bed of a Creek whare
water had run in times past. found a lot of little bushes
strait, from 6 to 10 feet high, about as thick as a man's

[26] Rich says they took a southwest course for the day, traveling down a
narrow valley.

thumb. I cut a back load of them and took to Camp
to make a wigwam to turn the rain, but by the time
I got to camp the Son was a shineing. I feel that the
Lord in great mercy sent this Rain to us. Some of our
party said they herd Capt. Smith say to Bro. Rich
that the finger of the Lord was in this. For my part
it is plain to me and I shall acknowledge the hand of
God in it.[27]

WE. 14th   Cloudy. 3 of our brethren started towards
a mountain to look for a camping place and water to
Camp at until it, the wether, becums clear for the
General is determine not to leave here until he can
get a view of the contry from the top of a high mountain west of the Camp some 15 miles. After a while
the Brethren returned. Reported found no water. by
this time some of Capt. Smith's men Reported that
they had been out and had found a small spring about
3 miles toward the South, but thought by diging a
little plenty of water could be had. orders was given
to pack up and go thare. lots of tadpoles in the spring,
it was cleaned out and we had plenty of water such
as it was.[28] Grass good and water standing about in
pools.

THURSDAY NOV. 15th, 1849   Clear except some
clouds that hangs about the top of sum of the mountains, after Breakfast the General with 3 other men
started for the top of the mountain west of our Camp [29]
in order to get a view of the country, in the evening

27 Others of the party looked upon this rain as having been miraculously
sent to save their lives.

28 Coyote Spring, about 40 miles from Glendale and a little west of highway 93, running to Alamo. They later called it Division Spring, because of
the dividing of the party here on November 16. George E. Perkins, in his
Pioneers of the Western Desert (Los Angeles, Wetzel Publishing Company,
1947), p. 47, identifies Coyote Spring as Division Spring.

29 Sheep Mountain range.

we sent out some mules to meet them, it was now near dark and Capt. Flake ordered a fire to be made on a high place near camp for them to cum to, for it was cloudy and heardely a star to be seen. the Boys returned about 8, reported they found them not, they went to the foot of the mountain and fired 10 rounds, but got no answer. about an hour after their return the General came. he got a prospect of the Country but said thare was no sight for water or grass as far as he could see, neither was there a chance in his opinion for a pass. he could see mountains piled one above another for 150 miles. thare was a valley over on the other side of the mountain at least ¾ of a mile higher than this, it looked like a perfect desert. he said thare was a valley southward that run west, that if thare was any pass it must be through it, but thare was not a good prospect for water that way. on Considering he give it as his Council for us to go the Spanish trail. his mind is not to go any other at present, and all that is a mint to follow him Can do so, if not they can go their own way. his heart has ached ever sence we left farm Creek [Beaverdam Wash] in fact he told Capt. F. at farm Creek he wanted to go farther south. Capt. F. said he acknowledged that he had not done as he was told.

FRIDAY 16th NOVEM, 1849 Clear. this morning Capt. Smith came and asked Bro. Rich what discoveries he made from the top of the mountain and what way he thought of going &. Bro. Rich told him what he had seen and give his opinion of the route, that it was his mind not to go that way any further, that he should make for the Spanish trail. Smith Said he would continue his course a cross the mountain, if he perished and if we never herd from him we mite know he was dead, had died with his face westward and not before he had eaten some mule meat too. at about 9 the 2 companies parted. 2 or 3 of Smiths men left him and joined us. we went a fiew miles and came to water & grass whare we rested a little and let our horses drink and eat, after which we continued our travils. our cours was South down the bed of a Creek[30] about 15 miles, and campted after passing through a ledge about ¼ of a mile. Grass and water plenty. this ledge is a Curiosity. it is an opening through a mountain more than 300 feet high on each side of a creek.[31] indians was liveing here. they run and left their Bows and arrows, Baskets, Knives and paints, &.

SAT. 17 OF NOVE 1849   Clear & fair, at 8 we was on the way. Continued down the River traveling mostly in its bed. after traveling about 10 m. we came to a greater curiousity than the one yesterday. the Bed of the River past through a mountain for about 3 miles, a solled [solid] mass of Rocks perpendicular to the highth of from 500 to 1000 feet high on either side of the Creek, the passage is about 10 yards wide, the bed of the Creek was dry, thare was several holes of water found standing. about half way through we found whare the indians had shot over head about 80 feet into a crivis as if they wished to pry off a large shelv in Rock. probable thare was more than 200 arrows sticking thare.[32] the bursting of a Cap in this passage

---

30 Pahranagat Wash.

31 Double canyon, shown on St. Thomas Quadrangle, U.S.G.S.

32 Thereafter called Arrow Canyon, shown on St. Thomas Quadrangle. It is about ten miles northwest of Glendale. On August 4, 1951, with young Perkins as guide, we drove from Glendale on U.S. highway 93 for about twelve miles, then turned left and down a gravel wash as far as our low-swung car could go. Then we walked the three miles to the head of Arrow Canyon.

The CCC boys, probably in the late 1930s, built a masonry dam across the canyon to make a reservoir for storing flood waters. We found the place dry.

sounded like the crack of a Rifle, everything seames to go write sence the General has took things in hand. we have no mountains to pass over, but pass rite through them, and the River Runs the rite way and we have water whenever we want it for ourselves and animals, in deed we feel like new men sence the masheen had been put in order. as we left the Canion we came to fine grass for our animals. we halted and let our horses eat a while. near hear is some warm springs, we past by some of them, and some of our road rather muddy in places caused by those springs. Came today about 15 mi and Campt. near the Creek. lots of water and good Grass. this stream is supposed by Bro. Fife to be Muddy Creek. Bro. F. had traveled the Spanish trail last year after being let loose from Uncle Sam [33] and judged this to be Mudy from the looks of the water.[34] tonight I stand guard, but what is worse than all I have left my pocket knife whare we eat breakfast back at our old Camp, lieing on the ground.

SUNDAY NOV. 18th, 1849   At 8 we was on the march. went 5 m. when we saw a smoke. in a fiew minutes we seen Cattle feeding on the other side of the Creek and some men with them. they told us Cap. Hunt was encampted just below us with a train of waggons. when we made up who did we find but Captain Hunt sure anough, with a large train of waggons on the Spanish trail just at the edge of the 50 m. drive. among the train was Bros. Pratt, Brown and Blackwell, still with the Roadometer, on their way to the islands. this fild our

I climbed to the top of the dam — about ten feet high on upper side and about twenty on lower — and looked down the canyon. It is only about twenty-five feet wide at the bottom and is crooked. The walls are of black rock. The road used to run through this canyon.

[33] Released from the Mormon Battalion after his term of service expired.
[34] The water of the Muddy has a milky color.

hearts with joy. indeed we was happily disapointed. we
did not expect to strike the trail for 2 days yet, this
reminds me of my dream, last night I dreamed of seeing
Bros. P. & Brown, we all felt to rejoice and thank the
Lord to meet with friends and provisions so quick
whare we could recruit we got some Crackers and I
thought it the best eating ever I had, I naturally like
to eat hard bread any how. we left Captain Smiths
Company just as some of his men was getting out of
provisions, and the word was that they ware threatening
us with their rifles if we did not divide with them for
we had agreed to let them have, when they got out.[35]
Capt. Hunt used us well and we got some provisions
from the train. Capt. H. says that a train of 100
waggons has started to follow us to go it or perish, and
they will perish if they dont back out for I am sure
they cant go it. as for Capt. Smith he is a goner if he
dont beat down south on to the Spanish trail.[36] This
evening Bro. James Brown wanted me to agree to go
with him & Bro. Pratt to the islands Saying that Bro.
P. wanted me to go and that he had heard Bro. Pratt
ask Bro. Rich how he would like to swap off one of his
men for Bro. Blackwell and that Bro. Rich had said
if it was agreeable between the parties he had no
objections. I told him I did not like to Consent to go.

Mo. Nov. 19th 1849   Laid by all day. Bro. Rich
sold a yoke of oxen and Bought provisions for our
Company,[37] tonight I stand guard.

Tuesday 20th   Last evening a dutchman got in who
had left Smith's train. he was Robed by the indians of

---

[35] Rich also indicates (Nov. 15 entry) that there was some threat or
danger that Smith's men would attempt to take food away from the Mormons.

[36] As indicated (part VIII: A), Smith did turn back, heading for Salt Lake
City, but was met and picked up by the Egan wagon train and brought
through to California.

[37] Explained in the Pratt diary, (see III: B).

nearly all of his provisions. At noon we took up our line of march, haveing a 50 mile desert before us. Sometime after night we Came up to whare Bros. J. Brown & Geo. Cannon was. they had wrode on a head and had found some holes of water and had stopted to give notice. we halted and watered our animals and then drove on having the train of waggons afollowing in our rear. The moon shone and we had good traviling, about 10 oclock we struck Camp having found a good spot of grass and plenty of water for our animals, standing in holes, that had fell dureing the late rains. this encampment was to the right of the road, and the water was over a mile still, far to the right among some bushes, the other water was near the road to our left. Came today about 25 m. [to Dry Lake].

WE. 21st this morning I seen plenty of water and is nearer 2 m. than one from the road. After breakfasting we took up our line of march, traveled up a gradual ascent for 10 or 12 m. and then descended for severel miles over rough road, then traveled on a bottom until we struck the abagus [38] whare we found plenty of water & Grass. today several horses give out among whom was one of Shelden Stoddards [39] and John Dixon's. made today about 25 m. The waggons did not get up until most morning.

THURSDAY 22nd It was thought to stay here today and let our animals recruit a little as thare was good feed but as it was known that thare was good grass a fiew miles ahed we gethered up and went to it, a distance of 4 or 5 m. Several warm springs here.[40]

[38] Las Vegas.

[39] Stoddard went with the Mormon colony in 1851 to found San Bernardino, California, where he lived the remainder of his life. *See* extract from his biographical sketch, part V: F.

[40] Head springs of Las Vegas creek.

FR. 23d   traveled about 12 m. and campt on a little creek [Cottonwood Creek]. the camping was poor as most all the grass had been eaten off by emegrants animals ahead of us. today was cool and windy. the contry over which we traveled was poor & rocky – tonight I stand guard.

SAT. 24th   Went 4 m. and campted on a good spot of feed that was found by Capt Hunt last evening, water tolerable, plenty. I spent much of the day in hunting Hairs [jack rabbits] but did not get the first shoot.

SUNDAY 25th   Clear & nice, went 8¾ by the roadometer and Campted at a spring [Mountain Spring] to the rite of the road in the mountain, grass scarse, fire wood in abundance, Cedar. here we found a note from a train that past on the 18th Requesting a Mr. Dallas a Capt of a train behind us to Cum a head as soon as possible, that their train was a starving, he had seen things that made his Blood run cold, they had killed several oxen and had sent some men to the Settlements for provisions.[41] Capt. Hunt makes it 220 miles from here to William's the first Settlment.

MO. 26th   Clear & fine, last night I stood guard. at 8 or 9 we was on the march, had a good Road all day, down hill for 27 miles by the roadometer to whare we struck the first water, 3 or 4 clusters of willow trees growing near by [Stump Springs] we thought of Camping here but what little feed there had been was eat off. we turned to the right about 4 m. and found plenty of bunch in a deep bed of a Creek, but no

---

[41] The train that passed Mountain Spring a week previous was the lead section of the Gruwell-Derr Company. From here the Gruwells, Derr, and two others had gone ahead to California for supplies. Dallas was of the same train, but had fallen behind. The Hunt company had caught up with him and some other wagons of the party at the Muddy. See Pratt's diary, Nov. 15 entry (part III: B).

water, and campted. it is now 7 oclock at night.
traviled today about 31 m.

TUESDAY 27th Clear and frosty. Bro. Fife found
some water about 1 mile and a half down the creek
below us. we went thare and took breakfast, after which
we traviled 20 m. and encampted at a spring. plenty
of grass and water [Resting Spring] the land round
about in places is saleratus. the Road today was not so
good, past over 2 hills. it is said some spaniard was
kiled here by the indians.[42] the fires of the formost
trains was not gone out. seen several dead oxen by the
way. 1 – one – live ox so poor he had give out. I
felt sorrow for him when I seen him standing alone
with no other Cattle about and was perhaps at least
5 m. from water. yokes and Kags was lieing along by
the way.

WE. 28th Rained in the night. Cloudy and cool
today. wagon got up last night at 9 oclock. laid by all
day. the provisions was examined. our mess has been
liveing on Rashions, we have but 4 days provisions and
it will be at least 8 days before we can reach the
Settlements. Bro. Rich let us have 23 lbs. of flower &
3 of hard bread, one man of the wagon train killed
a beef and we got 43 lbs at 8 cts per pound, so that
we now have 8 days provisions.

THURSDAY 29th Clear. at noon we left the waggons
and went about 7 miles and encampted on Saleratus
Creek at a spring.[43] good grass. today as we passed
along we could see the Saleratus white like snow about
1 or 2 m. distant. along here is the meanest looking
country I ever see, fit for nothing but hobgoblins to

---

[42] In 1844. See Fremont's report of the incident and the retaliation by
Carson and Godey.

[43] This is the spring that comes out of the hill on the east side of Amargosa
Canyon, about two miles below Tecopa.

live at. the water of this Creek [Amargosa river] looked like strong lie. We had to wach our animals vary carefully to keep them from drinking it. tonight I stand guard.

Fr. 30th   Clear. 2 foot man came in last night. had left the wagon for the Settlements carrying their provisions on their backs. Started early this morning, traviled down the Creek, Crossing it a great meny times for 8 or 10 miles, then left the Creek and turned a little to the left. traviled through sand which mad it harde for boath man and beast. we past through a narrow Rockey little Canion through a notch of the mountain, here is a weak spring of brackish water; here I saw signs for gold. about a mile further we came to Salt water [Salt Spring] and finding some grass we stopted to let our animals eat a little as we have a drive of 45 m before we Cum to water. Being vary thirsty and having no water with me I went to hunt water. after traveling back a mile to the right up a steep Canion I found fresh water in some rocks.

Just as I got back I seen the Camp driving the animals to water near the Camp. the like never was known before, for the animals was exceedingly dry, feeding over Saleratus land. I felt to Rejoice and praise the Lord in giveing water to our animals as well as for ourselves. this water was found by some of the camp a little to the left, standing in holes. we then took a good rest, eat our bite and let our horses eat, filled up our Canteens with fresh water and at 4 PM, was on the march. good smooth road and the moon shone bright and pritty. we traviled until about midnight, past a waggon that had been left & a Box and several dead oxen. we campted without any water for our animals, neither grass. our camping was at the head of a Short deep Canion. one of my horses nearly give out. one horse belonging to the mess did give out and was left. Came about 25 m sence 4 oclock makeing in all for todays travil about 35 or 6 m. I got vary tired. I do not know but I should of give out had it not been for Bro. Rich for I had no horse to wride, for Bro. Keeler and me had but 2 animals between us and they ware so poor and week we ware saveing them all we could. Bro Rich let me have his mule to wride in turns with him, which I feel was Cind and I truly felt thankful.

SAT. DEC. 1st, 1849 Clear & frosty. the horse that was left was brought in this morning. at Sunrise we ware on the march. went about 8 or 10 m. when we seen some wagons in Camp off to our left about 1½ miles. we sent to know who they ware and happly we learnt thare was plenty of fresh water thare standing in holes. they accidently had found it. we soon unpacked and let our animals to water & Grass and our Cooks was soon at work prepareing something to eat. after Resting 3 hours we packed up and went 10 m. further and encampted near the Bitter Spring. at the Road whare we turned off for the water this morning Bro. Rich left a note for Capt. Hunt. Bro. Cains pack horse gave out. plenty of fresh water and some grass, lots of emegrants here.[44]

SUNDAY 2nd Clear and frosty, at about 8 we was on our march. our Course is a Cross a mountain 15 m. to the summit and 35 to the Mohave River. the first water after Crossing the Ridge we stopted and let our animals eat a little. I went and prospected a little for goal, as thare appeared to be sign for it. it was 9 oclock at night before we made Camp, I was tired and hungry,

---

[44] Part of the Gruwell-Derr company.

the old Sierra Nevada is close by in front and as Capt.
Hunt says bold as tigers.[45] Some of our Companies
animals give out, one of our mess left his horse to
shift for himself. – Such tramps and fatigues as we
make sometimes will make men old before their days
is half gone.

Mo. 3d   I went out to hunt the horses before breakfast, came across a greap [grape] patch, the greaps was
sweet as Reasons [raisins].[46] I eat until I found myself
sick! here is a lot of emegrants & waggons. they have
been here for a month liveing on nothing but beef.[47]
the Company let them have some flower for their
wimen and Children – lots of timber along the River
but no Running water at this time, we found water in
holes. at 1 PM we left Camp, traviled up the River for
12 m. and Campted for the night.

Tuesday 4th   Cloudy, Sot off about 8 still going up
the River. Some of the Company went ahead to hunt
for deer. the mare we got of Bro. Flakes lost hur colt,
and this morning we had to help up the mare of Bro.
John Smiths. Bro. Rich advised me to leave hur which
I did at the first water & grass. I realy felt Sorrow
for the dum bruit to be left alone in the wilderness.
at 8 in the night we made Camp tired and hungry and
wet it haveing rained considerably to day which made
it still worse to travil. but those who had went ahead
had made good large fires for wood was plenty. Came
today 20 m. Bro. Keeler and I have but one animal
between us to Carry us through, our provisions is nearly
exhausted!

We. 5th   Snowing, laid by all day. Bro. Cannon was

---

[45] Book A says "bold as lions."

[46] He has reached the Mojave River.

[47] The advance group of the Gruwell-Derr train. It appears that they
had not been at this particular point for a month, but had lived on beef for
that length of time (*see* Farrer's entry of December 3, part V: c).

quite sick. Several Hunters went with myself went out to hunt deer but none was killed. Several was wounded but it Snowed and Rained so that they could not be tracked. while I was out thare came up a heavy Snowstorm, late in the eavening and I got lost and began to think I would have to lay out alone but fortunately I found Camp and was in before dark. I felt greatful to the Lord for I believe he guided me by his spirit or I should of had to laid out being all wet and Cold. this morning one of the Camp shot an owl and Cooked it and I helpted them eat it, went first rate. this evening a footman Came in and brought Bro. Smiths mare. She seamed so smart I gave the strainger a dollar for hur and will try if Possible to get her to the Settlements.

THURSDAY 6th. DEC. 1849 this morning it quit Snowing. thought best by Bro. Rich to lay by and hunt as our provisions is scarse and the Black-tailed deer seamed to be plenty. 6 hunters went out and brought in 3 fine deer which greatly increased our stock of provisions Bro. Rich was one of the 6 hunters, he found one dead that had been shot yester. we all felt to thank the Lord. last night Bro. Cains mess and ours joined together at evening prayer and asked the Lord to bless the hunters on the morrow and he has answered our prayers. I felt to rejoice and thank the Lord when I seen them coming in with their game.

FRIDAY 7th fair. at 10 oclock we took up our line of march. found soft traveling, the snow melting vary fast. traveled up the Mohava about 10 miles and campted in the timber near the Creek, here the Creek runs, one of our men kild a deer. the mare I gave the dollar for was found dead this morning, poor Creature it appeared to me that she frooze to death. this evening

Brother Rich called the Camp together and laide before them the propriety of dividing the Camp as he thought we ware with in 2 days travil of the Settlement, and thare appeared to be no sign of indians about. he thought it was not more than 6 miles to the head of the Mohava whare we would turn off for the Pass and from thare 20 m. to the Cahoon Pass. this could be traviled in one day by the strong animals and the rest had better make 2 days of it. those who went a head could leave more provisions for the hinder company and in so doing we mite get all our animals through by giveing the weaker ones more time. our mess and Bro. Cains volunteered to go behind. this was about half the crowd, it was voted that Bro. Rich go ahead.

SUNDAY 8th   last night was a vary cold night. this morning Clear – Bro. Rich & Company left early this morning and we followed soon after, went 6 m. Crost the Creek which is quite a stream at this place and campt on the opposite side, Grass scarse for our animals.

SUNDAY 9th   Made an early start on perpose to reach a Spring a cross the mountain about 18 m. We gained the Sumit [Cajon Pass] after traveling about 15 m. Before arriving at the top of the mountain we stopted a fiew minutes to rest whare the son shone warm and the snow was going off, while setting down I fell into a dose of sleep and thought I was eating bread, at this place Bro. Keelers and my only & last animial give out! We unpacked hur and put the pack on a loose mule. I made out to get hur a cross the mountain within about a mile of camp, when I could get hur no farther. after leaveing hur on our reaching camp to our joy here we finds a man with a wagon

load of provisions & beef from the Settlements to Sell.[48]
Some of the boys who was in the front Croud was here
bakeing *bread,* no sooner than we seen his bread we
helpted our selves without much coaxing either. this
was why I wrote my dream for it was precisely such
looking bread as I thought I seen, we ware not long
unpacking, neither was our cooks slow in getting a
good supper. – we learn that it is 25 m. to the first
ranch or Settlement.

MO. 10th this morning I went back and brought
in the mare I left yesterday. I felt in my vary heart
to pity the poor animal. thare appeared to be something
else the matter with hur besides fatigue. Seamed to be
stiff behind and about every 200 yards she would lie
down. So I am compeld to leave hur behind. after
eating a good hearty breakfast we took up our line of
march, traveling down the Canion, Crossin the stream
a great meny times, long at first it was remarkable
bad traveling, being so rocky. went about 12 m and
Campt in the edge of the Great Valley, the wind blew
hard down the Canion and it was cold passing long
don the Canion. I freequently see sign as I thought
for gold –

Nothing makes me feel more Sorrowful than to
leave a good faithful animal in the wilderness to perish
and die alone.

TUESDAY DEC. 11th, 1849. Clear, here the feed is
green. at 8 we left Camp, went 15 m. and Campt at the
CoComongo's Ranch. I recon thare was a glad set of
fellows when we found we was through an a possibility
of getting something to eat.

WE. 12th OF DEC., 1849 Laid by all day to hunt
for Bro. Fife's horse. Bought a bushel of wheat for 3

---

48 Mr. Davis, sent out by Isaac Williams of Chino Rancho.

dollars and ground it on the hand mill and will eat
the flower without boulting which is a Common thing
among the Spaniards of this Contry – took a fiew horns
of Good wine, 50 cts.

THUR. DEC. 13th   Found all the horses, at 1 oclock
we left for Williams Ranch [Chino] 9 m. whare we
found Bro. Rich & the brethren all quartered with a
room all ready provided for us to go into and plenty
of provisions. we will now begin to live, but the worst
of it is we have no wood to cook our groub and it looks
much like rain, here cums the boys with some wood –
we now will soon have something to eat for we get
flower & meat without money or price. Mr. Williams
has not been at home sence the General came and Mr.
W's agent & clerks seames to know nothing about the
price of anything, hence we know nothing about the
prices until he Cums home which is expected this
evening.

FRI. DEC. 14th, 1849   Commenced raining last night
and rains hard all day today. Mr. Williams got home
last night. everything is now regulated. Flower $12 per
fanager [49] which is about eaquel 100 lbs. or $2 per
alimo, Beef Cattle from $5 to 15 dollars per head.
Corn 6 dollars fanager, Salt 1 dollar per alimo, Coffee
37½ cts per pound, the same for sugar.

SAT. 15th   Clear. Colonel Williams gave us liberty
to take 2 yoke of cattle to haul some wood and let our
animals rest. Myself & 3 others got up the teem and
brought in a load of wood while some others got up a
beef and drest it, others kep house and Cleaned it out
and at night we had a fine Supper.

SUN. 16th   Fair. I went and got two alimo of flower,
herd by some men who have just arrived from the mines

---

[49] A *fanega* equals about 1.6 bushels.

that beef is worth 75 cts per pound thare, flower 1-25
per lb. $250 for a passage on a vessel from Pueblo
[Los Angeles] up San francisco. Boards worth $500
a thousand at the bay and in the mines.

Mo. 17th   Rained all day. Bro. Rich brought in
some books for us to pass of the day with – Bunions
dreames [*Pilgrim's Progress*] and some other religious
works, tracks &.

Tu. 18th   Cleared up this morning. Mr. Williams
wants Bro. Rich to buy him out. he asks $200,000.[50]
he says he has Cattle a nough on his ranch to pay for
its self. he says that Bro. R. with his men can pay for
it in 6 months out of the Cattle, he has more than
40,000 head of cattle on his ranch besides a 1000 head
of horses & mules. he says he is not satisfied and wants
to sell off and go to the states, that he is bound to sell
or leave it in some shape or other to be secured for
his Children. Bro. Rich says he is got [gave] the Book
of Mormon to [Williams to] read.

We. Dec. 19th 1849   Today our Company Commenced to work for Mr. Williams for provisions &
has sot us to clean out an old water ditch. at dark
[F. M.] Pomeroy arrived from the wagons bringing
4 horses that had been left by the way belonging to
the Company. he left Capt. Hunt some 30 m. down
the Mohava. This evening Bro. Rich called us together
and wanted to know how much wheat the Company
wanted &. 2 fanager each was the conclusion. Mr. W.
will let us have it or a teem to bring it with. can get
wheet for $5.50 per fanager and 50 cts. for grinding.

Thurs. 20th   Clear. Worked on the ditch, vary

---

50 This is the inception of the idea that culminated in the Mormon pur-
chase of land and the settlement of San Bernardino in 1851. When the
colony finally came the leaders expected to buy Williams's Chino Rancho,
but they failed to make a deal, and land was purchased from Lugo instead.

laborious work. Bro. Rollens & Keeler is appointed
Cooks for the Croud. Some of us have got a cold sence
we have been liveing in a house. about the middle
afternoon my back & head ached so that I left off work
for the day. I and Bro. Cain went to the Cain break
and cut some cane for brooms to sweap out the house.

FR. 21st OF DEC. 1849   Clear and vary warm. finished the ditch.

SAT. 22nd   Fair & warm. the Country is as green
as the month of may at home. Capt. Hunt arrived with
the train. the roadometer makes the distance from
Great Salt Lake City to this place 722 miles,[51] to the
pass 701.

SUNDAY 23d   warm and growing wether. I am
unwell haveing a cold. Washed my shirt and garment.
Some talk of Christmas.

MO. 24th   I was hunting for Bro. Whittles horse
today, in the evening Bro. Pratt came in from hunting,
brought in 2 ducks & 1 Curlew[52] for Christmas, a
bulock is also drest and Cooks appointed to Cook a
Christmas dinner.

TU. 25th   Clear & warm growing wether, the earth
is green with grass and wild oats, & had an excellent
dinner Considering the materials they had to make it
of. plenty of roast beef and potatoes, Baked ducks and
plum pooding. as for myself I did not enjoy myself
well haveing a severe pane in my left eye. I went to
the doctor, he said thare was nothing in it. it seames
as though something was sticking in it near the puple.
it panes me much. I Cant bare the light even to my
well eye. I am compeld to blindfold myself. this

---

[51] The mileage on the modern highway would be 710 miles from Salt Lake
City to the Chino Rancho (three miles southwest of the present town of
Chino).

[52] Pratt, above, says two ducks and a brant.

evening after prayers I got Bros. Rich and Pratt to lay hands on me When they layed hands on me their hands felt hot to my head, after which I felt easy and rested well all night.

WE. 26th Fogy from the ocean. My eye does not pane me any for which I feel thankful to the Lord. I worked on the mill race all day, at night Bro. Pratt sung us some good songs.

THURS. 27th Worked all day. the light I find is not good for my eye, yet it does not pane me but weakens it. I have a cold and I feel weak and feeble. Sent to the store for some sugar to sweeten my tea, after supper a fiew songs by Bro. Pratt.

MO. DEC. 31st nothing of importance sence the 27th. Capt. Hunt and Pomeroy left this morning for Mr. Lugoes [53] to buy oxen for the Company to go from here to the mines with ox teams. Cleaning wheat ready for the mill. today Bro. Pratt asked me if I would go to the islands should Bros. Rich and Amasa Lyman call on me to go. I told him I should if that was their council.

TUES. JAN. 1st, 1850 New years day. All hands cleaning wheat, haveing 34 fanagers, we hired 4 squaws to Clean with baskets, one of them will clean as much as 3 of us,[54] the wheat is full of gravel.

WE. 2nd Rained some. I have a severe cold. I caughed so much last night that my lungs is vary sore. Cleaning wheat all day.

THURS. JAN. 3d, 1850 Showery. Some of the boys hunting their horses. Capt. H. has not returned. the

---

[53] The Lugo's Rancho San Bernardino, a large tract that included present Colton and San Bernardino. *See* Beattie, *Heritage of the Valley, op. cit.,* pp. 51-55.

[54] The Indians had much experience in working at the missions and ranchos.

General is uneasy, they ware to been back yesterday. only 30 miles to Lugoes.

FR. 4th Showery. the Boys returned without finding their horses, in the evening Capt. H.&P. returned with 4 yoke of half broken oxen. $31 per yoke. I and Darwin Chase [55] was buisy in weighing up flower.

SAT. 5th Cloudy. turned our Cattle out with hobbles on, they run like so meny buffalo and broke a part and we was oblige to hire a yung Spaniard to take his horse and lassoe them for us while we made them fast a gain by the horns. Wet and vary mudy under foot.

SUN. 6th Clear. Herding the oxen, this evening Capt. Egan arrived from the valley.[56] Bro. Rich got a letter from Bros. Geo. Smith & E. F. Benson informing us that the Colery is Killing some of Uncle Sams fat ones and that the President of the United States had made a proclamation and sot a part a day of fasting to almighty God to take away the scurge, but if he is like themselves he "can do nothing for them." Bro. S. and B. want Brother Rich to rase them $5000 from the brethren who are now on their mishion to get goald [57] that their hands may be liberated and be able to return to their field of labour, and they will pray the Lord to lead the Brethren into some nook or corner whar it lays. as for my part I shall be glad to help rase it for them and have their prayers and blessings on my head.

THURSDAY, JAN. 10th, 1850 Nothing of importance since the 6th. it has rained considerable this week, all the horses is found but 2 belonging to Bro. Farrer. Late

[55] Chase had been a member of the Mormon Battalion in Co. B. *See* Daniel Tyler, *Mormon Battalion, op. cit.,* p. 120; and Jenson, *Latter-Day Saint Biographical Encyclopedia,* IV, 738-39.

[56] *See* below, Part VIII.

[57] Bigler, Cannon, and others were considered as having been "called" on a mission to do gold mining.

this afternoon we made a moove with our wagons for the mines, went 3 miles & campted. Stood gard tonight to keep the Cattle from running away. Bro. Rich did not start with us but will overtake us in a fiew days as he is going with a fiew that will go with pack animals.

FR. JAN. 11th, 1850 Sot off this morning about 9 oclock, the road being so soft we mired down and was obliged to unload in order to get the waggon out. went 6 m. and Campted on the bank of a Creek [San Jose] excellent ford, in about 1 hour after Camping Capt Haward Egan roaled up and Campt by us with instruction for us to wait until the General Cum up.

SAT. 12th Did not travil today. I and others ware hunting for Bro. Farrers two horses. did not find them. in the afternoon Bros. Rich, Pratt and Hunt came and this evening Bro. H. was made Captain for our Company. herd that the City of San francisco is burnt down and in consequence of it grocerys is vary high at the Puebalow [Los Angeles] the place whare we wanted to get our Sugar & Coffee &.

SUN. JAN. 13th, 1850 Rained this morning, at 10 it cleared up, when we struck our tent and was off, I and 4 others went to look for the 2 lost horses but could not find them, they are given up as being stold, when we came in to camp found we had Cum 10 m. Campted by a River. the contry over which we passed is nice, some splended Ranches,[58] the soil is vary Rich indeed, and I may say hundreds of thousands of Cattle feeding on the plains besides hundreds of heads of horses.

MO. 14th Clear and frosty this morning, struck tents at 9, went 8 m. and stopted at St. Gabriels Mis-

---

[58] The large Puente ranches of John Rowland and William Workman, who in 1841 led the first group of Americans over the Old Spanish trail to settle in California. *See* Hafen and Hafen, *Old Spanish Trail.*

sion,[59] it has been a fine building with 5 bells built of adobies & covered with tile, a large vineyard and beautiful gardens, we went in the orchard among the orange and lemon trees, got some of the fruit I did not like them being not quite ripe, the olive trees was bending with their fruit. I gethered a quantity of olive stones to take to Salt Lake to plant, after resting 2 hours we went 4 m. and Campted. Splended Camping except wood is vary scarse. Came today 12 m.

TU. JAN. 15th, 1850 This morning the Generals horse is misen and while the wagons went on I and some others turned out to hunt for him but could not find him. whe[n] we came in we found the Company encampted one mile above the Pueblow on River Sanpedro [60] haveing cum 2 miles, we shall lay here today and tomorrow to hunt for Bro. Riche's horse and buy some grocerys at the Pueblow.

WE. 16th Fair. the horse was not found.

THURS. 17th Fair. a general settlement was made this morning in camp as we had all been buying and liveing together & Sent down to town and bought our Sugar & Coffee &. at 9 we roaled out, went 9 m. and Campt above on the same River at the same old Camp ground whare I Campted the first night after I was discharged from Servis in Company with Capt. Evert & Company.[61]

FR. 18th The Camp this morning bought a fine beef Cow of a Spaniard $10. after dressing and dividing it went 10 m. & campt. fine food, plenty of wood, here lives a family of either or boath Spaniards or indians.[62]

---

59 A famous California mission, founded in 1771. The church building is preserved and in use today.

60 Now called Los Angeles River. Its bed is generally dry.

61 After discharge from the Mormon Battalion in 1847.

62 The journal continues, covering the further trip to the gold mines.

B: CHARLES C. RICH DIARY

[Charles C. Rich, one of the Twelve Apostles of the Mormon Church and a prominent leader of the sect, was going to California to help manage Mormon affairs there. His biography by John Henry Evans, is published as *Charles Coulson Rich, Pioneer Builder of the West* (New York, 1936). He was forty years old in 1849.

The original of this diary is in the Historical Library of the Mormon Church in Salt Lake City. The Church Historian's office kindly supplied us a typed copy of the journal as published here. Some punctuation has been added for clarification.]

OCTOBER the 8th 1849   2 o'clock p.m. left my home and the city of the great Salt Lake on a mission to Upper California having been appointed to assist Amasa Lyman in the presidency of that country by the conference held on the 6th. Staid at G. M. Flake on cottonwood 12 miles.[63]

TUESDAY 9th Took breakfast at John Bills then went to Utau [Provo] accompanied by James Brown. Staid at Alexander Williams, found some excitement with regard to the Indians some of them having fired on some of our people. 39 mi.

WEDNESDAY 10th Early this morning the Indians came down in considerable numbers to attack the fort as was supposed all had called out after some consultation they wished peace. I mad a speech to the brethren and organized them, gave the Indians some council and left about 10 o'clock, passing Hobble Creek, Spanish Fork, Petete Creek and camped on a small clear stream. 21 miles.

THURSDAY 11th   We passed the Springs, Willow Creek, Salt Creek, Toola, camped on a sage plain without watter, traveled about 50 miles.

---

[63] Since the route has been traced in some detail above, especially in the notes accompanying the journals of Sheldon Young, Addison Pratt, and H. W. Bigler, we shall not duplicate such informational notes here.

FRIDAY 12th   After traveling about 8 miles we overtook Capt. Hunt with the main train, camped on the Severe river, James Brown and F. M. Pomroy having traveled with me up to this place. here we overtook Br A Pratt and Hiram Blackwell with our team, took breakfast then started on in co with the train of about one hundred waggons, passed over low mountain then through a small valley, here we found plenty of hares, killed a great many, passed over another mountain, came into the Severe valley which was large, come to the cedar springs after night, 23 miles from the Severe.

SATURDAY 13th   We passed a small creek and camped on fine creek which we call Potters [Chalk] creek named from the abundance of broken potters ware found on it. 9 miles, good grass and watter

SUNDAY 14th   We lay buy. Mr. Granger [64] a Baptist minister preached

MONDAY 15th   Passed along the valley, camped on the willow Flats, good grass and watter. 159 miles from the city.

TUESDAY 16th   Passed over a mountain down a canion, camped at the emigrants Spring. 181 miles, good grass and watter.

WEDNESDAY 17th   at five miles passed a small creek, good grass and watter. Passed over a mountain, down a kenyon, camped on Sage Creek, 23 miles, poor grass

THURSDAY 18th   traveled 5 miles, came to Beaver creek 20 feet wide, camped. plenty grass and watter. good land for a small settlement. plenty timber in this vicinity

FRIDAY 19th   Lay buy. some men went down the

64 Lewis Granger, later a hotel man in Los Angeles.

creek to look out a new rout, returned and reported favorable

SATTURDAY 20th   also lay buy and explored

SUNDAY 21st   Started down Beaver creek, camped at the low end of the kenion. 12 miles. Br. James Brown and my self went up on the mountain to look at Little Salt Lake and did not get in till 9 oclock at night

MONDAY 22nd   Went 11 miles into the plain. Stopt at 3 o'clock P. M. Pioneers reported no watter near, some still in search for watter

TUESDAY 23rd   Camp in confusion, some for one thing and some for another. about 40 waggons went back to beaver creek, the rest remained, sent their animals back and teams to bring watter to the remaining part of the camp. Our waggon remained. I went back with the animals. met with Capt. Flake with a company of about 20 of the brethren on their way to the mines [65]

WEDNESDAY 24th   We took the animals back to the train, Capt. Hunt having returned and found no watter all the train returned to Beaver camp up and down in confusion.

THURSDAY 25th   I held a council with the brethren and Capt. Hunt. finding them anxious to go by the way of Walkers pass I concluded to take F. M. Pomroy with me and leave the train of waggons, Br Pratt Brown & Blackwell with the waggon train, after buying a poney and making some arrangements for packing we went up the river 5 miles and camped in company with the waggons

FRIDAY 26th   concluded our arrangements for packing. traveled 8 miles. camped near the top of the

[65] Captain Flake's company had just caught up with the Jefferson Hunt wagon train, with which Rich was traveling.

mountain, no watter, good grass, plenty of cedar wood

SATTURDAY 27th   crossed over the mountain into the valley of the Little Salt Lake, camped on the first stream putting in from the east mountain. distance 21 miles. good grass and watter. the soil not good that we passed over today, the valley is of considerable size say 40 miles long and 10 wide, the lake about 7 long and from one to 5 wide. On the east side and south end of the Valley there is some fine streams and good land and grass, high mountains on the east side

SUNDAY 28th   this morning we left the waggon train. after going 8 miles passed a good sized creek, 6 further we came to another beautiful running stream. Here we overtook Capt Smiths co. 28 men in number, who was going the same rout. we were each to manage our own concerns and travel near together for mutual protection. Here we camped and staid over night. 14 miles.

MONDAY 29th   after traveling 8 miles came to a good spring at the point of a mountain in the south end of the Valley, 6 miles further came to Little Muddy [Coal Creek] a good sized creek, plenty timber & grass 8 miles further where we came to some springs [Iron Springs]. here we found iron ore. 22 miles today. some waggons camped here also

TUESDAY 30th   at day light we discovered Indians peaking from behind the rocks in different directions, ten came out and came to the guard fire. we found they were Piutes and had been trying to steal our horses. after traveling 14 miles we passed near some springs, 14 further we camped on a small stream putting out of the mountain side. Peter Fife seen 6 Indians lurking near camp. poor feed. traveled 28 miles

WEDNESDAY 31st We traveled 6 miles and camped up in the mouth of the kenyon where the Spanish trail crosses the rim of the basin. camped on the account of rain

NOVEMBER 1st Here we left the Spanish trail and bore to the right. Struck a kanion and after traveling ten miles camped on the account of heavy rain. good grass and watter

FRIDAY 2 Continued up the creek, found some springs, passed over the rim and down a rough kanion about 5 miles and camped on good grass and watter. here we found an Indian had fire burning, also found corn cob, so we named the creek farm creek [head of Beaver Dam Wash] when on the summit there was one continued scene of mountains as far as the eye could extend. traveled 25 miles

SATTURDAY 3rd Lay buy till 12 o'clock to let our animals rest. we pass down the kanion some 2 miles, then followed a trail across some of the mountains, high and rough on both sides. here the creek had become a beautiful stream. here we found an Indian lodge pot on boiling, all their effects in and about the lodge, the Indians having fled, found corn cobs, pumkin seed, also specimans of stone coal. here we found hickory, asp, maple, box elder, muskeet &c, traveled ten miles today

SUNDAY 4th this morning dark and cloudy having rained through the night. we continued down the kanion, passed over some spurs and passed some precipices to avoid some narrow and abrupt passes in the kanion, it rained hard almost all day. camped after traveling 5 miles, little feed

MONDAY 5th this morning clear and beautiful. George Cannon found his horse dead caused by a fall

in passing a steep place on last evening. Passed down
the creek 11 miles, passed over an old corn field and
camped on one that had just been gathered, good feed
for our animals, they had raised corn, pumpkins,
squash, beans, morning glories, prince's feathers &c,
the frost had only slightly killed vegetation, crop had
been raised by irrigation

TUESDAY 6th   clear and beautiful, continued our
journey down the creek. mountains grow lower. met
some Indians traveling up the creek. they left all and
ran for the mountain, they had some cowhide which
shows they had been on the Spanish trail. we troubled
nothing. after traveling 15 miles, camped

WEDNESDAY 7th   We shod some horses, started at
noon, after traveling 1½ miles we concluded to stop
at a corn field. good feed, some wheat sowed, looked
well.[66] corn, pumkins, broom corn &c, had been raised
here. Br. Keeler had a spur accidentally stuck in his
foot which hurt him very much

THURSDAY 8th   Started at 8 o'clock, after going
down the creek 2 miles Capt. Smith, Flake, and others
thought we had best to bear more to the north and
leave the creek. I thought not and told them it would
be my advice to go directly west leaving some high
mountains on our right, but they bore north. After
traveling all day over a desert about one hour after
dark we came to a dry creek, some Indians camped
on it. when we drew near we fired off a gun, they put
out the fire and fled. here we lay all night without
watter. 6 men of Capt. Smith did not get up. traveled
32 miles

FRIDAY 9th   At day light I took two men and went
on a high rise 2 miles west to look for a prospect for

---

[66] Interesting to find a field of fall wheat growing here in Beaver Dam
Wash. The variety of crops produced here is notable.

watter, when I returned I found both companies
started up the creek without any council from me. we
traveled about 12 miles up the creek nearly east [more
north] and found watter. here we camped [Providence
creek, Meadow Valley Wash] and remained the rest
of the day. 2 of the six men came into camp, got watter,
returned to meet their companions, returned at night
without having found them. fear was entertained that
the Indians had killed as several parties had been seen
during the day

SATTURDAY 10th   continued in camp. sent out ten
men to search for the four men that was lost. they met
them four miles off, coming to camp. they had found
watter below

SUNDAY 11th   We continued my journey. I here
advised to go down the creek. Capt. Smith took north,
crossed some rough ground and quite a high mountain.
all seemed dissatisfied. here I made up my mind to
leave Capt. Smith and take those that would go with
me. after traveling all day hard we camped about 8
miles higher up on the same creek we left in the
morning. here I told Capt. Smith and Flake that I was
going to take my own course and those that would
follow me might, and those that chose might go some
other way. they both agreed to yield the point, the
men all having become dissatisfied with our course

MONDAY 12th   we started in a southwest direction
down a narrow valley, traveled till ten o'clock at night,
camped without watter, making about 30 miles

TUESDAY 13th   we started early and traveled the
same course till about 12 o'clock when it commenced
to rain. if ever I was thankful for a rain it was now.
also all the men. we had been one day and a half
without watter. we scooped holes and wattered our
animals and got plenty ourselves. here we camped and

made large fires of prickly pines [joshuas]. traveled 20 miles

WEDNESDAY 14th we removed our camp 12 miles south to a spring [Coyote Spring] good watter and grass here, we lay buy the remainder of the day. here I determined to ascend a high mountain which lay about ten miles west of us before proceeding farther as I had come to the opinion we would have to bear south to the Spanish trail.

THURSDAY 15th This morning in company with Darwin Chase, George Bankhead, and Mr. Adams [67] I started for the mountain, about 2 o'clock we reached the top, passing through thick cloud the whole way. when on top we found ourselves above the clouds with a good view to the west. here we saw a high mountain about 150 miles west, a high range south west about 80 miles, low hill or mountain north, after a few minutes view we started down, heard some hollowing below, some one of our company answered, they hollowed the second time, I advised the boys not to answer for it might be Indians. we missed the way we came up and went down 2 miles south of where we went up, it was after dark when we reached the foot of the mountain. passing down a small kanion near the mouth we saw a fire in a low place. we approached carefully and when within about 20 feet we saw an Indian sitting in a squatted position looking at us. we withdrew carefully and struck our camp about 9 o'clock. here I feel to acknowledge the hand of the Lord in our deliverance as there is no doubt the main party was way laying our path which we ascended. we traveled this day not less than thirty

---

67 Adams was doubtless one of the six non-Mormon packers who had left the wagon train at Mount Misery and had caught up with the Flake-Rich and Smith companies just before they left Beaver Dam Wash.

miles. After I got to camp I told a few of the company we would go south to the trail. Smith's company began to swear they would take their guns to get more game.[68]

FRIDAY, 16th We parted with Capt Smith's company and took down the creek. found plenty of watter and grass after passing a kanion, camped Indians just left, plenty of watter and grass, we left all their things undisturbed, traveled about 15 miles. Capt Smith had bore south west to try to cross the mountain [69]

SATTURDAY Nov. 17th Continued down bed of creek passing through lofty mountains forming a canion narrow sufficiently wide for the watter to flow through. about 1500 feet high of solid rock. it was about three miles through this passage which was from one to two rods wide [Arrow Canyon] after traveling 15 miles camped at some Indian farms, found wheat growing finely, plenty of warm springs making a fine creek [70]

SUNDAY Nov. 18th Continued down creek 15 miles where we came to Capt. Hunt and 7 waggons including the roadometer beside two small companies [71] which was ahead of Hunt's train. Here we met Bros. Pratt, Brown, Blackwell, the rest of Capt. Hunt's train having taken Walkers cut-off. here we found we were on the Muddy, the most favorable point we could have struck, we felt to acknowledge the hand of the Lord in our deliverance and rejoiced to see our brethren in the waggons. here we camped and rested

MONDAY Nov. 19th Remained in camp to recruit

---

68 Evidence of friction between the Mormon Flake-Rich party and the Smith Gentile company. For entries in Farrer's diary of Nov. 18, *see* part v: c, and in Cannon's narrative, see part v: D.

69 Here is the first indication of the Smith route after leaving Division (Coyote) Spring.

70 This would be about the location of the present Indian farms of the Moapa reservation on the Muddy.

71 Of the Gruwell-Derr wagon train.

our animals and replenish our provisions. we found that both watter and grass was so full of saleratus that it was injurious to our animals

TUESDAY Nov. 20th   Started about 12 o'clock having a fifty mile desert before us. after traveling about 22 miles camped on some good grass one mile to the right of the road, watter 1½ miles north of the grass

WEDNESDAY Nov. 21st   traveled about 28 miles and camped on the Vagus [Las Vegas]. today several horses sick with the saleratus, left some

THURSDAY Nov. 22nd   traveled 6 miles and camped on the head of the Vagus in co with the waggons

FRIDAY Nov. 23rd   traveled about 15 miles and camped at a spring [Cottonwood] poor feed

SATTURDAY Nov. 24th   traveled 3 miles and camped on good feed and watter

SUNDAY Nov. 25th   traveled 10 miles, camped at ceder springs [Mountain Springs] for feed

MONDAY Nov. 26th   traveled 27 miles and came to a spring under a willow tree [Stump Spring] found no grass, bore to the right 3 miles, on a creek found good grass and watter.

TUESDAY Nov. 27th   we traveled 22 miles and camped at the orchard [Resting Spring] good grass and watter

WEDNESDAY Nov. 28th   Lay in camp all day to recruit our animals

THURSDAY Nov. 29th   We left the waggons, traveled 7 miles and camped on the Magoch or Saleratus creek [Amargosa] at a spring to the left

FRIDAY Nov. 30th   traveled down Saleratus creek crossing it a great many times and stoped at Salt Spring to rest our animals. 15 miles. here we found some watter in holes. at 3 o'clock P. M. we started on across the desert, after traveling 27 miles we camped at 12 o'clock at night. many of the brethren being worn out did not get up till 2 o'clock, at Salt Springs Capt Hunt's company found gold

SATTURDAY DECEMBER 1st   traveled 6 miles. came to a camp of waggons, found grass and watter, let our animals graze till 1 o'clock, traveled 5 miles, camped at the Bitter Springs, found several waggons out of provisions, cattle worn out and in a suffering condition

SUNDAY DEC. 2nd   traveled 12 miles up hill, on top we had a full view of the Sire [Sierra] nevada. left one more horse. after traveling 23 miles farther we camped on the Mahovey, grass and watter, left some 2 or 3 animals, found more waggons out of provisions[72]

MONDAY DECEMBER 3rd   traveled up the Mahovey 12 miles and camped, but little to eat

TUESDAY DEC. 4th   Continued up the Mahovey 20 miles and camped, rained all night, it was cold and disagreeable

WEDNESDAY 5th   it snowed all day. stoped in camp, almost entirely out of provisions, some went out, shot some deer, did not get any

THURSDAY DEC. 6th   Stoped to hunt, killed 3 deer which helped us much

FRIDAY DEC. 7th   traveled up the Mahovey 10 miles, Capt Flake killed a deer. here I thought it wisdom considering the circumstances of some of the animals that those of the brethren that had good mules should proceed as fast as possible to the settlement, by doing so we could leave more meat for those that was left behind and if found necessary return with provisions

SATTURDAY DEC. 8th   half the company with myself started early. after traveling 5 miles we crossed the

[72] Lead wagons of the Gruwell-Derr wagon train.

Mahovey and left it on our left hand, after traveling 15 miles further camped at a spring in the cahoon pass. here we found a waggon loaded with provisions [73] here we supplied ourselves

SUNDAY DEC. 9th Traveled down the canion 10 miles, camped

MONDAY DEC. 10th traveled 15 miles and camped at the cocomongo ranch. got beef and such things as we needed

TUESDAY 11th we traveled 12 miles and camped at Colonel Williams. he was at Puebolo and did not come home for a day or two

WEDNESDAY 12th Remained in camp

THURSDAY 13th The rest of the company came up. we moved our camp and took shelter in one of Williams' rooms, from this date till the 12 of January we remained here in camp getting grain and getting it ground, fitting up for the rest of the journey. Capt. Egan and co also arrived. I went to Puebolo [Los Angeles] with Capt. Hunt, &c.

JANUARY 12th 1850 left Williams and traveled 10 miles, overtook the waggons which had started two days before and was camped on a small creek

SUNDAY 13th Traveled 10 miles and camped on San Graviell [San Gabriel] river, a fine stream, a fine body of land

MONDAY 14th traveled 7 miles and came to San Graviell Mission, the most beautiful location that I have seen in this country, the garden filled with oranges and olives and other fruit trees. we then traveled 3 miles and camped

TUESDAY 15th we traveled 4 miles and camped on St Pedro [Los Angeles] river about 1½ above De Los Angelos. my poney lost

[73] Sent out by Isaac Williams.

C: WILLIAM FARRER DIARY

[William Farrer, born January 26, 1821, in Westmoreland, England, accepted the Mormon faith in 1842 and migrated to America that year. After living in Nauvoo, he trekked with the Saints to Utah in 1847. For the journey to California in 1849 he was outfitted by Joseph Horne, who was to receive one-half the gold young Farrer obtained. Instead of returning to Utah from the mines, in November, 1850, he went on a Mormon mission to Hawaii. After four years there, he returned to Utah and settled at Provo. He married Elizabeth Ann Kerry in 1856. They reared eight children. Mr. Farrer died at Provo, February 17, 1906.

The diary published herewith was made available to us through the kindness of Mrs. Ramona Cottam of Provo, granddaughter of Mr. Farrer. Dr. Vasco M. Tanner of Brigham Young University generously provided us with a typed copy.]

THURSDAY. OCTR 11th 1849 There being a party got up on the west side of Jordon by Bro [John] Taylor on account of his leaving to go on a mission to France. There were about 1 hundred persons invited. an universal spirit of hillarity prevailed. we five or six of us took our parting Dinner with them. the table was spread with a profusion of every thing eatable. Stopped there all night.

FRIDAY. OCT 12th 1849 Detained rather late this morning on account of Bro [Joseph] Cain who had been taken sick on the road last night as soon as he got ready we started on and traveled about 4 miles South and crossed Jordon & camped on Willow Creek[74] rained nearly all night but we slept comfortable considering the weather.

SATERDAY, OCT 13th '49 I morning started from Willow Creek after traveling five miles came to the ridge of mountains runing between the two Vallies Salt Lake & Utah we could not see much of the Vally

---

[74] Site of Draper. Places enroute having been identified in connection with the diaries published above, we shall not repeat geographical explanations.

from the ridge: but after traveling a few miles farther
we came more into the Valley and could see the lake
in the distance: we crossed the dry bed of a creek in
our days travel, and after traveling about 16 miles
from Willow Creek we came to the American Fork,
where we camped for the night. the creek was about
a rod wide a very prety stream and very good water:
it rained during the night.

SUNDAY, OCT 14th '49 we rose before day we
intended to reach the settlement as soon as we could
and remain there the rest of the day. The mountains
on the East side of the Valey are higher than in the
upper Valley: but not so much snow on them. About
noon we crossed small spring branch and in a few rods
arrived at the Provo river it was a large rapid stream
about 3 rods wide: the settlement is on the banks of
this stream they had a fort [Fort Utah] built it is a
very prety situation there is a good deal of timber on
this stream scattered thro the bottom in the vally
principally Cedar and Cottonwood: they have a City
[Provo] laid out East of the Fort a very prety
situation. Bros. Parks an Orr live here sister Parks
cooked for us supper and breakfast, we slept at Bro
Orrs.

MONDAY, OCT 15th '49 We started prety early this
morning 20 in all and had chosen Bro J. M. Flake for
Captain: after travelling 8 miles we reached Hobble
Creek: & 8 miles farther crossed Spanish fork: 6 miles
further Creek. 3½ miles came to Clear Creek a creek
in the prairy without timber or brush of any consequence, where we camped, the feed excellent.

TUESDAY. OCT 16th '49 Started about 8 o'clock
and reached summit Creek after 3½ miles we soon
entered Yohab [Juab] Valley we passed some springs

on the prairy 5 miles from the last creek & reached sick creek after 5 miles travel. We traveled 10 miles and camped on Salt Creek.

WEDNESDAY. OCT 17th '49 Started very early this morning left the Yohab Valley by crossing a low ridge and entered into a pleasant Valley no water though a very little timber the hills were covered with scrub Cedar: we stopped at noon and unpacked about 2 hours on a creek very clear called Chicken creek: we traveled untill after Sun down and Camped on the Severe River, the road in the afternoon was hilly & dusty.

THURSDAY. OCT 18th '49 crossed the Severe it was prety deep but we crossed without any great difficulty. it was a very rough barren country during the morning and prety hilly: after about 8 miles travel we came to a small Valley after 2 miles travel we crossed the dry bed of a creek, & then ascended a hill & then up a Canion about 1½ miles no water in it after crossing the ridge decending we came into a large wide Canion feed growing very luxuriently. we came into an extensive Valley little water sage Brush plentiful feed prety good: about 25 miles from the Severe we came to some mountain springs which we called Cedar Springs.

FRIDAY, OCT 19th '49 Captain smiths company started with us this morning they had traveled with us since we left [Fort] Utah. good feeling prevailed between the two companies. After starting passed some springs under the bluffs near our camp ground, crossed a small creek after 1½ miles travel, 4 miles farther crossed another wider creek a little timber growing on it. traveled thro a good deal of Sage after 12 miles travel we came to a creek spread on the bottom, & soon came to another branch of the same creek where we concluded to stop, 11 of us being together. the Captain and 8 others having gone ahead. Bro Fife who was in our mess had been on this road before & told us there was no water for 25 miles ahead, this caused us to stop.

SATERDAY. OCT 20th '49 Traveled up this valley 8 or 10 miles and then crossed ridges, and traveled through Vallies for several miles & came to a very steep hill, to descend we then struck a valley about 2 miles wide, we traveled several miles through a rough country & came in sight of some willows growing in a valley from which we judged there would be water & upon close observation we discovered some camps: they proved to be Smiths & ours, we were glad to arrive at Camp as we had traveled about 27 miles without water.

SUNDAY. OCT 21st '49 Started in the morning and traveled about 3½ miles & came to a small creek in the same Valley we passed through a fine patch of Rye grass in this valley: crossed a ridge & went down a kanyon: crossed several ridges & thro a barren country & struck a creek with some little timber in it but very little grass. we unpacked & cooked & eat supper packed I started calculating to travel untill we reached grass. Captain Smith staid at the creek & drove his animals some distance to some feed under the bluffs. We traveled up a ravine and Camped on the bluff about 1½ miles from the creek: feed rather thin but a good kind of grass called mountain bunch grass.

MONDAY. OCT 22nd '49 Started this morning early came to a small prety creek about 1 mile from where we camped: about ¼ of a mile further came to another where we found an upright stick with Bro Richs name on marked 208 miles from Great Salt Lake City, also telling us to keep down the creek [Beaver]: it was a beautiful stream tolerably wide and rapid: we traveled down the creek thro the Canyon & crossed it four times came out into a Valley we could see the waggons ahead some distance: we stoped at some feed to bait awhile: but afterwards concluded to stay for the night first rate feed having been found on the creek, we were about 1½ miles from it on the bench.

TUESDAY. OCT 23rd '49   Did not start very early on account of our animals being in the best feed we have had: traveled about 2 miles from our camping ground and met some men returning from the waggons saying there was no water ahead & the waggons were returning: Capt Hunt had started on the previous evening on his horse & had been out all night on the search for water, and had returned completly exhausted without having found any. Upon receiving this information we thought it best to turn down to the right to the creek: where we unpacked & concluded to remain that day until we could hear some news: we expected to see or hear from Bro Rich: Bro [J. H.] Rollins & another of the boys having gone to see him. In a short time after camping Bros Rich, Pomeroy, & Brown rode up they were very glad to see us: Bro Rich explained to us the cause of the stoppage. Capt Hunt had been told that by keeping down Beaver Creek and then striking across to the left it would save travel and be a better route: he had told this to the officers of the camp, who were formed into a council at the under the title of the Grand Council & said that if they chose to take the responsibility of going that route they might, but he knew nothing about it himself only what he had been told: They resolved to go the route and exonerate him from all blame that might be attached to the officers in case of failure: this we were glad to hear as we were afraid the Capt might be brought under cencure for taking this route he being the Pilot

of the company. Capt Smith camped up the creek about
½ mile from us. Gen Rich & Capt Flake went to see
Capt Smith about going Walkers cut off (as it was
called) a route that struck west thro the unexplored
region laid down by Fremont on his map & South of
the range of mountains described by him as running
East & West having seen them from the Northern line
of exploration. This route was said to be practicable.
Capt Smith & some of his men having seen Barny Ward
a mountaineer who lives among our people in the
Valley, who told them he had been thro on the route
3 times,[75] & had got a diagram of it from him. Upon
examining the subject as laid before them by him, they
thought they would go it, but still did not bring themselves to a positive determination on the subject:
calculating to call the Brethren together and lay it
before them. and let them chose for themselves expecting that the spirit would diricet us on the right course
to pursue: if we concluded to go Walkers cut off Capt
Smiths company and ours would travel in Consort &
camp close together so that in case of an attack we
would be ready to unite & we were not to leave one
another (Capt Smith) was resolved to go that route.

WEDNESDAY. OCT 24th '49 Started this morning
with the expectation of having to travel 35 miles to
get to water it having been thought that distance: we
traveled about 10 miles & met Capt Smiths company
returning they having started in the morning before
us who told us that Capt Hunt had been out again and
traveled 40 miles and found no water & had returned

75 Barney Ward, old mountaineer, was already closely associated with the
Mormons. Manly says the information about the cutoff came from a Williams.
His reminiscent account is not so reliable as this and other contemporary
accounts ascribing it to Ward. Whether or not Ward had actually been over
such a route it is difficult to say.

used up having traveled on foot: upon hearing this we thought best to return to the creek until some route was found. Camped on the creek close by Capt Smith above where we started from: feed very good. Bro Rich spoke to the brethren about going this new route & it was unanimously voted that we go that way. He was busy trying to get animals to go with us. Bro Pomeroy had two. while on this creek I got one of the fore feet shoes set to the mare which had come of.

THURSDAY. OCT 25th '49   There were two waggons along with us & 3 horses to each & 3 men with one & two with the other & it had been thought best for them to pack from here: they were very busy getting ready fixing packsadles &c. Bro Whittle Joseph Peck & Peter Hoagland were with one waggon [76] & Bros Bigler & Keeler with the other. Started with the intention of going up to where we cross the creek the first time & camp for the night: & from there strike of to the left on the Spanish trail for the Little Salt Lake: we reached the camping ground after dark: good feed.

FRIDAY. OCT 26th '49   Started in the afternoon and traveled 7 miles & camped in a canyon without water but feed excellent.

SATERDAY. OCT 27th '49   Traveled up the canyon & crossed some ridges and down a steep hill thro a cedar grove & came on to a bottom traveled thro the sage for several miles & crossed 1 or two spurs of the mountains & came into the Little Salt Lake Valley it was very barren for several miles, after entering came to several springs [Buckhorn] in the bottom after 15 miles travel from our camp in the morning: we traveled 5¾ miles further & struck a creek went up ½ a mile and camped,

---

[76] These three who gave up a wagon here and joined the packers for the cutoff were not named previously.

tolerably good. This day one of Henry Phelps horses
gave out: he traded it for another by giving the price
of a tolerable good horse with it.

SUNDAY. OCT 28th '49 Took leave of Bros Prat &
Brown who remained with the waggons. traveled 6
miles and came to a prety clear creek [Parowan]
banks steeper than usual with those streams. Kept on
& reached another after about 4 miles we found Capt
Smith camped here he had crossed the mountains from
Beaver Valley & came on the north side of the Lake
(the Lake is about 7 miles long and 1 wide) we came
down the south side: we camped here the remainder
of the day.

MONDAY. OCT 29th '49 Traveled down muddy
creek valley on entering the Valley We crossed a spring
on the side of the ridge as we decended this so as 6
miles from morning camp: thence 8 miles to Muddy
creek [Coal creek] abundance of timber: after traveling 9 miles to the West we came to a prety large Spring
[Iron] creek banks very high and steep: we had good
dry cedar to burn Plenty of Scrub Cedar on the surrounding hills. feed rather scarce.

TUESDAY. OCT 30th '49 Started this morning
expecting to travel 28 having to go that distance before
coming to water of any consequence: there was a spring
about 14 miles from where we started in the mountains
to our left a little way from the road Capt Hunt called
it the Willow Springs 14 miles further we came to a
small creek called lost [Pinto]creek it did not run any
distance in the bottom before it sank. feed scarce we
found a little feed about half mile from the creek on
the side of the mountain. This evening Bro Rich called
a meeting of the company to know their feelings
regarding the new route, and whether they were to be

governed by all the men of the company by half or
one man: he had found out already that there were
different opinions about our treatment of the indians,
& he wanted that there should be no room for feelings
on any subject hereafter. The feelings of the brethren
were that we go the cut off & that we be governed by
him in all things. Bro Rich said that he wanted to have
two persons appointed to keep a record of our proceedings that he might have a record of the route &
proceedings to hand when he returned to the Recorder
of the Church. Bros Rollins & Cain were appointed
one to write & the other to assist & take notice of every
thing worth noticeing on the road. On Sunday the 28
In the evening Bro Rich called the company together
to know who should be Captain of the Company it was
his mind that Bro Flake remain as Capt of the company
It was motioned and unanimously carried.

WEDNESDAY. OCT 31st '49   Looked very much like
rain: we passed over a good many ridges it comenced
raining while traveling: camped at a creek about 15
miles from the place of starting. we were now in the
vicinity of the place of turning: raining very heavily
and continued all afternoon & night, which made it
very disagreable.

THURSDAY. NOV 1st '49   we arose this morning we
arose perfectly saturated. cleared away and promised
to be fine. after drying our blankets &c that they might
not be so heavy we packed up & started: turned back
about half a mile and then struck over the ridge to the
Westward after about a mile travel crossed a small
spring branch had to climb a good many ridges: struck
South [North?] west to a gap in the mountains
crossing a valley diagonaly of several miles width. we
soon arrived at the gap we aimed for and in time to

get into the [rain] which was falling on the mountains:
traveled some distance up of a creek: struck of to the
right over some spurs of the mountain raining very
heavy: very bad traveling in concequence it was very
cold & we were unable to keep our selves warm by
walking the rain beating in our face: we were thoroughly drenched and our bedding and every thing
we had was perfectly wet through: upon rounding
the point of a rock we perceived the forward part of
our company dismounting and preparing to camp; it
was an agreable sight & we soon drew up under some
rocks with caves in, which we named the rock of
refuge [four miles west of Enterprise]: after traveling
about 15 miles from the place of starting in the
morning: the rain soon subsided after we stoped and
we made large fires and dryed our things and made
ourselves as comfortable as possible for the night.

FRIDAY. NOV 2nd Continued up by the side of a
dry Creek called Dry Sandy. the same we struck the
previous evening after about 1 miles travel came to
Capt smiths camp ground: after 2 miles travel came
to a small strean impregnated with iron this sinks in
the bed of the sands: our course still continued up the
bed of the [Shoal] creek 10 miles from the Rock and
came to a beautiful spring [near the Terry ranch] on
our left: before reaching this spring we (passed) thro
a fine patch of grass: kept on in S W [N W?] direction
untill we came to a narrow pass in a Canyon about 3
miles from the spring & here found plenty of water
which arose and sunk in about 300 yds. (The Valley
up to this point affording plenty of feed and good land.
the mountains destitute of any timber but Cedar &
scrub Pines & Sage) continued our course up the
Canyon we came to a small Valley surrounded by hills

or low mountains: we still continued our course S W for about 1½ miles we then Struck southward still continuing up the bed of the creek for ¾ mile. then entered a narrow Canyon on our right filled with Cedar: we traveled up this canyon about 1 [mile] then turned our coures south ward over the dividing ridge of the Great Basin: here considerable snow had fallen during the night: some still continued on the ground, after crossing we came to a large Canyon running West S W down which we went untill we came to the Devils offset as it was called by our boys, where we found we could go no farther, after hunting round for some time we found the trail where some of the company who were ahead of us: when they came to the Rock they turned back about ¼ mile & struck over the hills to the southward about 3 miles, then struck the same Canyon about 100 yds below the offset: continuing down the Canyon some time the road tolerably bad we came to a flat of about 50 acres of grass [77] at the lower end of which we found some good springs which supplied us with plenty of good water: this days travel amounted to 25 miles. There was an old corn cob found near an Indian Lodge just vacated the fire in which had just been covered up: Some indians were seen at a distance. Several Pitch Pines found. The animals were much fatiguede with this days travel. Bros Cannon Cain & Bigler were behind the Company this evening having been detained with Bro Cannons Pack horse which gave out on the dividing ridge & they had staid to endeavour to drive him to Camp: they arrived in camp just as some of the brethren were starting to meet them.

SATERDAY. NOV 3rd '49 Remained encamped here

---

[77] Here Bigler scratched his initials on the white cliff.

to recruit our animals after the fatigues of yesterday:
we expected to reach a Valley to camp in this evening.
Traveled down the Canyon crossed the creek several
times, had some bad places rather miry Canon narrow
& the mountains on each side perpendicular and
Rocky. climbed a mountain the Canyon being im-
passible sides covered with cedar ascent very difficult
for our pack animals. traveled thro some Cedar ridges
& ascended a steep rocky mountain extremely difficult
of ascent: upon reaching the summit we found Capt
Smiths company stoped busily engage fixing the road
to descend the mountain. this was extremely difficult
they made it to wind round the side of the mountain
to a spur that descended more gradual to the creek
below: great care had to be taken in decending for
one false step would precipitate animal & pack down
the mountain without any prospect of escaping with
life. all arrived at bottom of mountain without any
acident. Crossed creek a great number of times it had
increased in size very much since we left it. arrived
at a large bend with a tolerable suply of grass in it.
concluded it best to camp for the night as there was
no prospect of us reaching the Valley: day had been
cloudy & we could not see by the sun the course we
had been traveling looked very much like storm:
rained very heavyly during the night: found Indian
wigwams close by camp recently vacated by the[m].
Pot made of earthen ware being on the fire a bow
laying close by the inhabitants had left upon hearing
us. We are now in the Pah Utah teritory & as they
are notorious for their depredations, we had to be very
vigilent.

SUNDAY. NOV 4th   Arose this morning & felt very
uncomfortable with wet: it still continued raining &

was very cold. When I arose I was told that my mare
had cast her colt I went to see & found a colt about half
grown this I attributed to the crossing the mountains
and to the storm the animals all looked very bad in
consequence of the storm. After rain had subsided
packed up and started. Still kept down Canyon
crossing & recrossing creek a great many times &
some places very bad: upon rounding a point we found
the company all stopped not being able to go any
farther in the opinion of some: Surrounded by high
mountains upon all sides impracticable to cross:
several men were sent to the tops of those surrounding
us to reconnoitre & see if there was any possible outlet,
all returned with unfavourable reports, nothing to be
seen but mountains: Capt Flake & one or two others
then decended the Canyon to see if there was any
possibility of our being able by laboring to make a
practicable route for us to decend: the men that had
been on the mountains stating that the Canyon grew
wider a little lower & that if we could surmount the
obstcles immediately ahead we could proceed. The
Capt returned stating that it was extremely rough
being very Rocky & a precipice to ascend, but thought
we would be able by roling a few rocks out of the
way to go on: we were glad to hear of this for we had
now been standing for about four hours in a drenching
rain every thing we had on us & on our packs being
completely drenched. We commenced our decent of
the Canon found it as represented by Capt Flake. got
thro it all without any accident until we reached the
precipice: the animals with some help from the men
& very little unpacking succeeded in reaching the top
without any accident with the exception of Bro
Cannons pack horse. he suceeded in reaching nearly

to the top of the steepest part, when he fell and would have roled down if he had not caught hold of him. he cut the cap of his knee on a sharp rock in his fall, by helping him he was got into the Cannon again. after about 1½ miles [Bigler and Rich say 5 miles] travel we reached a place we thought best to stop at: feed tolerable good for animals.

MONDAY. NOV 5th This morning found Bro Cannons horse in the creek drowned. Started early crossed creek a great many times expecting to see a Valley, every headland we rounded, but were disappointed until the afternoon about 3 o-clock we came into a small Valley about 20 acres of cultivated land soil sandy old cornstalks standing round evidences of last years cultivation we traveled about 3 miles and came to another small valley with a standing cornfield, ears of corn taken off stalks standing. Beans, morning glories, Squash vines, &c &c. all in a good state of cultivation. large drains being made for irregating shewing industry and perseverance, the corn stalks affording good feed for our animals.

TUESDAY. NOV 6th Canon more open than it had been pleasanter traveling after traveling about 12 miles came to a beautiful grove of Cottonwood [Motoqua] making a fine shade on the banks of the creek which had considerably decreased so as scarcely to run it had been sinking for sometime. in our days travel we passed an Indian camp which they had deserted on our approach: several things of Indian manufacture being lying round & some peices of ox or cow hide which had recently been taken of: also a number of bitter squash seeds spread out to dry which we thought they had been preparing for food: this days travel called 12 miles:

WEDNESDAY. NOV 7th '49   as we were going to continue here a part of the day I thought it best to get the shoes set on the hind feet of the mare as her feet had got wore considerable with traveling over the rocks and through the creek so much. I got a Blacksmith in Capt smiths company to set them on: this evening we traveled about 1½ miles to a corn field which had been found and camped for the night.

THURSDAY. NOV 8th '49   This morning 6 Emigrants with 5 horses overtook us from the waggons. the people with the wagons had all determined to come this route. Traveled down the creeck about a mile & struck over some high hills to the West, & kept in this direction nearly all day. Camped in the dry bed of Creek after dark with no water or feed for our animals after 32 miles travel: animals very much exhausted for want of feed & water: many of the men suffered very much for want of water Cap Smiths men many of them offering any thing they had for it they appeared to suffer more for the want of it than our company. The prospects were not very promising for finding any for a good distance.

FRIDAY. NOV 9th '49   Traveled up the bed of the creek to the Northward expecting to find water at the mountains: after 10 miles travel we came to the canon after a little travel up which we came to water both men & animals drank greedily for all had suffered. I suffered more this morning than I had suffered on the road for water. Several animals have given out. This was called Providence creek [in Meadow Valley Wash] on account of finding it so Providentially. Upon the foremost of the company seeing the water they shouted it was answered back the length of the line with rapture. This afternoon two of the men who had overtaken us yesterday morning came in the other 4 were behind with the animals. They started back after eating dinner with 4 canteens of water for their comrades but were not able to find them: we were afraid the Indians had laid in ambush & killed them as they had som narrow cannons to descend, & two of Smiths men had been back for some horses but could [not] find them saw 22 or 23 Indians three of them had rifles.

SATERDAY. NOV 10th '49 This morning there was a call for men to go back to find these men if possible five from our Co. & five from Capt Smiths Co. making 12 in all with the 2 men belonging to the Co. armed themselves and started taking a canteen of water apeice with them & met them coming about 4 miles from camp: they had found water about 8 miles below our old camp ground upon this creek bed.

SUNDAY. NOV 11th '49 Started this morning & traveled down bed of creek about a mile and then struck off to the Westward over some low mountains. This days travel was an uninterupted succession of hills very fatigueing for both men & animals we did not seem to make much headway as we had to tack round considerable to avoid heavy hills. After traveling till near night we saw a creek to our right down in a canon a long distance from where we were by searching a while we found a place, where we could descend. upon examination we found it was Providence Creek & that we had only gained about 3 or 4 miles by our days travel. Bro Rich said this evening that he was not going to be led round in this manner any longer we should all perish in the mountains if there was not an alteration, if he could not have his way he should go back to the wagons as quick as he could. He said that if his councel had been taken we would not have been there. I was glad to hear him talk in this way as I felt that Cap Smiths opinion had been taken in preference to the Generals [Rich's] : it had been his mind to travel in the table land & keep out the mountains & if we could not go that way we could not go at all. two or three horses gave out today.

MONDAY. NOV 12th '49 Started this morning with the intention of striking for the bottom we took all the water we could carry with us in case we did not reach any this evening. Traveled until evening & stopped & fed on excellent grass. Capt Flake went ahead to see if he could find water and grass for feed to camp. We traveled until about ten o'clock & camped without water grass. We traveled 32 miles.

TUESDAY. NOV 13th '49 Started this morning at daylight Bro Rich started ahead with two or three going with him on foot we traveled on until afternoon we began to feel very hungry & thirsty having Started in the morning without breakfast. it began to [rain] a little & increased. Bro Rich stopped the animals on a spot of good grass thinking that the hoot [wet] grass would help them. Bro Rich got at some hard bread he had in his pack and gave us all an invitation to eat this was very acceptable as we were most of us hungry. We started again after about an hour it still continued raining as we went along every rock that had a hollow in it with water was greedily devoured by the men. it soon began to stand in puddles on the ground & we soon got satisfied as well as the animals. We camped in a hollow & cooked our supper with rain water & filled everything that would hold water for the morrow Capt Smith said to Gen Rich that the finger of the Lord was in this, for we must have suffered very much had it not been for this & probaly have perished for to all appearances there was no water any nearer than Providence creek. Ceased rained in the evening.

WEDNESDAY. NOV 14th '49 Capt Smith sent out men early this morning to search for water. three of our men started for a range of Mountains West to see if they could find any water, or any signs of any coming from them, but could not find any. Capt. Smiths men found a small spring in the bottom to the Southward and thought by digging we might get to water: Started in the afternoon to the spring [Coyote, or Division Spring] it was very weak furnishing enough for us, the animals finding water enough standing in pools. Grass was good.

THURSDAY. NOV 15th '49 Bro. Rich started this morning for the mountains West calculating to see what chance there was to go on the other side he was gone all day. he had three men with him & did not return till after night fall. The prospect from the mountains was very dull for us going this route: the country westward was considerably higher than this & very sterile; he thought there was not enough grass for one animal to subsist upon & he did not see any signs of water, the land was undulating spurs putting out from the range north; to the Southward there was a valley running to the west that he thought if any route went this way it must be through it. but there was not a good prospect of water, through it. He saw a range of mountains about 80 miles as he supposed from the range he was on. beyond this he saw a large Snowy peak looming thro the clouds but whether connected with a range or not he could not tell on account of the fog. he judged it to be 150 miles distant. Upon mature deliberation he did not think it would be wisdom for him to take the company thro & he thought he would strike for the Spanish Trail. The brethren were unanimous in their feelings to go the Spanish Trail.

FRIDAY. NOV 16th Capt Smith came up to our camp this morning to hear the result of Bro Rich's view. Bro Rich stated to him what he had seen & his opinion of the route. Capt Smith expressed his determination to persevere & swore that he would go if he died in the attempt, & said that if we did not hear from [him] we might know that he had died with his face westward & not before he had eat some mule meat with a good appetite. All the men with the exception of one or two that joined our company not belonging to the Church left & went with Capt Smith. We parted with the best of feelings. each one beleiving his way the best. Traveled until afternoon stopped & fed about half an hour. started and traveled thro a narrow canon thro a mountain sides rising precipitously to several hundred feet. Camped about ¼ mile from the mouth of the canon feed tolerably good.

SATERDAY. NOV 17th Traveled down the bed of the creek until we came to a Canon [Arrow] about three miles long sides of solid rock rising perpendicularly several hundred feet it was good traveling down the Canon upon emerging from it we came to good grass & some warm springs of water: we fed our horses an hour & again started the springs soon formed a creek with considerable water in it. Very bad traveling in consequence of mire. Camped on the bank of creek good feed. Bro Fife who had been the Spanish Trail home from California thought it was the Muddy Creek from its appearance. Our course yesterday & today had been South East [78] with the intention of intersecting the Spanish Trail.

[78] Pahranagat Wash, which they followed, runs slightly east of south.

SUNDAY. NOV 18th   Traveled about 5 miles down the creek & came in sight of some cattle grazing on the other side of the creek & seen some men who told us Cap Hunt was here with seven wagons the rest having left him & gone our trail: we were glad to hear it & felt to return thanks to our Heavenly Father for this: we had all been seperated from the Train Capt. Hunt with enough men to go thro in safty & we had seperated from Capt. Smiths Company just as some of them had run out of provisions and they were threatening to use their rifles if they could not get it any other way: [79] and our agreement with them was to divide with them when they were out. Capt. Hunt was glad to see us and we got some provisions enough as we thought to last us through.

MONDAY. NOV. 19th   Remained camped all day to recruit our animals.

TUESDAY. NOV. 20th   Started to day about noon, we had before us the fifty mile desert: we travelled until after night fall when we came to some puddles of water to the left of the road, where we watered our animals: the moon shone brightly and made it pleasant travelling: we reached a spot of grass to the right of the road about 25 miles we thought from Muddy and found water among some bushes about a mile and half from feed it was in puddles from the last rain.

WEDNESDAY. NOV. 21   We had this morning a gradual ascent of about 12 miles and then descended for a few miles over very rough road & then travelled on a bottom until we struck the Vegus [Las Vegas] where we camped. We had rough rocky road, several horses gave out to day. We did not reach camp ground

---

[79] *See* Rich's reference to the same situation in his entry of November 15; part V: B.

till after dark. The wagons did not come up untill near morning.

THURSDAY. 22nd '49   As there was good feed here Bro Rich thought we had better stay here & let the animals recruit but afterwards thought we had better travel about 6 miles to the head of the springs

FRIDAY. NOV 23rd   Very Windy & cold this morning it made it very tedious traveling it seemed a long 14 miles, and we were glad when we struck the creek upon which we camped: it was formed by springs rising immediately above where we were encamped they were rather warm. The country we passed through today was barren and rather rocky: feed this evening was very poor having all been eaten out by the travelers animals who were ahead of us.

SATERDAY. NOV 24th   Concluded this morning to go about 3 miles further and encamp for the day on some good feed that Capt Hunt had found last evening: we found good grass & a weak spring of water affording sufficient to supply Capt Hunts Co. & ours.

SUNDAY. NOV 25th '49   Fine pleasant morning. Todays travel was rough we camped at a spring [Mountain] to the right of the road upon a grassy ridge affording rather poor pasturage for our animals having all been eaten off: we found some good feed on the side of a mountain about ¾ mile from camp.[80] We had an abundance of wood this evening having plenty of Cedar & Pine all around us.

MONDAY. NOV 26th   We had thirty miles travel before us today but the road was good & decending: we came before we knew it to some very large willow

---

[80] This is where another spring oozes out of the side of the mountain, north of the spring on the road. Today there are several such springs and the present owner told us in 1951 that most of them developed at the time of the San Francisco earthquake of 1906.

trees in a bottom where we found a spring of water [Stump Spring]. this the roadometer made 27 miles when we came there we did not think it was more than 22 or 23 miles but when the wagons came along they informed us different: there had been some feed but it was all eaten. We went to the right Northward when we left this spring & after traveling about 3 miles we struck a bottom & after traveling westward about a mile, we came to some bunch grass of excellent quality: but did not find any water.

TUESDAY. NOV 27th   Bros Fife & Gibson went out this morning & found water still further west: we went down to it & cooked breakfast. We traveled about 7 miles & crossed a ridge rather bad descending. traveled in the Valley about 12 miles & turned to the right & crossed a steep ridge & traveled about 5 miles & camped upon a spring [Resting] with very good feed but strongly impregnated like all the grass in this country with saleratus.

WEDNESDAY. NOV 28th '49 Remained encamped here all day. bought some provisions & beef from the wagons dried the beef.

THURSDAY. NOV 29th '49   Started about noon to the spring on saleratus creek a distance of 7 miles: to our right as we traveled we could see about 1½ miles distant the banks crusted white with alkali: we had some very steep descending to get into the bottom where the creek ran: the water was poisonous looking like strong lye more than water. We found the water where we camped passably good: we had to be careful with the animals in crossing and recrossing the creek to prevent them from drinking.

FRIDAY. NOV 30th '49   Started very early this morning & traveled down the creek about 10 miles crossing

& recrossing repeatedly: when we emerged from the canon we turned to our left & rounded the point of a mountain we traveled some in very heavy sand making it toilsome for man & beast we passed through a Rocky Canon very rough traveling in which we found a weak spring of water not fit for use: about ½ a mile further we came to grass & some very strong salt springs not fit for use: we remained here until 3 oclock when some of the boys found some pools of standing rain water to our left where we watered our animals: this stretch we called 14 or 15 miles. We traveled this evening & night we had a beautiful moon to travel by the light of about 28 miles: part of the road was hard & level & part was quite rough & rocky we traveled up a canon about a mile & camped no feed & had to tie our animals to the bushes: we arrived in camp about 1 oclock: I felt very much fatigued this evening & was not very well I had walked nearly all the distance as my horse did not appear very well & I had packed the mare today to rest him. I had walked considerable for some time back to save my animals which had been failing for some time. this days travel we called about 43 miles

SATERDAY. DECR 1st   Started this morning & traveled about 6 miles when we observed a camp of wagons to the left about a mile and a haf: we found standing water besides the wagon & we unpacked & stoped until about 10 oclock: when we again started and reached the Bitter Spring as it is called, we found some grass about a mile from the spring. Bro Cain & Henry Phelp's Pack animals gave out today.

SUNDAY. DECR 2nd   We traveled about 16 miles ascending this morning: when we came to the top of the ridge we caught the first sight of the Sierra Nuvada: after passing over the top of the ridge we stopped and fed for about 2 hours. We then started again & traveled until about 10 oclock when we struck the Mohahve where we camped. plenty of feed & water.

MONDAY. DEC 3rd '49   Did not start until late this morning intending to go about 10 or 12 miles: there were some emigrants wagons here who had been living the last 4 or 5 weeks upon beef: we let them have what flour we could spare for the women & children. There was considerable of timber on this stream & an abundance of grass. There was no running water in the bed of this creek what water we had we found standing in pools. We traveled about 12 miles & camped on the Mohahve which was considerable of a stream at this place.

TUESDAY. DEC 4th   Our previsions begining to be scarce some of the men went ahead to try & kill some deer they being said to be plentiful on this stream. It rained prety freely today making it very bad traveling we arrived in camp this evening wet & tired having traveled about 20 miles: we built very large fires this evening to dry our clothes wood being very plentiful. It ceased raining before we went to bed but commenced again towards morning.

WEDNESDAY. DEC 5th   Commenced snowing this morning we built a shanty of blankets over our beds to try to keep them Dry & kept a good fire in front Bro Cannon was unwell today. Several of the Brethren were out trying to kill some game but were unsuccessful.

THURSDAY. DECR 6th   Ceased snowing during forenoon. Bro Rich started out this morning with some of the rest of the brethren & found a deer lying in the bushes dead: it had been wounded yesterday and had laid down in the bushes & died. soon afterwards some of the rest of the brethren came in with two. This meat came in very opportunely as we were almost out of every kind of provisions: & we felt to return thanks to our heavenly Father for his goodness to us in this our need.

FRIDAY. DECR 7th Traveled about 10 miles today very bad traveling & camped in the timber the creek was runing here nearly over the bottom. The night was very cold. This evening Bro. Rich called the company together to consult upon the propriety of part of the Company going ahead & the remainder travel more slowly & try to get the weak animals thro: he thought that it would be about 6 miles up the creek to where we would turn off for the pass & about 20 miles from there to the pass. this he thought could be traveled by the strong animals in a day. & he thought the weaker would be better to travel it in two: those who went ahead would be able to leave what provisions they had to spare with those who remained this was the principle object in proposing the seperation one half of the company comprising Bro Whittles mess & ours volunteered to stay & travel slower, it was unanimously agreed that Bro. Rich should go ahead.

SATERDAY. DECR 8th '49 Bro Rich & those with him started early: we started soon after & camped across the creek: which was quite a wide stream here. This evening some of the men who had been sent to the settlements for provisions by the wagons short of provisions arrived here this evening bringing some provisions: but would not part with any.[81]

SUNDAY. DECR 9th 1849 Started this morning for the Cahoon Pass in the Mountains the ascent was very gradual scarcely perceptible: a short time before

---

[81] The two Gruwell brothers returning to their families. *See* Pratt's entry of Dec. 9, part III: B.

reaching the top we met H & E Gibson who told us that there was a wagon in the canon with provisions to sell. that Bro Rich & the rest had gone to the settlement & they had stayed to come back after a sadle they had been obliged to leave yesterday on account of one of their mules giving out. [The diary ends abruptly here.]

D: GEORGE Q. CANNON NARRATIVE

[George Q. Cannon, whose parents came from the Isle of Man, was born in Liverpool, England, January 11, 1827. While the family was migrating to America in 1842, George's mother died at sea. His father died two years later, leaving six orphans. George, the eldest, lived for some years with his uncle, John Taylor, from whom he learned the printer's trade.

George migrated to Utah in 1847. He went reluctantly to the California mines in 1849, having been outfitted by his uncle. The next year he sailed to Hawaii on a Mormon mission. Returning to Utah in 1854, he soon became one of the prominent leaders of the Mormon Church. In 1866 he launched the *Juvenile Instructor,* a magazine designed primarily for use in the Mormon Sunday Schools.

Until his death in 1901, Cannon continued high in the councils of the Mormon Church. He served as First Counselor to three Presidents in turn; and as Delegate from Utah Territory to Washington. He was principal executor of the estate of Brigham Young; was author of a number of books; and was a successful leader in business affairs.[82]

His serial "Twenty Years Ago; a Trip to California," appeared in the pages of his *Juvenile Instructor* in 1869. This story of his 1849 journey we republish herewith.]

The gold discoveries in California, and the events which occurred here [Salt Lake City] in 1849, had their influence in prompting the calling of myself and others to go to California. It was in the fall of that year that we were selected. We formed a company, and were

---

[82] For a sketch of his life *see* Andrew Jenson, *Latter-Day Saint Biographical Encyclopedia,* I, 42-51.

joined by some few whose only motive in going was to enrich themselves by digging gold. It is the account of this trip that I propose to write for the *Juvenile Instructor,* and though it may not be so exciting as the descriptions of some adventures, it has one merit – it is true. The writer kept a journal, and therefore does not trust to memory alone, though every event is firmly imprinted there.

There was no place that I would not rather have gone to at that time than California. I heartily despised the work of digging gold. I thought it very poor business for men to be running over the country for gold. I was quite young then, and though nearly twenty years have elapsed since that time, I still think so. There is no honorable occupation that I would not rather follow than hunting and digging gold. My instructions were to go to California and be guided by the counsels of Elders Amasa M. Lyman and Charles C. Rich, two of the Twelve Apostles.[83] The former was already in California, having been sent there in the spring of 1849, and the latter was on the point of starting there, having been called at the Conference to go on a mission to that country.

It was decided that we should go to California by what was known as the Spanish Trail. To go by this Trail we had to go south as far as Little Salt Lake Valley, then travel in a south-westerly direction to the Cajone Pass, in the Sierra Nevada mountains, which was near the part of California that we wished to reach first. At the time of which I write, this route had not been traveled much by wagons. Captain Davis (after whom Davis County in this Territory is named) had brought one through from California on that route

---

[83] The Twelve Apostles form a quorum of high authority in the Mormon Church, ranking next to the Presidency.

when he and a number of brethren came here in the winter of 1847-8, on their discharge from the "Mormon Battalion." [84] It could have been made a pretty good wagon road, but we were mostly in favor of packing. Many of my little readers [85] have seen men with pack trains riding through the streets of this city and other settlements where they live, on their way to the mines. Mules are the most suitable for this service, though horses are also often used. A pack-saddle which has horns at each end, is securely fastened on the animal that has to carry the pack. On this the load is hung and then carefully lashed; for if it should get loose, there is danger of the animal getting frightened and running away and losing its pack. The men have horses or mules on which they ride, and they generally drive the pack animals ahead of them. Five of our company, [86] however, thought they would rather not pack, so they started with two wagons. My Uncle, who procured my outfit, [87] bought two animals for me, both of which had been highly recommended to him. The one which I selected for my pack horse was a crop eared, iron grey. He was a good-sized, stout-looking animal, and it was thought he would endure the fatigues of the journey very well. As we proceed you shall know more about "Croppy," as we learned to call him. My riding animal was a cream-colored mare, with a black mane and tail. She was young, and therefore not so tough as she would have been had she been two years older, but she proved serviceable.

[84] *See* account of this trip above, in the Historical Summary.

[85] The *Juvenile Instructor* was planned primarily for young readers.

[86] Henry W. Bigler and James Keeler in one wagon; Thomas Whittle, Joseph Peck, and Peter Hoagland in the other (*see* Farrer's diary entry of October 25, part V: c).

[87] His uncle, John Taylor (who later became President of the Mormon Church), "grubstaked" Cannon.

Thursday, October 11th, was the day selected for starting. The excitement of getting ready prevented me from feeling any sorrow at the prospect of leaving, though I dreaded it. I had never been absent from home more than a night or two in my life, and when I had been under the necessity of staying away a night in the kanyon to get a load of logs or timber of any kind, I had hastened home the next day with great delight. But when the hour of parting came I could not control my feelings. For upwards of a year after this I could not think of home without being homesick. Our grand mountains and beautiful valleys, with the sweet and peaceful spirit that prevailed here, had such an attraction for me that I could never think of them without wishing that the time had come for me to return to them.

We traveled easily for the first few days. There was no necessity for hurrying, as the company was not all together. There was a novelty about packing that, in those days, I liked. But I soon found that that mode of traveling had its inconveniences. Before we reached Provo it rained upon us two nights, and we felt the want of water-proof blankets with which to cover our beds—a want that we seriously felt at many times before we reached California. We arrived at Provo on Sunday morning, the 14th, and remained there that day. None of the settlements that now dot the road from this city to Provo had been then made. From the Cottonwoods to Provo the entire country was in a state of nature. Not one house of the many flourishing settlements that are now to be found on the various streams south of Cottonwood was in existence when we passed along. At Provo a small settlement had been formed, and the people lived in a fort; it was then the most distant settlement from this city.

While we were at Provo we found there were twenty
of us who were prepared to go through in company.
A meeting was held and Bro James M. Flake was
chosen Captain. On Monday, October 15th, we left
Provo. I felt somewhat as I would if I were pushing
out to sea. Before us lay a country through which we
intended to travel of which we knew but very little.
At that time very few of the Saints had traveled south
of Provo. Bro. Peter Fife, who was with us, was the
only man in our company who had ever been over the
ground. He had been in the "Mormon Batallion," and
after it had been discharged had traveled by this route
from California to Salt Lake City. On many occasions
we found his knowledge of the country of very great
use to us, though sometimes his memory would fail
him. It was customary with us, in spreading our beds
on the ground of an evening, to place our riding and
pack saddles at our heads. I think it was the first
morning after we left Provo that when I arose I found
the coyotes had been at work during the night at my
pack saddle. They had gnawed and carried off the raw
hide straps with which I fastened it. This was on
Peteetneet Creek, where Payson now stands. These
creatures were very numerous through that country at
that time; but I scarcely thought they would be so
daring as to come into camp and commit their depredations. We had a guard; but it is probable that Mr.
Coyote had noticed that they were either asleep or
engaged in attending to the animals. I knew I was a
sound sleeper, loud thunder often failing to awake me,
but after that occurrence I had a much bigger opinion
than before of the sleeping qualities of my bedfellow,
as their gnawing had not disturbed him.

Nothing of importance occurred to us in traveling

through Juab, Round and Pauvan valleys. I found before we had left home many days that I had not enough clothing for my comfort. By some means I had got the idea that in traveling on this southern route the weather would be so warm that we would need but little clothing, and to make my pack as light as possible I had not brought much with me. This was partly true after we crossed the rim of the Basin; but I learned then, as I have had occasion to remark many times since, that in this mountainous country every person who travels should go prepared with clothing for cold weather.

When we reached what is now known as Beaver Creek, and on which the settlement of Beaver is now built, we found a stake with Brother Charles C. Rich's name upon it, and marked "208 miles from Great Salt Lake City." Our trail lay across the creek; but Brother Rich had written on the stake for us to keep down the creek.

Brother Rich was traveling with three Elders who had been appointed on missions to the Society Islands. Their names were Addison Pratt, James S. Brown, and Hiram H. Blackwell; Francis M. Pomeroy was also with Brother Rich. They were going through with wagons, and they had traveled in the company of a large number of gold-seekers. These latter had reached Great Salt Lake Valley too late in the season to go through to California in safety by the northern route. But they could not content themselves to spend the winter in this valley, when there was so much gold in California waiting to be dug by them. So they resolved to hire a guide, and go through by the southern route, or as it was then called, the Spanish Trail.

Captain Jefferson Hunt was the most suitable man

they could get to be their guide. He was recommended to them by President Young, and they employed him. He was the senior captain in the "Mormon Battalion," and when that body was discharged he came to the Valley by this southern route,[88] and was, therefore, familiar with it. This company started from the city several days ahead of us. Before leaving the city an odometer had been put in the wagon in which Brother A. Pratt and the other brethren traveled. This is an instrument fastened to the wheel of a carriage or wagon by which the distance traveled can be measured by counting the number of times the wheel turns. Every ten miles they had placed stakes, on which the distance was marked. It was on one of these stakes that we found Brother Rich's name written at Beaver with directions to keep down the creek.

I have not been down the Beaver since the time of which I write; but we found it a beautiful stream, tolerably wide and rapid. We traveled down the creek, through the kanyon and crossed the stream four times and came out into a valley. We could see the wagons some distance ahead. We found fine feed and we camped for the night about a mile and a half from the creek. Our animals being in excellent feed we did not start very early the next morning. There is a settlement called Minersville on the Beaver, and I think that we camped somewhere near where it now stands. After traveling about two miles from our campground we met a number of men returning from the wagons. They told us there was no water ahead and the wagons were returning. Captain Hunt had started the previous evening on horseback, had been out all night searching

---

[88] His return from California in 1847 had been by the northern route; but he had gone to California again in the fall of 1847 by the southern route and returned in the spring of 1848 over the same trail.

for water, but without success, and had returned completely exhausted. Upon hearing this news we turned down to the creek, unpacked and concluded to remain the day, or until we could see General Rich, who was with the wagons.

Brother J. H. Rollins and another of the boys had gone to find Brother Rich. Shortly after we had camped these brethren returned, bringing with them Brothers Rich, Pomeroy and Brown. The meeting was a joyful one. They were as glad to see us as we were to see them They, with Brothers Pratt and Blackwell and Captain Hunt, were the only Latter-day Saints [Mormons] in the company, and they did not like the society with which they had to mix.

From what I saw of the company they were traveling companions from whom I should have separated as soon as possible. Some of them were rough, swearing men, and when we met them returning they did not appear to advantage nor impress us favorably. They were not all, however, of this kind. I now number among my most intimate friends one who was in that company. He was but a boy at that time, but he has since traveled extensively as an Elder of the Church of Jesus Christ of Latter-day Saints and has been the means, in the hands of God, of doing much good.

From General Rich we learned the cause of the stoppage and turning back of the company. Captain Hunt had been told that by keeping down Beaver Creek, and then striking across to the left, a shorter and better route could be found than by passing through Little Salt Lake Valley. He told this to the officers of the company, who were formed into a council at the start under the title of a Grand Council. He said if they chose to take the responsibility of going this route, he would do what he could to pilot them through; but he knew nothing about it himself, only what he had been told. They resolved to go the new route, and in case of failure, Captain Hunt was to be clear of all blame. We were pleased to hear this explanation, as we had been afraid that the Captain, as pilot, might be brought under censure for leaving the regular trail.

Up to this time I had never known much about organizations among outsiders [non-Mormons]. My experience had been confined to the church. I naturally enough, therefore, took notice of what I saw in this company with which we had met. The contrast between their Grand Council and the Councils held among Latter-day Saints struck me. Our people never murmured against authority; but they honored and obeyed those who were placed to lead and govern. Not so this company. We found many who spoke out loudly in condemnation of their Grand Council for leading them on that route, and they cursed and swore about them in round terms. It was very plain to be seen that they were full of discord, and I did not think they would go to California without splitting up. The stragglers from this company kept coming all day on to the creek where we were.

There was a company of packers who had traveled with us from Provo to this point. They were principally outsiders, though some few of them had joined the church in the Valley as they were passing through. They numbered about as many as we did, and were going to California in search of gold. The captain of the company was named Smith. In traveling he had several conversations with our captain, Bro. Flake, and others of our company, about a new route that

E. Barney Ward, the mountaineer, (who was killed
by the Indians in Salt Creek kanyon, Sevier County,
near Gunnison, in April, 1865)[89] had described to
him and several of his men.

Smith was fond of dwelling upon the advantages
of going by this route, which was called "Walker's
Cut-off." [90] He wanted to go by that way himself and
to have our company go also, as he knew that if we
should travel with him, he could go through without
fear of attack from Indians. One of his arguments in
favor of the "cut-off" was that the gold mines on the
Stanislaus river could be reached by that route before
the rainy season commenced; but by the Spanish Trail
we would only reach the Cajon Pass or Los Angeles,
by that season, and then from this latter point we
would have to travel some hundreds of miles through
the rain to reach the "diggings." Those who conversed
with him were persuaded by his reasoning; it sounded
very plausible; and it seemed as if we could do no
better than to go that way; for who would not prefer
a direct road to a roundabout one? Every one who
knew anything about the points of the compass was
satisfied that if we could go directly across the country
westward to the Sierra Nevada, and find a pass through
that range of mountains by which we could descend
into California, it would be a great saving of travel
and the route might properly be called a "cut-off." If
any one ventured to express a doubt about being able
to travel by it, they were silenced by the statement
that Barney Ward had said that he had traveled

[89] Ward was killed during Utah's Black Hawk war (*see* footnote 27).
Just where Capt. Smith met Ward is not reported.

[90] This cutoff may have been traversed by the famous Mountain Man,
Joseph R. Walker; it may have derived its name from the Ute Chief,
Wakara; or it may have been so-named because it headed for Walker's
Pass in the Sierra Nevadas.

through that way three times, and there was a paper which he had given them and on which the route was marked.[91] The route struck west through the region laid down by Fremont on his map as unexplored, and south of a range of mountains described by him as running east and west, he having seen them from his northern line of exploration.

There was no doubt about the shortness of the route; it was direct; it ran due west; if we could go by it we would save time and several hundred miles of travel, which at that season of the year was valuable. In fact, there was everything to be said in favor of it, and there was really only one objection against it. That objection it took subsequent experience to reveal to us. But I can now tell you what it was: *it was not a practical route.* The country through which it was said to run was a desert, with grass and water to be found only in spots and at long intervals, and there was no certainty that men traveling through there for the first time would find them.

When General Rich came to our camp the brethren who had conversed with Captain Smith on this subject told him about this new route. He soon saw that they were in favor of it. The wish was very general in our company that he would fit up and go through with us, as our provisions were not sufficient to admit of our traveling through as slowly as the wagons would. Though he had a good outfit to go through with the wagons, he felt led to arrange his affairs so that he could travel with us. He was impressed with the idea that if he did not do so, some of us, if not all, would perish. Before I have finished my account you will see that this impression was a correct one. He was a great blessing to us, and I think the company could not all

---

[91] Several other accounts also make this statement

have got through alive, if he had not been with us.

In the afternoon of the day that we were camped on Beaver Creek General Rich and Captain Flake went up to see Captain Smith and converse with him about this new route. Smith was so confident about his ability to go by the route, and his information from Barney Ward appeared so reliable, that the General thought very favorably of the proposition to go that way. But he and Brother Flake would not decide positively that they would travel on it until they had laid the matter before our company. They wanted us to choose for ourselves. Captain Smith and company had made up their minds to travel the new route. If we concluded to go also the two companies would travel in consort and camp close together, so that in case of an attack we would be ready to unite.

The next day we started westward again, expecting to travel 35 miles to get to water; but we had only traveled 10 miles when we met Captain Smith and his pack train returning. They informed us that Captain Hunt had been out again on the desert on foot in search of water, but had found none, though he had traveled 40 miles. When we heard this we returned to the creek and camped. As I have told you I have never visited that part of the country since the time of which I write; but I am told that our people who wish to go to settlements west travel down the Beaver, and water has been found where Captain Hunt searched for it. After we reached the creek Brother Rich asked us our feelings about the new route, and we all voted to go that way. He already had a mule, so he bought a horse; this gave him one to ride and another to pack. Brother F. M. Pomeroy had two horses which he used for the same purpose. You can imagine how glad we were to have them join our company; for with Bro. Rich to counsel and guide us we felt that we could travel in safety.

Five of the brethren of our company had traveled to this point in two wagons. Their names were Henry W. Bigler, James Keeler, Thomas Whittle, Joseph Peck and Peter Hoagland.[92] They had two animals apiece, and they resolved to leave their wagons here and pack through. To travel with wagons in company with a pack train is not very pleasant on a good road; but we were going to travel on a route over which no wagon had ever crossed that we knew anything about, therefore, it was deemed wisdom for these brethren to change their mode of traveling.

We turned back up the Beaver to the point where we first crossed it and then struck off on the Spanish trail to Little Salt Lake valley. The company of wagons, of which Captain Hunt was the pilot, also took this route. At Red creek, about where Paragoonah now stands, we took leave of Brothers Addison Pratt, James S. Brown, and Hiram H. Blackwell, who remained with the train of wagons. Some of the men from the wagons were desirous of traveling with us; but their horses were poor and they had only enough to pack without any to ride. A committee from our company examined their outfit, and decided it was unsuitable. It was a duty we owed to ourselves to see that none should join us who had not good animals and enough of them; for if their horses should fail the company would have to carry them and their provisions; we could not leave them on the deserts. But these men were resolved to travel with us any how; they said they could walk themselves and their horses could carry their packs.[93]

[92] See the same information in Farrer's Journal on October 25, part v: c.

Already there was a diversity of opinion among the members of the company about the best manner of treating the Indians, and of traveling. Brother Rich heard enough to show him that something should be done to check this division of sentiment. He called us together one evening and told us that he wanted to know whether we were to be governed by all the men in the company, by one-half, or by one man. He thought it necessary that this should be understood before we went any further. We were about to enter upon a new route, and, to be safe, union must prevail. There should be a head to dictate. As Latter-day Saints there was but one way that we could travel and be prospered, and all were in favor of that way: we were all willing to be controlled by him.

It was the last day of October, and we had a fine rain. At home with houses, or even covered wagons to sleep in we would not have minded it; but we had neither. Our covering was the heavens; we did not have even a tent to shelter us. It rained when we laid down, and when we arose in the morning our bedding and clothing were thoroughly soaked. We concluded that, however pleasant packing might be in fine weather, it was far from being agreeable when it stormed.

On the first of November we left the trail and struck off on the cut-off. The morning was fine when we started. We crossed a ridge to the westward and after traveling about a mile crossed a small spring branch, then crossed a number of ridges. In passing through a cedar grove we found two or three Indian wick-e-ups very comfortably made out of cedar limbs and tops. They had not long been untenanted. We saw

93 No other account seems to mention this. Whether or not any others besides Rich and Pomeroy joined the pack train is not known positively.

a gap in the mountains to the south west of where we were; in making for it we crossed a valley diagonally several miles in width. In the meantime we could see that a storm was in progress in the mountains, and when we reached the gap it was still storming. We traveled up the dry bed of a creek and over some spurs, the rain descending heavily all the time. It was so cold that we had to dismount and walk. Even then our animals had a hard time, the ground was so miry. We walked along without speaking, each of us absorbed in his own reflections, which probably were not very pleasant, for the rain beat in our faces and we were very cold, and, with our bedding and everything we had, were thoroughly drenched. It was a very acceptable sight, therefore, when after traveling about fifteen miles we, towards night, came to some rocks containing caves, which we named the Rocks of Refuge. As we stopped, the rain ceased, and we soon had large fires burning, before which we dried our clothes and bedding, and made ourselves as comfortable as we could. We had no idea of obtaining such good quarters for the night, and cheerfulness took the place of our former gloomy feelings.

The next morning we traveled for a long distance up the dry bed of the creek which we struck the day before. We called it Dry Sandy. We passed a small stream, impregnated with iron which sinks in the bed of the Sandy; also a beautiful spring which was on our left. About three miles from the spring, in a south-westerly direction, we came to a narrow pass in a kanyon, and found plenty of water which arose and sunk within about three hundred yards distance. Up to this point, I find my journal says, the valley afforded plenty of feed and good land; the mountains had no timber that we could see but cedar and scrub pine; sage also grew on them. Traveling some distance further we came to what we called the dividing ridge of the Great Basin, where the water instead of flowing into the Basin, as all our creeks and rivers do in this part of the territory, runs into the Pacific Ocean. Considerable snow had fallen on this ridge during the night, and some still remained. We then went down a large kanyon until we came to a place which some of the company called the Devil's Offset.

My horse "Croppy" had been gradually failing for some days. To-day he failed so much that he did not keep up with the company, consequently I was left behind. There were two of the brethren, however, who would not leave me – Brothers Joseph Cain and Henry W. Bigler. When we came to this Offset we were alone. The trail which the company had made led directly to it; but here they had stopped; they had found it impossible to pass there, and they had scattered in every direction to find a better route. We were very much puzzled to tell which way they had gone. After searching some time we at last got on their trail again. They had gone back about a quarter of a mile, and made a circuit over the hills to the southward for about three miles, and reached the same kanyon about one hundred yards below Offset. After we got into the kanyon again we hoped to see the camp fires at every point we rounded; for it began to grow dark, and we had to watch closely to keep the trail. But we, finally, began to think that we would have to camp for if we kept on in the dark we would lose the trail of the company and wander out of our way. We were, therefore, gladdened when Bro. Bigler, who was ahead, shouted that he smelt the camp. I presume that we must have been half a mile distant from the camping ground at the time. You may think it strange that he should be able to know by his nose at that distance that the camp was not far off. But in a kanyon the currents of air are confined to it, and the smell of the sage brush, of which the company built their fires, and which is very strong, was carried towards us. We found Capt. Smith's company and ours encamped upon a plat containing about fifty acres of grass, at the lower end of which we found some good springs. There was an Indian lodge found close to the camp. It had been deserted by the Indians when they saw us coming; for they had been seen in the distance and the fire had just been covered up.

We found the Indians all through this country very shy; they would run away from us like rabbits, they were so scared. We were convinced that many of them had never seen white men before, and our appearance in their country terrified them. White men had been on the Spanish Trail, and some of them might have seen them there, but only at a distance.

In traveling down the kanyon we fully expected to reach a valley. In fact, the hope of finding a valley extending westward, in which we could find water and feed, and could travel without having to cross mountains, was always present with us. If the difficulties of the day were very great, and the mountains hemmed us in, we were cheered by the expectation that on the morrow it would be all right, for we should soon reach a valley. In going down the kanyon we had to cross the creek a number of times, and found some of the crossings rather miry. The kanyon was narrow and the mountains on each side towered up perpendicular and rocky. There were a number of caves in the sides. We

soon found the kanyon impassable, and were compelled
to climb a mountain, the sides of which were covered
with cedar. The ascent of this mountain was very
difficult for our pack animals. We then traveled over
some cedar ridges, and found ourselves in a position
where, to get any further, we must climb a steep, rocky
mountain. It was difficult for a man on foot to make
the ascent, and, of course, the pack animals had a hard
time to reach the summit. But we all finally reached
the top. There was but little satisfaction in this; for
we were no sooner up than we had to prepare to
descend. This was more difficult and dangerous than
climbing. We made as good a road as we could by
winding round the mountain to a spur that sloped
gradually to the creek; but, even then, great care had
to be taken; one false step would have precipitated
an animal and pack down the mountain without any
prospect of escaping with life. We all reached the
bottom of the mountain without accident. The creek
had increased considerably in size, and after crossing
it several times we arrived at a large bend in which
we found a tolerable supply of grass. We concluded
it best to camp here, as there was no prospect of
reaching that valley for the sight of which we strained
our eyes in vain. This day had been cloudy, and in
the evening we were threatened with a storm. I dug
a trench around the bed of myself and bedfellow;
but it did not save us from a drenching. It rained
heavily all night, and we arose in the morning, in the
midst of the rain, feeling very uncomfortable. We
found an Indian wigwam not far from our camp. Its
occupants had evidently ran away upon hearing our
approach, as a pot made of earthenware, containing
some food, was on the fire.

Our animals had suffered as much as ourselves during the storm. They looked badly in the morning. As soon as the rain ceased we started. We still kept down the kanyon, crossing and recrossing the creek a great number of times. But after a few hours we came to a place beyond which it seemed impossible to pass. We were hemmed in by high mountains, impracticable to cross, and the channel through which the creek ran was so rocky and precipitous that our passage by that way seemed to be barred. Several of the company climbed to the tops of the mountains surrounding us to examine, if possible, the country ahead of us. All returned with unfavorable reports; there was nothing to be seen but mountains. We were in a bad fix. Further progress seemed impossible. If we should turn back to the point where we left the regular trail, and endeavor to go through on that route, we would not have half enough provisions for our use, and there was no way of obtaining more short of Salt Lake City or California. If we were to return up this kanyon, and strike off to the right or left, what assurance had we that we could get through these mountains any easier than by the route we were then traveling? These were anxious moments, but none of us could think of returning. We must proceed at all hazards. Those who had climbed the mountains to reconnoitre, had reported that the kanyon grew wider a little below where we were, and if we could surmount the obstacles right before us, we could still proceed. There was a gleam of hope in this. Captain Flake and one or two others concluded they would try and descend the kanyon on foot. After some time had elapsed they returned and informed the company that they found the passage exceedingly rocky; the creek took a leap over a precipice ten or twelve feet in hight, and at this waterfall the mountains which rose on each side, were steep and slippery; but on one side, they thought, a passage might be made with some labor. This intelligence relieved every one. It promised action, and that in the circumstances we were in then would be a relief. We had been detained here several hours in a pouring rain, the animals were chilled, the packs were well soaked and the men were wet to the skin. We commenced our descent of the kanyon. By rolling rocks out of the way we succeeded in getting along tolerably well until we reached the precipice. At this point we took the packs off many of the animals; and then by the men fastening lariets round their necks and pulling them up, they made the ascent without accident. "Old Croppy" was the only exception. He had been gradually failing, and was not very strong. By pulling and pushing him he succeeded in nearly reaching the top of the steepest part of the ascent, when his hind feet slipped and he fell. We had considerable difficulty in keeping him from rolling to the bottom and carrying us along with him. We tried to get him on his feet again; but without avail. He was too weak, and the place was too steep. We had to roll him over on to a more favorable place, and then he got up. With more help the next attempt was successful, and we all got over into the kanyon. "Croppy" had his knee badly cut in his fall, and was much shaken. He acted as though his fall had crazed him. A sensible horse would, when turned loose, have followed the others. "Croppy" would have done so before he had this fall; but now, when we drove him ahead of us into the kanyon, he seemed determined to get into the creek. In despite of our efforts to prevent him he rushed down the steep bank into the water. The bottom on the side of the creek which we traveled was probably two or three hundred yards wide; and the Indian trail which the company followed ran close at the base of the mountain. Between that and the creek there was a dense growth of willows, wild rose bushes, and other brush.

To drive "Croppy" ahead it was necessary to pass through this under-growth; and, as night had spread its mantle of darkness over us, we found this very disagreeable. Bro. Joseph Cain remained with me to assist in getting my horse into camp. We were afoot, and as we were scrambling along through the brush we suddenly came on to an Indian wick-e-up. The first notice we had of it we were at its entrance. We had heard so many tales of the treachery and cruelty of these Indians that we had a wholesome dread of exposing ourselves or animals to their attacks or depredations. You can imagine, therefore, how startled we were to find ourselves so near to one of their dwellings at such a time and under such circumstances. I fancied I could distinguish in the gloom an Indian inside; but I might have been mistaken; at any rate we did not stop to satisfy ourselves on that point, for the company was a long way ahead of us and our riding horses had kept with the company, and my rifle was fastened to my riding saddle. I was unarmed, unless my butcher knife, which I carried, Spanish fashion, in my legging, could be called a weapon. Bro. Cain had his rifle; but, unfortunately, in trying to load it a day or two before he had used too thick a patching, and the bullet had stuck half way down the barrel. There it was, immovable; he could neither get it up nor down. Neither he nor any of the rest of us had dared to fire off the rifle for fear of it bursting.

If there were any Indians in or near the wick-e-up, they were probably more frightened than we; for our company had come upon them unexpectedly, and they must have been at a total loss to know what our object could be in coming through that part of their country, where probably no white man had ever been to their knowledge before. We were glad to get out of the brush and to get "Croppy" out of the creek on to the trail again, and before long we were gladdened still more by seeing the light of the camp fires in the distance. There was considerable interest felt in camp about "Croppy." The fear was very general that he could not hold out much longer, and in our circumstances the loss of a horse or a mule by any one of the company was a general loss. We were dependent upon one another, and we, therefore, were compelled to look upon ourselves to some extent as one family. Whether "Croppy" was determined to commit suicide by drowning or not I can not say; but the creek seemed to have great attractions for him. If the weather had been warm, I might have thought that he sought its waters to cool himself; but it was November and the nights were cold. Sometime in the night I was awakened by my friend, Bro. Joseph Cain, who wanted me to get up. "Croppy" was in the creek, and help was needed to draw him out. He had been in the creek before; and it had taken three of the guard to bring him to the bank. With some trouble we managed to get him out and on to his feet; but he was chilled through, and I thought it very doubtful about his being able to live. I led him away from the creek and left him under the shelter of some brush, in a place where he could get feed and be warm. I then returned to bed. He soon wandered off again to the creek, and there I found him the next morning stretched out stark and cold. He was drowned! Under some circumstances my position would have been a very disagreeable one, left with but one animal at a distance of nearly five hundred miles from any point where I could obtain supplies; but the only feeling of unpleasantness that I had arose from my being dependent. The brethren of my mess were very kind; they divided my pack and carried a portion on each of their horses. Their doing this still left me my mare to ride.

Every headland we rounded in our travel down the kanyon the next day we expected to see a valley; but we were disappointed until about the middle of the afternoon, when we came into a small valley containing about twenty acres of cultivated land. The soil was sandy, and from the cornstalks lying around we judged the Indians had raised good corn there. About three miles further down we came to another small valley. There was a corn field there also, in which the corn stalks were standing; the ears had been stripped off. Morning glories, and beans, squash vines, and other vegetables had grown in the field, and had been well cultivated. Large ditches had been made for irrigating purposes, which gave evidence of industry and perseverance. Though this was November the fifth, there had been no frost to nip vegetation. As we continued our travel down this creek the kanyon became more open, the surrounding mountains were lower and receded from the creek, and the water almost ceased to run. We came to another corn field. It was surprising to us to see the foliage so luxuriant and green as it was here; to have judged by that we should have thought it July rather than November.

Had we continued on the course we were then

pursuing we should have struck the Spanish Trail
before long, as we were traveling in a southerly
direction, and this [Beaver Dam] wash on which we
then were doubtless led into another wash or stream
which crossed the Trail on its route to the Colorado
river. This, of course, would not have suited those who
wished to go through by "Walker's cut-off." We
remained a day in the vicinity of this last corn field,
and while there were joined by some men from the
main train of wagons, of which Captain Hunt was the
pilot. There were six of them with five horses. They
informed us that the people with the wagons had all
resolved to follow us, and had started on our track.
Up to this point we had been traveling on no trail; we
had followed the course of streams, and were only able
to know what our general course was by the compass.
There were plenty of trails; but they ran in all directions over the country, being made by the Indians to
suit their local convenience. In starting again we struck
over some high hills to the westward and traveled in
this direction nearly all day. We estimated our day's
journey at 32 miles. We camped in the dry bed of a
creek, but could find no water. The animals were very
much exhausted for want of feed and water. There was
much suffering from thirst among the men in camp
this night; many of Captain Smith's company offered
to give anything they had for a drink. Gloomy and
despondent feelings prevailed with a great number, as
the prospect of finding water without going a great
distance was not very promising.

To the northward of where we camped were some
mountains, and, as the dry bed of the creek came from
that direction, it was hoped that by following it up we
might find water there. In the morning, therefore, we

started. The weather was very warm for the season, and, after the sun arose, its rays felt oppressive to both men and animals. Before we reached the mouth of the kanyon one of the brethren became almost crazy with thirst, and I had serious fears for him. I understood afterwards that he had recourse to the dreadful expedient of drinking his urine, in the vain hope that he could, by that means, quench his thirst. Instead of it having that effect, it had the very opposite, as he ought to have known it would; it made him more thirsty, and almost maddened him. There were several of Smith's men also whose reason was nearly upset through their excessive thirst. There were a number of the animals belonging to Captain Smith's company which "gave out," as well as some of ours.

It seemed as though we would never reach the kanyon for which we were aiming. The distance was not very great; and men with plenty of food and drink would have soon traveled it; but we were all weak, as we did not like to eat for fear of increasing our thirst, and we found it difficult to drag ourselves along through the sand in the bed of the creek. The travel of that morning tested the endurance of all very thoroughly; and the company straggled along in a broken condition. The men on the lead reached the kanyon a long time ahead of those who were behind. After proceeding up the kanyon a little distance they found running water. As soon as they saw it they shouted *"Water, Water"* at the top of their voices. The cry was caught up by those behind, and was rapturously repeated the whole length of the line. This delightful news infused new life into the drooping frames of the men, and they pushed forward with increased energy. Some of them were so long, however, in reaching the water, that an impression began to prevail among them that they had been deceived. But they reached it at last. Pure, sparkling, cold water was there, gurgling as it ran over the rocks in the channel. Oh, what music to our ears was in the sound! How ravishing the sight! It was not a large stream; but it was sufficient; and a body of water as large as Lake Superior could not have produced more joy or thankfulness. I thought that morning, and many times during that journey, that I would never cease to be thankful for the precious gift of water. Though nearly twenty years have elapsed since then, the impression still remains; I cannot bear now to see water wasted. We rushed eagerly to the stream, and, stretched at full length on the ground, slaked our thirst by copious draughts, taken at such intervals as not to hurt us. What more appropriate name could we think of for this place than "Providence Kanyon?" [Meadow Valley Wash] for the finding of this water had indeed been providential.

During the afternoon two of the men from the company behind, who had overtaken us a day or two before, came into camp in a suffering condition for the want of water. They had left their four comrades behind with the animals, while they pushed ahead with the hope of finding water that they could carry back to them. After eating, they started back with four canteens of water; but at night they returned with the word that they could not find them. The worst fears prevailed among us respecting the fate of these men. Two of Smith's company had been back for a horse, which they had left behind; they could not find it; but they saw, they said, a band of Indians, about twenty-two or twenty-three in number, three of whom had rifles. Supposing that these men had told the truth, we were afraid the Indians had laid in ambush and killed the four men as they passed through one of the narrow kanyons which were on their route.

The next morning a call was made for five of our company, and five of Captain Smith's to go back with the two men and search for some traces of the missing ones. We armed ourselves and started afoot, taking with us a canteen of water apiece. We also took a spade with us, hoping that, if murdered, we might, at least, find their bodies, and give them as decent a burial as we could. But, to our great relief, we had not proceeded more than four or five miles from camp when we met the men and their horses alive and well. They had wandered from our trail in search of water, and had found some in a cave eight miles below the place where we had camped in the dry bed of the creek. This had saved their lives. We were so pleased to find them that, when we neared the mouth of the kanyon, we whooped, and some fired off their guns, with the intent of informing the companies that the men were safe. But the companies, recollecting what the two men, who went back for the horse, had told them about seeing Indians, supposed the camp was attacked, and they seized their guns and took such measures for defense as suggested themselves to them in the excitement. Fortunately, they were able to distinguish who we were before they fired upon us; but it was a lesson to me not to do the like again. We ought to have known that our firing and whooping would only create alarm.

The day's travel after leaving Providence Kanyon was very fatiguing to the animals and men. We traveled up and down hill all day, yet we did not seem to make much headway in a straight direction; for, to avoid climbing the hills which were steep and high, we frequently had to make considerable of a circuit. We met with no water through the day, and when night approached we saw a creek in a kanyon a long distance off. After searching awhile we found a place where we could descend to the water; but we camped on the high land. An examination revealed to us the startling fact that we had been traveling all day, over a most fatiguing road, to gain three miles! We were only about three miles farther up Providence Kanyon than we were the day before! When this became known the most of the company felt low spirited. And no wonder they did; for, after our recent experience, it seemed that, unless there was a change in our mode of travel we must inevitably perish in the midst of this wilderness. Since we left the regular Trail we had been wandering about in these kanyons, mountains and deserts for eleven days. Our progress in the direction of California had been very slow. But we had excellent appetites. Our provisions were disappearing, our clothes wearing out, and our animals would soon be too thin to afford much sustenance, if we had to kill them.

Our precarious condition aroused Gen. C. C. Rich. The time had come for him to speak and act. He had been led to travel with the company to save us from just such a fate as then threatened us. Up to this time he had not taken a very active part in the guidance of the company. Captain Smith's opinion had been taken in preference to his. But this evening he told the company that he was not going to be led around in this manner any longer. If there was not an alteration in our mode of travel, we should all perish in the mountains. He was determined now to have his way, or he would go back to the wagons as quickly as he could. We were relieved by his remarks. They made us feel glad; for we knew that he, not Captain Smith, had the right to lead us, and that if we should be saved from our perilous circumstances, it would be through him. It seemed as though the Lord had permitted us to wander about on that 11th day of November, without making any progress, to arouse everyone to a sense of the peril we were in, that he whose right it was to lead us might be justified in the eyes of all in dictating our future movements.

Smith's company soon learned that there was to be a change in our plan of travel, and that if they traveled in our company they must follow our lead. You may be sure that some of them sneered at the idea of the "Mormon" apostle leading them. They would now see how successful we should be in finding feed and water and a good route with an apostle to dictate. I was young and inexperienced then, and did not realize, as I have since, the responsibility which Brother Rich felt. When Smith was on the lead nobody blamed him if we did not make much progress or did not find feed or water; but with Bro. Rich it was different. These men would not acknowledge that he had any more authority or knowledge than they had, yet they expected more from him than they did from one of themselves. In their hearts they felt there was an authority which their mouths denied.

As if to test our faith, the next day's travel was a hard one. We struck for the low lands, and it was fortunate for us that we had followed Bro. Rich's counsel in taking with us all the water we could carry, (which, however, was not much) for though we found excellent grass for the animals where we stopped an hour about sun-set, we traveled until ten o'clock in the evening without finding either water or grass, and, being tired out, were compelled to camp.

Before daylight we were stirring. Bro. Rich and two or three of us shouldered our rifles and started out ahead on foot. We did not eat anything, thinking we should not be so likely to get thirsty. To the westward of where we were we saw a number of ridges or hills rising suddenly out of the valley. By ascending them we hoped to be able to see where we could find water. But, though we climbed several, we were disappointed. The prospect was dreary. As far as the eye could reach, there was a desert on every side of us. There was a range of mountains lying to the westward, where we thought it likely we should find water; but they were far distant, and as there was no sign of water that we could discover this side of them, it became a question of some anxiety whether we and our animals could hold out to reach them. We had nothing but our canteens to carry our water in, and our supply was already exhausted.

We had kept ahead of the company through the forenoon. By one or two o'clock in the afternoon we began to feel faint for the want of food. From the top of the last ridge or hill which we climbed we saw the company winding along in the distance, and we took our bearings so as to meet them. About the time we joined them, which was in the middle of the afternoon, a sprinkle of rain commenced to fall; and, as it fortunately happened, we found a small patch of grass. The animals were both hungry and thirsty, and as this wet grass was what they wanted, Brother Rich had the company stop for awhile. He and those of us who had walked ahead with him, had been without food about twenty-four hours, and traveling as we had, you may well suppose that we were ravenously hungry. An invitation, therefore, from him, to eat some hard bread, which he had got off his pack mule, was gratefully accepted, regardless of the thirst which oppressed us. I have always given him credit since of furnishing me the best meal that I ever partook of.

An hour had scarcely passed before the small, scattering drops of rain became a regular shower. Then we resumed our journey. I rode on horseback, and I turned up the rim of my hat, and made it something like a dish. By carrying my head very steady I contrived to catch some rain, to which the hat gave a smoky flavor; but it quenched thirst. The ground over which we traveled was covered with rocks; as the rain continued to descend it settled in the hollows which were in the surface of them, and from these the men soon got all they wanted to drink. The animals also were able to satisfy their thirst from the puddles which covered the ground. We camped that night in a ravine, and cooked our supper with rain water. We did not have many vessels that would hold water; but we filled everything that we had; we did not suffer a drop to go to waste that we had any means of keeping.

I have always believed that this shower of rain was sent to save our lives. We all felt very grateful, for the providence of the Lord was very visible to us in this timely relief. Even Captain Smith deemed it providential; for he told Gen. Rich that the finger of the Lord was in this rain. It is very probable that some of us, and perhaps all, would have miserably perished in that desert if the rain had not fallen. If there was water near, we did not know where to look for it; there were no indications of its presence to guide us in our search for it. We did think we should obtain it at the mountains west; but three of our men went there the next day and could not find any. The day was spent in searching for water. A small spring was at last found in the bottom to the southward of where we were. It was very weak, but it was thought that, by digging, we might obtain sufficient water for ourselves, and the animals could be supplied from the clay puddles near the spring. Had we found this spring before the rain fell; it would have given us very little relief. Its flow after the rain was barely sufficient to supply the men, and there would have been no water for the animals, for it was the recent rain that had made the pools at which they drank.

We moved to the spring that afternoon. The next day Gen. Rich and three of our company started for the mountains, with the intention of taking a view from them of the country westward. The day wore away and, as night approached, we looked eagerly for their return; but it was long after nightfall before they reached our camp. In the descent of the mountain they had heard holloaing, which the men wanted to reply to, thinking that it must be some of our company searching for them; but Brother Rich checked them, and it was well he did so. They were Indians. Shortly afterwards they saw a fire, and when they got within a few feet of it, there sat an Indian. It was so dark he could not see them.

This view from the mountain satisfied Brother Rich that this was not the route for us to travel. He came back to camp with his mind fully made up to strike for the Spanish Trail. The country westward was high and sterile, with, to all appearances, but little grass. After hearing the description of the country and Brother Rich's feelings, our company were unanimous in their decision to turn in the direction of the Spanish Trail. The next morning Captain Smith came over to our camp to learn from General Rich what he had seen and his opinion about the route. When he learned our determination it did not shake him in the least. He swore by the gods he would go straight ahead, if he died in the attempt. Said he: "If you do not hear from me, you may know that I died with my face westward, and not before I have eaten some mule meat."

These were brave words, and were designed to draw a contrast between what he thought was our lack of perseverance and courage, and the pluck, energy and unyielding resolution which he and his men possessed. They had, however, but little effect upon us. To our minds it was no evidence of bravery in a man to plunge himself into the midst of difficulties, to expose his life unnecessarily, or to brave starvation and dangers when they could be honorably avoided. It was with no disposition to flinch, or to back out that we came to the conclusion to no longer pursue this route; but prudence and wisdom alike forbade our persistance in that direction.

We called this spot "Division Spring"; for here we separated. With the exception of one or two, all the men not belonging to the Church, who had joined our company, left us and went with Captain Smith. Some two or three of his men, who had become members of the Church, at Salt Lake City, left him and joined us. We parted with the best of feelings, each one believing his way to be the best. As it will be interesting to my readers to know what became of Captain Smith and his company, I will here relate what I afterwards learned respecting them. The morning we separated they pursued their way westward, and after traveling that day and part of the next without finding water, they became alarmed, and concluded to return to "Division Spring." They reached there in a very exhausted condition, and some of them would likely have perished before arriving there, had they not killed a mare and drank its blood! By this time Smith had either forgotten his oath, or thought dying with his face westward was not so pleasant as he had imagined it would be; for he and some of his men decided upon taking the back track.

The route over which they and we had traveled in company, bad as it was, they preferred rather than encounter the horrors of the unknown wilds west of "Division Spring." They might have followed us, but their pride revolted at this. They never stopped going eastward until they met a company of our people – I think it was Major Howard Egan and party – who were on their way to California. This was after they had got inside of the Rim of the Basin.[94] They furnished Smith and his men provisions and carried them through to California, where they arrived some time after we had been there.

When Captain Smith and his company reached "Division Spring" on their return from the desert, some of the men who had been following up our trail, determined they would not go East. So eleven of them, including some members of Smith's company, resolved to form a company of their own. Their destination was California, and in that direction they were determined to travel at all hazards. They packed up all the provisions they had, which was not much, and a

[94] Egan picked up four men at Iron Spring back on the Old Spanish Trail, and took them on to California. (*See* Egan's diary, entry of December 2, 1849, part VIII.

little bedding, and their guns and ammunition, and left everything else and started out to the westward on foot. As you can readily imagine they suffered terribly. Had they known the country their sufferings would have been comparatively light; but they had to trust to chance to find water. Their food soon failed and they were reduced to the verge of starvation. They were as far from all human succor as if they had been in the midst of the ocean. On every hand desolation reigned supreme, and their only hope consisted in pushing on. When they reached the vicinity of Owens Lake they saw the mighty Sierra Nevada rearing its towering summits to the skies. It then became a question of some importance what course they should take to surmount this formidable barrier. If they could only succeed in finding an easy passage over it, and their strength did not entirely fail, they might hope to live. But at this point they could not agree upon the route to take.

Nine went in one direction and two in another.[95] The nine never reached the settlements. No tidings of their fate ever came to white men's ears, that I have heard of. How they perished, whether by starvation, by Indians, or to what horrible extremities they were reduced, we can only imagine. The two succeeded in crossing the Sierra Nevada mountains and reached the settlements in California. When they neared the mountains they were so fortunate as to find some acorns which the Indians had *cached* for winter use. This discovery probably saved their lives. During that winter I met with one of these men in the Mariposa mines, and from his own lips learned the story of their

[95] These men were of the Death Valley party, rather than of Smith's party. Pinney and Savage were the two who reached California. *See* Stover's account in part VI.

dreadful sufferings. While I listened to him, and thought how narrowly I had escaped a similar fate, I felt thankful to God for His kindness in placing me in circumstances where I could be led by the priesthood; for to the presence of Bro. Rich in our company I attributed our deliverance from severe privations and hardships and probably death in the desert.

Following in the trail of these eleven came parties from the company which had broken off from Captain Hunt. I cannot write all the particulars of their fate; but they pushed on west, determined that kanyons and deserts should not stop them. Before them to the westward lay California, the land of gold, the El Dorado which they sought, and they were resolved to overcome every obstacle to tread its golden sands, hoping, in the wealth which they should gather there, to obtain a reward for all their sufferings and toils. Whether they met Smith and his party or not as they returned I do not know; but they came to Division Spring and still pressed on.[96]

There is a valley away to the westward of Division Spring which bears to this day the name of Death Valley. It is said to be wholly destitute of water, and though it is some fifty miles long by thirty in breadth, save at two points, it is wholly encircled with mountains, up whose steep sides it is impossible for any but expert climbers to ascend. I can scarcely believe all that is told about this valley, for it is said that no vegetation grows in it, and that shadow of bird or wild beast never darkened its white, glaring surface. But

[96] These Jayhawkers and other Death Valley parties did not meet Smith; in fact, they had taken a different road from Mount Misery than the one followed by the Smith and Flake-Rich parties. The Death Valley parties did not go by Division (Coyote) Spring.

whether this description of it be true or not, there is no doubt about it being a very horrible place. This valley, many of these people who followed our trail reached, lured into its treacherous bosom by the hope of finding water. They reached the centre; but the glaring desert and the dry, barren peaks met their gaze on every hand. Around the valley they wandered, and the children, crying for water, perished at their mothers' breasts. The mothers soon followed, and the men, with swollen tongues, tottered and raved and died. After wandering some time, it is said, the survivors found water in the hollow of a rock in the mountains, and a few finally succeeded in getting through. I have heard it stated that eighty-seven persons, with numbers of animals, perished in this fearful place, and since then it has been called DEATH VALLEY.[97]

Having given you a little idea in my last chapter of the result of Captain Smith's attempt to die with his face westward, also the misfortunes which befell those who perished in trying to push through on that route, I now return to our party. It was with a great sense of relief that we changed our course in leaving Division Spring on the morning of November 16th, 1849. We had been traveling directly West as nearly as we could; but that morning we started in a south easterly direction. As if to encourage us, we all felt buoyant and cheerful, so much so that we spoke of our feelings one to another. Smith's men were not the most pleasant company in the world for us. They were of the usual type of gold diggers, and their manners were not improved by the privations to which they had been subjected. They had not been careful with their provisions, and though our supply was small, I think

---

[97] Cannon's information about the Death Valley parties is very inaccurate.

we must have had more than they; for some of them said they were nearly out. If they could not get food any other way, however, it had been said, so I was told, they would use their rifles to obtain it. In other words, they would kill somebody rather than to go short. There would have been no necessity for them to have tried to kill us for any such purpose, for if they had behaved themselves, we should have shared with them as long as our provisions would have lasted. Had any of them tried force they would have found us a most difficult party to manage; we were united and resolute, familiar with the use of arms and numbered about as many as they. By our separation we were saved from all difficulty with them.[98]

We had no further trouble about obtaining water on the route we had chosen. In the afternoon we passed through a narrow kanyon which ran through a mountain, the sides of which towered up very steep to the height of several hundred feet. We camped about a quarter of a mile from the mouth of the kanyon [Double Canyon]. The next day we continued our journey down the bed of the creek, and came to another kanyon, about three miles long, with sides of solid rock [Arrow Canyon], which rose abruptly for several hundred feet. We found it good traveling down the kanyon. Upon emerging from it we came to splendid grass and some warm springs of water. These springs soon formed a creek of considerable size for that country. The traveling was bad in consequence of the mire. We camped on the creek that night in good feed.

Brother Peter Fife, who, as I informed you, had traveled on the Spanish Trail from California to Salt

---

[98] For Rich's entry of Nov. 15, and that of Farrer's of Nov. 18, relating to this question, *see* part V: B, C.

Lake Valley, was still with us. We had many questions
to ask him about the country, and were particularly
anxious to know whether he saw any points which
looked familiar to him. He knew of no creek so large
as this, excepting the Muddy, and it had every appearance of that stream. His conjecture proved to be
correct; for we had not traveled more than about five
miles down the creek in the morning before we espied
some cattle grazing on the other side, and directly
afterwards saw some men. These men informed us that
Captain Hunt was here with seven wagons, all the rest
having parted company with him, and followed our
trail. Our meeting with the Captain and his fellow-
travelers, Elders Addison Pratt, James S. Brown and
Hiram Blackwell was a joyful one. We found them
camped near where the Spanish Trail crossed the
Muddy.

It was with a feeling of great relief that we reached
the Spanish Trail. We were tired of traveling on a
"cut-off," and to say that a certain road was a "cut-off"
to any one of the company during the remainder of
that journey was sufficient to prejudice him against it.
To this day I have a dislike to "cut-offs." I prefer
traveling on roads that I know something about. We
had been traveling for eighteen days in a country of
which we knew nothing. Our animals were failing
every day, and our provisions were rapidly disappearing. While in this condition we could not divest
ourselves of the feeling of anxiety about the result.
The fact is I, for one, did not feel at ease respecting
our position and mode of traveling at no time after we
took the cut-off until Brother Rich avowed his determination to lead; and I felt still better after we left
Division Spring with the intenion of going to the
Spanish Trail.

We remained one day in camp on the Muddy. Captain Hunt and the other brethren spared us some provisions, with which we hoped to be able to reach the settlements in California. Between the Muddy and the Los Vegas, there is a stretch of fifty miles, which is generally called desert. When about halfway across we found feed, and some standing water among a patch of bushes, a mile and a half distant from the feed. This water had gathered in puddles from the last rain. It proved acceptable, as we camped there that night, and occupied two days in traveling the fifty miles.

I shall not attempt to write the details of each day's journey from this point to California. Many of our horses failed, and their owners had to perform the remainder of the distance on foot. By walking, and permitting my only animal to run loose, I had hoped to save her; but she failed and could not travel with us. Brother Francis M. Pomeroy had concluded to stop and travel through with Captain Hunt and the ox-teams, and kindly proffered to take charge of her, and drive her through with his animals. When we parted with Brother Pomeroy I did not expect to ever see her again. But he succeeded in bringing her through, and she afterwards did me considerable service.

When we struck the Mojave River we found some men with their wives and children encamped in wagons there [Gruwell-Derr Company]. They were moving to California, and for four or five weeks previous to our meeting them, they had been living upon beef only. Though we had but little flour our-selves, we let them have nearly all we had for the women and children. The next day several of the brethren started ahead with the hope of killing deer, which we had been told were to be found on this stream; but they were unsuccessful. It rained heavily all day. The next morning the rain changed to snow.

Our position was a disagreeable one; we had scarcely a mouthful of food, our clothing was very scanty and we had no tents to shelter us from the storm. My constant walking had worn out my boots, and for some time I had been compelled to use moccasins; but these were so badly worn that my feet were bare. To add to the painfulness of my position I arose that morning very sick. By putting the bedding together the brethren contrived to spare a blanket or two to cover a little shanty which they raised over our sleeping place, and I was very glad to crawl under this and lie the greater part of the day.

The snow continued to fall steadily, and it was useless to think of moving, yet hunger gnawed at our vitals, and any kind of food would have tasted sweet to us. Several hunted game with great perseverance; and though they saw and shot at several black-tailed deer, they were unable to secure one. An owl came within the reach of the rifle of one of the men and it was shot. A well-fed man or boy would turn up his nose at the bare mention of eating an owl. But I can assure you, my little readers, that it is not bad eating — when one is starving. Being sick, the privilege of drinking some of the soup was accorded me as a favor. It was the nicest dish of soup I had ever tasted. No chicken soup had ever been relished like this, and it did me good. Sharp hunger makes food taste wonderfully sweet; a piece of a donkey or of a dog eats very well when one is very hungry. I know this, for I have tried them both.

Through the night the snow continued to descend, and our surroundings gave a much greater degree of earnestness and fervor than usual to our prayers. The next morning as soon as we had attended to prayers, Brother Rich started out from camp, feeling led to go in a certain direction. He had not been gone long when he came back, carrying on his shoulders a good-sized deer, which he had found lying dead in the bushes. It was one that had been shot the previous day. Two more were also found by other brethren and brought into camp. A feeling of thankfulness to the Lord, for the supply which He had given us, filled our hearts, and universal cheerfulness prevailed.

The next day we moved on, and that night it was decided that those of the company who had the strongest animals should push on ahead, as it was thought that from the point where we then were they could travel to the settlements at least one day quicker than we could possibly do with the weaker animals. By so doing there would be more provisions for those who remained. Brother Rich offered to stay with the hinder part of the company; but all felt that he should go in ahead.

There were eleven of us left to travel as the hinder part of the company. In those days cattle roamed over the plains of California in countless herds. The chief value of a beef was his hide. We knew this, and had made our calculations that if we should come within shooting distance of cattle we would not hesitate to kill a beef, and settle for it with the owner as soon as we reached his ranch. But we were spared the necessity of doing this. As we were trudging wearily along, ascending the Cajon Pass of the Sierra Nevada, we met Brother Henry Gibson, who had gone ahead with the other part of the company, coming back to hunt a mule which had strayed off.

He told us the welcome news that we would find a wagon loaded with provisions at the camping place in the kanyon on the other side of the Pass. The wagon had been loaded and sent out by a Mr. Williams, for the purpose of selling food to the people who were coming in. This intelligence imparted new strength to us, and made us almost forget our fatigue.

A fire was speedily kindled after reaching the camping place, and while the bread was being baked, numerous slices of beef were cut off and broiled. Luckily the flour was unbolted, for had we eaten fine flour as freely as we did that, it might have killed us. I cannot state positively what quantity our mess ate; but I recollect that the other mess, five in number, bought fifteen pounds of flour, and in the morning they had none left for breakfast! Besides the flour, they had eaten a large quantity of meat! We were as hungry as they, and I think that we must have eaten as heartily.

We soon reached Williams' Ranch, distant some few miles from the town of Los Angeles, where we found Bro. Rich and the other brethren who had preceded us. Brother Rich secured us a job, and we remained there about one month, working. Food was plentiful; we could buy a fat steer for three dollars; and we soon got satisfied, and were contented with an ordinary meal. After we reached Williams' Ranch I was taken sick, and narrowly escaped death. I fully believe my life was saved through the Elders laying hands upon me and administering to me.

Through the kindness of Brother Rich and Captain Hunt, ox teams were bought on credit, with which a number of us, under the leadership of Major Howard Egan, proceeded up the coast. Those of the company who had mules went up as a pack company; they were accompanied by General Rich and Captain Hunt.

My "trip to California" is now ended, and I do not purpose to carry my readers any further, at least at present. My description of this trip might have been embellished and made more exciting; but I have preferred to give a simple recital of incidents which actually occurred, leaving to my readers' imaginations the labor of supplying the details.

I have been much interested in traveling in my mind over the ground again. I find it more pleasant to travel to California in this manner, than to travel with pack animals or to walk. May I hope that my readers have found the journey, which we have made together in this manner, interesting and profitable? There is one lesson which I trust has been impressed upon all by the perusal of this narrative, – that when a company or people follow the guidance of an inspired servant of God they can rely upon the protection and deliverance of the Lord.

E: James H. Rollins Recollection

[James Henry Rollins was born in Lima, New York, May 27, 1816. He had been in Utah one year before setting out on the 1849 journey to California.

The following account of his trip is copied from an autobiographical sketch dictated in 1898. This extract was kindly supplied to us by the Utah State Historical Society in July, 1945. Mr. Rollins was a member of the colony that founded San Bernardino, California. Returning to Utah, he served as Bishop of Minersville, 1860-69. He died at Bridger, Wyoming, January 7, 1899.]

In October of 1849, President Young called several missionaries to the Sandwich Islands and George Q. Cannon being one of them;[99] Charles C. Rich and

[99] As related above, in Cannon's account, he went to California to mine; but after working there some months he went to the Islands on a mission.

myself and others accompanied them as far as California. George Q. Cannon was then about 20 years old. When we arrived at Provo from Cottonwood, where we stayed for a few days waiting for General Rich. During this time we organized. James Flake as captain, which was not altogether satisfactory to General Rich.[100] At about this time a company of men with pack animals, and a great many other animals from New York,[101] joined us here. Their captain was a Mr. Smith. They went with us and we followed the road by Captain Hunt, who had agreed in Salt Lake for $1,000 to lead them through to California by the Spanish trail, which we had traveled over previous to this. We overtook them at a place called Minersville on the Beaver River, where they were camped. Captain Hunt spent all the day before we arrived searching watering places for a nearer route to the Antelope Springs.[102] He returned not finding any, very much exhausted; then our companies together turned our horses out to graze. One man of the New York Company by the name of Blodgett had a very fine horse, which he turned out in the evening with our horses. The next morning when he found his horse, his tail and mane was shaved closely. We remained here one day. Brother Addison Pratt and those that were with him, with a wagon, made pack saddles out of a wagon and packed their horses and went with us.[103] As we turned up the river and across the mountains to a place called the little Salt Lake. It is now called Parowan.

---

[100] General Rich was not in the party yet; but later he was dissatisfied with Flake's decisions, and assumed leadership himself.

[101] Here is our first indication of the region from which the main part of Capt. Smith's company came.

[102] Near the northern point of Iron Mountain.

[103] Rollins' recollection here is at fault. Pratt continued with the Hunt wagons; Bigler and four others gave up their wagons and joined the packers.

We stopped on Little Creek 2 or 3 days, there being excellent feed for our animals at that place. We then traveled on to Summit Creek, where we layed over one day. I was here taken very sick with the flux. I went up the stream about ¾ of a mile and layed there alone for some time. Brother Rich and another one of our brethren made a search, missing me from the camp. They found me laying under the bushes; they administered to me and then took me back to camp. One of the men in the New York company had some cholera medicine he had brought with him. He gave me some, which helped me. After taking two or three doses, I was able to start out the next morning. We then followed the Spanish trail to Pinto Creek; there a consultation was held and it was determined that we should leave and travel directly west through the mountains, for the Mariposa mines, thinking to cut off a great deal of travel by going that way. We found our way in places by mountains and gulches. At one place in the mountains we could see a stream and open country just beyond. Our mules and other animals slid down the mountains to a small hollow or valley. When we were down on this flat place, we built large fires and prospected our route through the short canyon, which we found impossible for our animals. There came on at this time a rain and snow storm, which caused our animals to shiver with cold. The mules warmed themselves by the fire like men. We found that we were caught as it were in a trap, and we could not go back the same way we came down in this little basin. We found by tying ropes together we could assist the pack mules to climb up the point of the mountain, which led down the gorge. After the first mule had got to the top, others followed without help.

When all was over, we were in summer, no frost had appeared as yet. We camped on this very creek [in Beaver Dam Wash] and George Q. Cannon lost his horse that night, by its falling off the bank of the creek, and was found dead the next morning. We stayed there the next day, then we continued our journey over a very rough country without water or grass. We traveled that day 30 miles or more, and camped near an Indian corn field, which was in the night, and the next morning our animals were missing, and were found at the place where we started from, about 5 miles from where we camped. We started from this point when the animals returned. We then went on 36 miles that day night, and found no water and feed for our animals. We tied up our animals that night, and started out bright and early the next morning to try to find water. Brother Rich took the lead and Captain Smith and myself were sent to prospect for grass and water. We discovered a mountain summit some 3 miles distant. While on this mountain I discovered a small cloud rising in the southwest. I said to Cap. Smith it is going to rain. He answered and said, "Why, it hasn't rained here since Noah's flood." I said to him we must get down from here to our mules, as we saw the train going in the same direction that we wished. By the time that we arrived to where our mules were, they being tied at the foot of the mountain, it began to rain very hard. Our hats both being just alike, we turned them up so as to catch the water in them. And when the water was gathered sufficient a swallow, we drank. He drank it off, and I also gave him what was on my hat. All the water that gathered in the holes in the rocks, he would lick out like a dog, until he got sufficient to quench his thirst. By the time that we arrived at the train, it was pouring rain and we stopped and scooped small holes that was filled with water, and our animals got sufficient water to drink, being 36 hours without water, and we would have perished if it had not been for this rain at this time.[104] We piled up dead Joshua's and made a great fire to dry our blankets. Some of the men dug holes under a bank that was near by, and slept in them at night. It ceased raining so we were able to dry our blankets and ourselves by these fires. The next day we passed over the place we had seen the day before. Here we found a small spring, and we camped at this place, and by constant labor, we got water for our animals. It was at this place that our company determined to take another course to the left. We also made it known to Cap. Smith and his company, that we would travel no more this direction, but would take our own course, the other company begging us not to go that way, but to go with them west. But we did not think so, and when we started from this point, we traveled in a south-easterly direction, and when about 3 miles from where we started from we came to a small lake of water. We had left the other company behind us. Here our mules drank sufficient water to satisfy them. We filled what vessels we had, and passed on. We could see a high mountain, or ridge, which we would have to pass over if we kept on our course. As we came to the foot of the mountain we discovered on the rocks many figures of animals engraved on the high rock. We also discovered an open path through the mountains. We entered therein and found no obstruction to hinder our passage. We saw in passing through

---

104 This was in Pahranagat Wash, a little above Coyote (Division) Spring. The foregoing account is somewhat jumbled, being a reminiscent report.

a large number of arrows shot into a crevice by the
Indians directly above, about one hundred feet. They
must have accomplished this, hence it is called to-day,
Arrow Canyon. This canyon is just wide enough for
a wagon road, and is about 3 miles in length, as near
as I can recollect. As we came to the east end of this
canyon, we saw many footprints of children, and could
hear them playing, but could see no one, as we came
out, and we traveled and camped that night several
miles from there, East. The next morning we traveled
on our course and camped again at night, and the
following [morning] early, some of our party discovered below us two or three miles, wagons and smoke.
We throwed on our packs as soon as possible and
discovered when we arrived there, Capt. Hunt, with
seven wagons of the company which he left Salt Lake
with, the rest following our trail that we left from
Pinto Creek, Utah. They were afterwards lost in
Death Valley.[105]

We were much rejoiced to find Capt. Hunt and
wagons there, which was at the old trail crossing at
Muddy. We bought flour of a man by the name of
Deallas,[106] at 22 cts. per lb., which was a little sour,
but we managed to eat it, as we had lived on very
short rations for several days before this. We also
bought an ox and killed and jerked its meat for our
future travels. At this place, our mules were badly
alkalied. From this point, where we stayed 2 or 3 days,
we proceeded to cross the desert to the Vegas, 50 miles,
at which we arrived very late in the night. Our mules

[105] Most of the wagons turned back from Mount Misery and followed
Hunt to California.

[106] Dallas appears to have had several wagons and a quantity of supplies.
See Pratt's diary, part III: B. W. L. Manly (*Death Valley in '49*, p. 100) had
sold his horse to Dallas in Utah Valley.

continued braying when we were 3 or 4 miles from
the Vegas; they quickened their pace, the night was
very dark, but we could discover water and green
grass. We picked a dry place and camped. When we
left this place, our next camping place was Upper
Vegas, or Cottonwood Creek; our next was at Stump
Springs and next at Resting Springs, being plenty of
grass and water there. We rested one or two days.
After leaving Vegas we traveled up Amagosh Creek
[down Amargosa], passed the Salt Springs. James
Brown found some gold and passed on to Bitter Spring,
and from thence to the top of Cajon Pass. In going
up the Mahava previous to this we camped near a
grove of cottonwood. That night it snowed 5 or 6
inches upon us. Some of our company in the morning
went hunting and killed a couple of deer. Altho they
were not fat, we ate them with good relish, as we were
pretty hungry, as we were nearly out of everything to
eat;* and stopped at the upper crossing of the Mojave
River. The next day we traveled and descended the
mountain into the Cajon Pass. Here we found a wagon
which had been sent up that far loaded with sugar,
coffee, flour, chopped wheat, meat and other things.
We bought some 25 lbs. of chopped wheat, and a
quantity of beef for our suppers. We were so very
hungry we ate very ravishingly, Gen. Rich advising
the boys not to eat too much for fear of making them
sick. But we could not resist, but were much distressed
during the night. The next morning we bought 18 lbs.
of chopped wheat and a lot of beef for our breakfast.
I hardly remember whether we stopped there that day
or not, but when we left there we did not take provisions enough with us to last two days; hence we

---

* Twelve of us went ahead that day.

camped in the Cajon Pass for the night, as the wind was very cold and severe. The next day, after a scant breakfast we traveled and came about 4 o'clock p.m., at which place we again camped. We there found beef and grapes, but no flour; and wine there was near where we camped, a ranch called Comingo [Cuca-monga]. There was plenty of wild grapes in trees that was gathered by us and ate, and also Tunies, which we had eaten before this on our road previous to satisfy our hunger. Wine and wild grapes caused many of the boys to shake as with the ague. The next morning we pursued our journey over to Williams' ranch, and as we were picking a camping place, and had stopped to unpack, it began raining. Williams sent word by a Spaniard for us to come to a certain fort that he had and put our things there, as it was liable to rain for several days, which we did with pleasure. The room we lived in for the next 30 days was nearly 100 feet in length. It rained continually night and day, more or less, for 31 days and nights.

There were sloughs near the place and his team and cattle were mired in them, and we were called on to help pull them out. Our animals were recruiting fast, so we were able to help them. The green clover was very plentiful at this time.

About this time, Capt. Hunt, with the others he had left on the Mojave arrived at the rancho. Williams gave us a nice fat cow for our Xmas dinner. Our dinner was very much enjoyed by all hands. When the rain receded, great preparations were made for our departure. Wheat was washed and ground, other provisions were obtained and loaded into the wagons that were to proceed on their journey up the Pacific coast.

FORT UTAH ON THE TIMPANOGAS, 1849
Site of the present-day city of Provo, in Utah Valley.

F: SHELDON STODDARD SKETCH

[Sheldon Stoddard was born near Toronto, Canada, February 8, 1830. After his trip of 1849 he went to the mines of northern California and then returned to Salt Lake City. There he married Jane, a daughter of Captain Jefferson Hunt, in March, 1851. The next month they started for California with the Mormon colonists that founded San Bernardino, the town which thereafter was his home. For many years he was engaged in carrying mail and freighting between San Bernardino and Salt Lake City. He crossed the desert twenty-four times with mail. In 1865 he took a freight outfit from San Bernardino to Montana, some 1300 miles, six months being required for the trip. The next year he freighted to Pioche, Nevada. In 1903 he was President of the Pioneer Society of San Bernardino.

In L. A. Ingersoll's *Century Annals of San Bernardino County* (Los Angeles, 1904), 653, is a sketch of Mr. Stoddard which tells briefly of his trip in the Flake-Rich company of 1849, and which we reprint here.]

Sheldon Stoddard started for California in 1848, coming via Council Bluffs and the North Platte to Salt Lake. Here a party of about thirty men, under the guidance of Captain Flake, started for the placer diggings in 1849. Among the members of this party were Chas. C. Rich, George Q. Cannon, William Lay, and Sheldon Stoddard.[107] They rode pack animals and followed a trail as far as Mountain Meadows, expecting to take a northern route via Walker' Lake [Pass] to the placer diggings. They traveled westward from Mt. Meadows for eighteen days without guides, compass, or maps. They found no water, and were saved from perishing by light showers when they caught water in their rubber blankets and drank it with a teaspoon. At last they turned eastward [southeastward] and struck the head of the Muddy River,

---

[107] This naming of Lay and Stoddard as members of the Flake-Rich party of packers is an important contribution.

which they followed down until they found a trail and soon afterward came up to Captain Hunt in camp with the seven wagons that had remained with him when the rest of his party had taken the route that led them into Death Valley. By the southern route they reached Chino Rancho, where they remained for a month to recruit their stock and were hospitably treated by Col. Williams.

Part VI

The Stover Party of Packers

Jacob Y. Stover was a member of the Sacramento Mining company that set out from Iowa City for the land of gold in May, 1849. Stover names twenty-six persons who were in this group. They appear to have traveled together as far as Salt Lake City, and most of them continued in the Hunt train as far as "Mt. Misery" on the "Walker Cutoff." Then the party broke up. Some took the Captain Hunt route to California, some followed Captain Smith on the cutoff. Of the latter group a few went through Death Valley and others accompanied Stover.

Stover finally became leader of some packers who followed Smith beyond Division Spring. When Smith turned back and the Pinney-Savage group pushed on westward, Stover's group went southwest, intersected the Hunt wagon trail, and followed it on to California. Stover's is the only story we have of the experiences of this last-named party.

Although a reminiscent account, lacking the day by day veracity of a diary, Stover's narrative carries important information and is full of human interest material. Dr. John W. Caughey, who edited the "Jacob Y. Stover Narrative" and published it in the *Pacific Historical Review* of June, 1937, gave permission for its re-publication here. We are reproducing only that section devoted to the trip from Salt Lake to Los Angeles.

THE JACOB Y. STOVER NARRATIVE

Nothing happened worth relating till we came to Salt Lake on the 10th of August [1849]. Our cattle's feet got very sore. Some of the emigrants were coming back; some had been out fifty miles [1] and said the grass was burned and there was nothing for our stock to eat. So we held a council. Our leading men were Masons and they came across a brother Mason by the name of Captain Hunt, who lived at Provo, forty-five miles from Salt Lake City south at Utah Lake. Says he, "If you will go up home with me, on good grass and water your stock will get fat by October; then you can go to Southern California. I brought a drove of cattle in the winter.[2] I will pilot 100 wagons for $10 apiece."

We looked around for a few days, found 100 wagons that would go, so we moved up to Utah Lake. We found Provo all right for us and our stock, a town of about 100 inhabitants. We coralled our wagons on the banks of Provo, a nice stream of water – a good camping ground. The Mormons were very good to us. They had log cabins built in or around a square of about one acre of land; inside of it, in the center of this lot, they had planted forks, putting poles overhead and brush, straw and dirt, and had planted a cannon on top of the dirt to protect themselves from the Indians. [Fort Utah].

Brigham Young was coming up there for a "blow-out" or to see his wives, or both. So four or five men got at the cannon as Brigham Young came out of the timber to cross the creek. They were going to fire a salute. They touched her off, went to load her again;

---

[1] Toward the Humboldt River.

[2] Hunt had helped bring cattle from southern California in the spring of 1848, as stated above, in our Historical Summary.

the man who had his thumb on the touch hole, when it burnt him, took his thumb off. The two men that were ramming the powder down were blown off and killed. One man had his arm blown off up to the elbow.[3] Our doctors came in good play. Dr. McCormick and Dr. Downer took it off above the elbow. I was watching and stood it pretty well till they commenced sawing the bone off; the man commenced to quiver; I had to leave, I got pretty weak. The men took care of the two dead men and while some were receiving Brigham Young, the little village was in great excitement.[4] But in the evening things became quiet.

By this time I had become acquainted with all the youngsters in Provo. The boys told me I must be around about dark, they were going to have a big dance in such a place. So I went into the square, met the boys, went to the place dictated.

Old Brigham was sitting in there by the side of a young lady, the school ma'am of the village, who my partner had been going with to all the dances since we had been there. The boys said, "We will tell you something. She is one of Brigham's wives; if you will go with us after the dance, you will see them go in that little house over yonder; that is where they will sleep."

We went into the dancing room. Brigham got up, gave out a hymn, and sung; made a long prayer, and led out the school ma'am on the floor; three couples came out. One of my friends urged me to take a partner and go out, so I did and had the honor of dancing in a set with Brigham.

[3] This was George Washington Bean. See his *Autobiography* (Salt Lake City, Utah Printing Co., 1945), pp. 57-61, for a more accurate account of the incident. Lieut. William Dayton was killed, Bean was badly mangled and lost his left hand, which was picked up in Jefferson Hunt's dooryard.

[4] According to Bean, Brigham Young's visit occurred about three weeks after the accident.

I didn't think much about it at that time but since I thought it worth mentioning.[5]

We traded our oxen off for horses, which was a bad trade. In a few days the time came around to start, the 10th of October,[6] which made two months we had spent with the Mormons. So we rolled out southwest on the Spanish trail. Our next point was Little Salt Lake. Captain Hunt led us to wood and water and grass every night. Nothing of any importance occurred. He took some four or five men with him on the trail every morning to go ahead and dig down the banks of creeks and cut the brush, as this was the first wagon train that had ever been through this country.

When we got down some two or three hundred miles south in some rolling hill country, I saw pieces of crockery were sticking out of the ground, pieces of jugs in large quantities, so I came to conclude there had been people here before us.[7] I spoke to Captain Hunt about what I had seen. He said, "I could take you south of here where there are old remains of stone foundations and relics, showing that there have been people living here hundreds of years ago. They have become extinct." So we got down to Little Salt Lake.

The next place was the Mountain Meadows, as

---

[5] John B. Colton, one of the gold seekers who set out with the Hunt wagon train and was later the chief advertiser of the Jayhawker party, later described Brigham Young: "He was a big, fine looking young or middle aged man at that time — sandy hair and beard, and, taken all in all, a very good looking fellow. At the time of our visit, he had, I think, seventeen wives, none of them over 18 years old and as pretty as peaches, to my young eyes at least. Old Brigham looked every inch a commander." — "Jayhawker Scrapbooks," I, 17 (Huntington library); quoted by Caughey in his notes accompanying the Stover narrative, *Pacific Historical Review*, VI, 171.

[6] As stated above in Sheldon Young's Log, some wagons started on October 2.

[7] In the vicinity of present Fillmore, Utah. (*See* Addison Pratt diary, III: B).

Captain Hunt called it; got there on Saturday and rested over Sunday. A man by the name of J. W. Brier had fallen in with us at Provo, who had with him his wife and two little boys, one five, the other three perhaps.[8] He called us together to preach for us. He was a Methodist preacher who used to preach in Iowa City and Pleasant Valley, a tall, slim man. All the old settlers will recollect him.

This Mountain Meadow Spring changed its name the next fall (in 1850) to the Mountain Meadow Massacre.[9] An emigrant train camped there and were all murdered by the Mormons and Indians. John B. [D.] Lee headed the company that did the horrible deed.

We travelled on a few days and one night a pack train came up and camped with us for the night. Soon the word came like fire on the prairie that this pack train was headed by a man by the name of Captain Smith, who had been through by a short route through the mountains, could go in twenty days into new mines into California.[10] Some men went around telling the good news. In a few minutes the whole train was brought together to see and hear what Captain Smith had to say.

He told us he had been through on a pack train.[11] He thought we could get through with wagons by digging and chopping a little. We called a meeting on

[8] Reverend Brier, his wife, and children were later prominent in the Death Valley adventure.

[9] The massacre did not occur until 1857. *See* Juanita Brooks, *The Mountain Meadows Massacre*. Stover came only within about ten miles of Mountain Meadows.

[10] Capt. O. K. Smith had caught up with the wagon train back at Beaver Creek, as related previously.

[11] Apparently Smith had not traveled the cutoff. He reported the information and map as having come from Barney Ward.

the spot to see how many wagons would go after Smith's pack train. I think about 80 voted to follow Smith.

The morning came, Captain Smith rolled out.[12] Captain Hunt made us a little speech: "Gentlemen, I agreed to pilot you through and if only one wagon goes with me I will go with it. If you want to follow Captain Smith, I can't help it, but I believe you will get into the jaws of hell; but I hope you will have good luck."

But notwithstanding, we rolled out after Captain Smith and had for about two hundred miles [13] good travelling. We came in sight of a high mountain, got to it, found a creek running parallel with the mountain, and Smith had gone down into the canyon,[14] which was very steep to get his ponies down. We coralled our wagons and sent men to look out a crossing up and down the canyon. The men that went up found a place to cross some ten miles above; the men that went below said Smith went in the canyon as far as they went, the trail still going down.

We were here I think three days. We had a very sick man and he died and we buried him in as good style as the circumstances would allow.[15] We broke up again; those that had ox teams went up ten miles to cross the canyon,[16] the horse and mule teams made pack saddles out of our wagons. We called this place Mount Misery. This man's grave will never be seen again, I suppose.

---

[12] Smith and the packers were four days ahead of the wagon train.

[13] From the point of departure from the Old Spanish trail to the place where the wagons were stalled near Mount Misery was only about twenty-five or thirty miles.

[14] Of Beaver Dam Wash.

[15] W. L. Manly also mentions the death of this man, in his *Death Valley in '49, op. cit.,* p. 110.

[16] These were the ones who went through Death Valley.

Our horses and mules started down the canyon after Captain Smith. We followed down I would think twenty miles when he crossed over on the west side of the creek. We followed his trail till we overtook him at the foot of a big mountain which was covered with snow. He was packing up to go to Salt Lake to winter.[17]

Some of our men started back with him. We were getting hard up for something to eat. Our twenty days were up. We camped for the night at Dead Horse Springs, as we called it. In the morning we killed our first horse to eat here, an old gray one of mine. After breakfast, nine of our company concluded to shoulder their guns and take it afoot over the big snowy mountain.

I studied the matter over. I came to this conclusion: there were two men in the nine that I would not like to travel with but would be glad to get rid of them both. Both of them were from Iowa City, John Adams, who had a wife and small family here; the other was Willy Webster, the man I helped out of the Platte River. All the way crossing the plains they were on the wrong side every time – that was what saved me from being one in that crowd.

John Adams lost one of his boots that night, we supposed a coyote stole it to eat; so he skinned the old gray horse's hind leg and stretched it on his foot and leg.

---

[17] The Stover party did not catch up with Capt. Smith for about three weeks and not until about two days after he and the Flake-Rich company had parted at Division Spring. Just which range was the "big mountain which was covered with snow" it is difficult to determine. West of Division Spring there are several parallel ranges running north and south. From east to west these are: Sheep, Desert, Pintwater, and Spotted ranges. Cannon, above, says Smith continued westward from Division Spring for one day and part of the next, and having found no water he began his return journey. According to this report he must have reached the foot of Desert Range or Pintwater Range before turning back.

They cut about ten pounds apiece of the old gray horse. I took their names and where they lived – can give four of their names, five of them lived in Illinois and Missouri; Webster and Adams from Iowa City, Savage from Illinois, Pinney from Ohio (these last two I will speak of later).[18]

I had a journal of every day's travel, what happened every day, the distance, and camping ground. I will tell you later what became of all the earthly goods that I started with.

We rolled out from Dead Horse Spring directly after the nine men went. We went back on our trail that day and camped for the night and held council on what we should do. They concluded to follow me, so I was captain to lead them out of the desert and mountains. Next morning I started and left all trails, made one of my own southwest.[19]

One night we camped in between two mountains and started quite early in the morning. About nine o'clock, I mentioned to one of Lawrence Hudson's messmates, "Where is Lawrence Hudson this morning?"

He replied, "We left him at the camp."

"Why did you leave him?"

"He said it wasn't worth while to try to go any farther, he was so sick and weak that he might as well die there as any other place."

So I called a halt, told him this would not do. Dr. Downer had the best horse. I said, "I will go back and bring him into camp."

When I came in sight of him he was sitting with his

18 This was one of the parties that crossed Death Valley and was the one of which Pinney and Savage were the survivors. Stover gives their story below.

19 Stover's report is too general and vague for one to identify his route with accuracy. The fact that he traveled several days in a southwest direction and that he reached Hunt's wagon road in the Amargosa River region indicates the general course taken.

head leaning forward with his old slouch hat hanging down all around his face. He looked up at me with surprise. I said, "I came after you. Can't you ride?"

"I don't know," said he.

"Get on here and try."

I helped him on and we started. We got into camp after dark. Dr. Downer took charge of him, let him ride his horse till he got able to walk.

In three days we came to a small creek, a good place to camp. I told the boys I would take with me Jim Dixon and go to the top of a high mountain peak. So in the morning we started, got on top of the mountain. It was one of those beautiful mountains. We could see in every direction. We were sitting looking and I saw a whirlwind at quite a distance making the dust fly; it would stop and then commence again. The wind came from the southwest and the road run the same direction, so we reasoned; if the whirlwind struck the road, the dust would fly and when it left the road the hard ground would show no dust. So we came to the conclusion that this was Hunt's trail. We went back and told what we saw. They all felt glad.

In the morning, after breakfast of horse meat, we started around the mountain, about twenty-five in number. Three New York boys had some mules, one three years old that could not travel good; they shot him next morning for breakfast – that beat any horse meat that I ate – and taking a few pounds with us, rolled out with the hope of finding Hunt's trail that day. But we did not go far till we came where a train had coralled their train of forty wagons, set them afire and burned them up and nothing but the irons left.[20]

20 The Burned Wagons site is located by Dr. Margaret Long in *The Shadow of the Arrow*, pp. 113-116, as about five miles west of modern Death Valley Junction. She says the trails of the various groups of Death Valley parties came together near Death Valley Junction.

We found some papers showing us it was a train from Arkansas that had travelled behind us and had called themselves the "Jahawkers." What became of them I never heard. We thought they had burned their wagons to keep the Mormons from getting them. We came to the conclusion that Captain Smith was sent out to decoy all those wagons out there so as to get them.

I will go back to the Hunt train. We struck for the place where we saw dust rising; late in the evening we struck the trail, sure enough it was Captain Hunt's trail. About sundown we came to a camping place where they had camped and had driven a stick in the ground, split the top, wrote a letter and stuck it in the top of the stick, stating when they camped there. The camp ground was on the bank of the Severe River.[21] There was a spring of boiling water, another cold, running into the river, and about one rod below a cold spring of good water.

We got up in the morning and started on the double quick. We made good time that day, you may be sure. Next morning we started but had not gone far before Jim Dixon and I, who were ahead as usual, ran on to a steer that had given out. We had him shot down and were skinning him when the rest came up. We would cut a chunk of beef, run a stick through it and hold it over the fire and broil it and then "go for" it. We took what we could carry and went on.

We could travel ten miles further in a day than we could in the mountains. We went in one day as far as Hunt went in two. We commenced to lighten up by throwing our guns away. I felt pretty bad over that but it helped us in walking. We hung on to our pistols. In a few days we came up with the tail of Captain Hunt's

---

21 Undoubtedly the Amargosa River. The hot springs on the river are about two miles above the present town of Tecopa.

train [22] – four or five wagons that had stopped to recruit their teams. We camped over night with them, glad to see them and have a talk with them. I left a sack of clothes, the only valuables I had left, with a man by the name of Stockton from Tipton, Cedar County, Iowa. I never saw him or my sack of clothes since. My journal was in the sack. He gave us some white soup beans and said, "That is all I can spare you, I must save something for my wife and children." The other wagons gave some food to the rest of our foot train (I think about twenty-five in number).

This was the last stream this side of the "Ninety Mile Desert," as it was called then. Since so many of our train perished there it was called "Death Valley." [23] I remember John Earhart was one who died in this valley.

We went in the evening on the desert and travelled all night. Next day it rained on us, it gave us water to drink but made it slippery to walk. The second night I shall never forget. We were sleepy, tired and hungry. We went five to ten miles and stopped to rest; we burned grease wood and then lay or stood around to get warm. This was in December.

We at last got to the Mojave River. The third night, which was dry, we found a deep hole that had water in it; we drank and what horses we had left drank. We lay down on the sand and gravel and slept good. Next morning we got up and ate a bite and started up the river. It had been a little cloudy and misty down

[22] Addison Pratt mentions a party of about twenty footmen who caught up with his wagon on December 9, and another group of similar size that came on December 15. (See Pratt's diary, part III: B). One or the other of these parties was undoubtedly the Stover company.

[23] This was not Death Valley, which is farther north. The so-called "Ninety-Mile Desert" was the stretch from the Amargosa River to the Mojave River.

where we were; we hadn't gone more than a mile or so
when all at once we saw the water coming three or four
feet high abreast, carrying with it sticks, brush and
logs, and on top six inches of foam.[24] We ran to the
nearest bank and just made it. Part of our men were
way down below. We hallooed to them so they got out
on the same side that we did.

We traveled up the stream all day but did not make
very good headway, there being so much brush on the
mountainside. Hunt's trail we could see now and then
on the other side. Night came on we were on the wrong
side of the river. The river was getting down. We went
to the water edge, stripped off our clothes, waded over,
got some wood, made a fire, warmed ourselves, and
slept there for the night. We came to the conclusion
that a cloud had bursted. We could see the mountain
covered white with snow.

Next morning we started on Hunt's trail, got two
or three miles when Jim and I (ahead as usual) came
on to two fine fat steers, drove them a few rods, were
thinking of having some fine beef when we met a man
hunting them. He said he was sent out with provisions
for us.[25] He took us up to his wagon. We saw some
tallow where he had been frying his fat beef. I think
it was half an inch thick and as big as the bottom of
the frying pan. We got hold of it about the same time,
broke it about the middle I guess – we didn't measure
it, but ate it down and looked for more. That tasted
as good as pie did at home.

But we did not stop at that; we took our butcher
knives, cut off chunks and put them on the coals and
broiled them, wet up corn meal, put on flat rocks, and

---

[24] The Mojave River has large floods on rare occasions, as the present
stream bed testifies.

[25] This was Mr. Davis, sent out by Isaac Williams from his rancho.

were in the business by the time the rest got there. They followed suit as quick as they saw what was going on. The man sat and looked on. We filled ourselves, then we commenced to ask him how far it was to California. He said, "Oh, you can get there tomorrow."

You better believe we felt good to think that only one more day and we would see that long-looked for place. He told us to take what meal we wanted and meat, so we did. The man went on out to meet more hungry people.

We started down the creek, crossing the creek every few rods, then wading in water, till we began to get hungry again. We stopped and baked on stones and cooked the meat on sticks and ate everything he had given us, then started on.

About sundown we got out of the canon to the loveliest place I ever saw; everything looked so nice and warm; the frogs were singing and the birds too; it seemed like we had passed into a new world. We went about one hundred and sixty rods and came to an oak grove; the wind had blown the leaves up against a log and made us a bed; we thought we would not reject the offer. We spread our blankets and turned in for the night. We were up at daylight on the road, the birds were singing; I can't describe the joy and happiness we all felt. Everything seemed so lovely.

In the afternoon we got to the first ranch, it was called Pokamongo [Cucamonga] Ranch in Spanish; in English, Negro Ranch. The owner was a negro. We came to the house, stacked our blankets in a pile, and went up where he was making wine of grapes and in rather a novel way to us. He had a beef hide with a hole in the center of the hide, four forks planted in the ground and four poles run through holes cut in the edge of the hide, which bagged down so it would hold two or three bushels of grapes. He had two forks, one on each side of the skin, and a pole tied from one fork to the other. Two buck Indians, stripped off naked, took hold of this pole with their hands and tramped the grapes. The wine would run. We ate grapes then went at the wine, caught it in our tin cups, as we all had one apiece. The old negro stood and looked on. We drank it as fast as the Indians could tramp it for awhile. The old negro after awhile said, "Gentlemen, you have had a hard time of it, I know, but de first ting you know you will know noting. You are welcome to it."

The old negro was right. They began to tumble over and the wine came up as fast as it went down. He got a spade and gave it to me, told me to dig holes at their mouths. So I did. Finally Dr. Downer and I were the only ones left on our feet. The sun was about one hour high was the last thing I recollect. Sometime in the night I waked up and found myself lying on my back, the stars shining in my face. I felt cold. How came I to be lying on the grass? I felt around for my blankets. I began to realize my situation seeing the rest of the company lying as I had left them. I looked around, found my blankets, went to bed.

Now this spree was on Christmas day. In the morning when we all got up we felt pretty good but awfully hungry. The old negro sent two of his buckaries [vaqueros] out to fetch in a beef for us. They brought in one. We soon had beef and corn meal, ate what we could, thanked him and started for Los Angeles. We had a good road to travel on, went to Roland's Ranch and got some more food there. He was from Pennsylvania, had married a Spanish woman and had children

SALT SPRING, NEAR THE AMARGOSA RIVER

LOOKING DOWN ARROW CANYON
North of the head of Muddy Creek

grown. We went to St. Gabriel's Mission, there stopped till after New Year.

We went down to Los Angeles to get something to eat, a distance of about four miles. We camped on the little creek that runs through the town. I got up quite early one morning and started for the butcher shop. Before I got there I ran on to a man cut all to pieces, a horrible sight. I walked around him and went on and told the butcher what I had seen. Said he, "They had a fandango last night. They generally cut or shoot one or two."

I got my beef and went back to the camp. We began to think we were in a bad place, so we went back to the Mission. The Spaniards were having a good time. They would lay down a dollar on the ground. A row of men were on each side with whips. The Spaniard would come on horseback, galloping, reach, pick up the dollar. He paid so much for the chance.

The next day I started back to hunt my clothes. I thought Stockton would be in by this time. I got up to William's Ranch. I found Hunt and part of our train in camp. They said Stockton, the man that I left my clothes and all my earthly effects with, had gone over to San Bernedeno and I would have to go there for them. I was about naked, and dirty and greasy, had a pair of buckskin breeches on and two shirts.

About four or five o'clock Jacob Gruel [26] came to me with a stranger and introduced him to me. Gruel was from Montrose, Iowa, and had his family with him. He was a Methodist preacher and preached for us when crossing the plains. He said, "This man says he is from San Francisco and wants a man to carry a letter to his partner in San Francisco, and I recommended you to him." The man wanted me to start at

26 Of the first wagon train. (*See* part II).

six o'clock that evening. I said, "You see how dirty I am. I can't go till I go up and get my clothes." Said he, "I have to get a letter on the ship at San Pedro by nine o'clock tomorrow morning."

I asked him how far it was. He said, "Seventy-five miles, but I have a good horse for you to ride. See here, you go. I will give you forty dollars to pay your passage. I and my partner have a store there, you can get a suit of clothes from head to foot. Now can't you go? I will write you a letter." He read me the letter.

I said, "I have not had anything to eat lately."

Said he, "Come down to the hotel."

I went, got my supper; he had the horse ready by the time I was done. He said, "Now take those letters and ride fast; if the horse gives out, go to a livery stable and get another one. The letter must go."

So I got on and started off, put him on the lope, went to Los Angeles in the latter part of the night, found the route he had directed me to go; then I had twenty-five miles to go yet. About eight o'clock I was in San Pedro. The "Little Hololula" stood out in the ocean a half mile or so. I got my breakfast and went down to the beach. They were loading her. Went aboard, gave the captain his letter. He gave me a ticket. I found my old friend McWilliams and family on board. They were as much surprised to see me as I was to see them once more. We had parted out on the plains where Captain Smith had led us off. They had stuck with Captain Hunt and had been in two or three weeks. We had a good time telling each other what had happened since we parted. . . .

[Stover delivered the message at San Francisco, and continued to the mines. At Deer Creek, where Nevada City now stands, he found old friends of his travels.]

I met Pinney and Savage [27] in Nevada City. They gave me the history of those travels after leaving us at Dead Horse Spring, as follows:

We went over the mountain and travelled through a rough country, nothing to shoot, not a living thing to be seen, till our horse meat was all gone, and we came one night into a camp on a big desert. The boys said we would have to draw cuts in the morning who should be killed to eat. As we did not want to be killed to be eaten or eat anybody, when we thought they were asleep we got up and travelled till day; then we took our butcher knives and dug holes in the sand and covered up all but our heads till night when we would come out and travel all night again. By this time we did not fear them and were recruited. This sand was what saved us. We think we kept westward more than we did before we left those seven men, they bore northwest too much to suit us. We had almost given out when we thought we saw water and smoke. That cheered us up and gave us encouragement till we made the lake. It was Owen's Lake. The Indians were there catching fish and drying them. They saw our condition and put a guard over us. We would have killed ourselves drinking water and eating fish, which they had lots of dried. They kept us three days and then put us on a horse apiece and sent an Indian to guide us into California. That is how we got in. Now tell us how you got through.[28]

So I did. I was in California about two years before I got started home. I left there the last day of May and got home about the 21st of June 1852. At San Francisco I got on the steamer called the Golden Gate (which was sunk the next trip or two after that), came by boat to Panama, walked across the Isthmus, and from there came on a steamer to New York, and then by rail home.

[27] Of the Death Valley company that Stover had parted with previously.
[28] For variation of the story as told by George Q. Cannon, *see* part V: D.

Part VII

The Pomeroy Wagon Train

The Pomeroy train set out from Salt Lake City on November 3, 1849. The core of the company was the wagon train of the Pomeroy brothers, merchants and freighters from Missouri. After selling some of their goods in Salt Lake City the Pomeroys decided to continue to California, taking the southern route. They employed some Utah men as teamsters and were joined by some through emigrants, such as Walter Van Dyke.

The four reports of the trip published below, are sketchy, reminiscent accounts; no diaries of the journey have been found.

A: PORTION OF THE EDWIN PETTIT BIOGRAPHY

[The Pettit account of his trip to California in the Pomeroy train of 1849 is taken from the *Biography of Edwin Pettit* (Salt Lake City, 1912). *See* this volume for additional biographical material.]

Early in November, 1849, my brother-in-law [David Seeley] and myself enlisted with Pomeroy to help him take his big ox train through to California. Pomeroy brought an ox train through from the eastern states with merchandise and sold out what he could, and traded the remainder for cattle. He took me along to drive his cattle on horseback. There were about forty or fifty head of cattle that I had to take charge of. He had about twenty wagons with two men and two yoke of oxen to each wagon. These men boarded themselves, but were paying their way to California by driving these teams. During the day I drove the cattle, and had to corral them at nights to keep them from the Indians. I was always the one to turn out the cattle every morning to let them eat while we had breakfast and got ready for our move. Then I had to bring up the cattle and eat my breakfast after every one else was done. The cattle got tired and footsore – so much so that they began to give out and lie down, and when I could not get them up any longer, I would have to leave them. I would leave two a day; five a day, as they gave out, and the last day I was with the company, I left nineteen head of cattle, as they could not go any further. When we reached the Muddy Desert, our teams were so reduced and the cattle so nearly gone that we put the wagons off to one side, using them for kindling wood, and packed everything up into as few wagons as possible.

About two weeks after Pomeroy left Salt Lake, there was an independent company started out for the gold mines of California, and they got out on the desert and got lost.[1] They were without water or food and were about to perish. They could not agree on which way to go, and some started out afoot – alone. They reached the Muddy Desert just at the time that we did – ragged, starved, and almost perished.[2] When this

[1] The party he is telling about, as shown below, was made up of the Flake-Rich and O. K. Smith groups, which started for California ahead of the Pomeroy train.

[2] This may have been a part of the Smith party that left their leader at Division Spring and came south to the trail crossing of the Muddy. The Flake-Rich company had reached that point previously, on October 18, and had there joined the wagon train headed by Hunt.

company were out on the desert and did not seem to
agree, Apostle Chas. C. Rich started out from the camp
one morning, and the boys asked where he was going.
He said he was just going out for a short distance and
would be back soon. They thought probably he was
out of his mind. He said: "I am just going over here
to pray for rain." They waited for him to come back,
and just as he arrived in camp the clouds were seen
to arise from the southwest and the rain poured down
and soaked up the ground. They got all they could
in buckets and cooled off their cattle and horses.[3]
Ponds of water were left on the ground and they were
all revived. Some of them later came up with Pomeroy's company near the Muddy.

I left Pomeroy's company here and joined this independent company. We bought a yoke of oxen and the
front wheels of a wagon and made them into a cart.
Packed all our goods on that, and in order to save
the cattle, I took a bundle of our goods, tied them
together, and carried them on my shoulders across the
desert. One man belonging to our company died crossing the desert. We arrived in San Bernardino, recruited
our stock, and then made our way down to Los Angeles.
I reached here during the rainy season, when the
streets were pools of water from the heavy rains; had
to sleep right on the ground, and many a time was
soaked before morning. We disposed of our cattle for
a good price, and went down to San Pedro where
there were a few adobe huts standing. Here we found
mostly Mexicans who killed cattle for the hide and
tallow for shipment. As it was considered a very
dangerous harbor, a vessel would only stop there once

---

[3] This is a subsequent and expanded account of the timely rain of November 13 that saved the Flake-Rich party.

in a great while. Here we engaged passage in an old
sailing craft for San Francisco at $25.00 each.

[He landed in San Francisco twelve days later, worked a few
days to get a grubstake for the mines, and went by steamboat up to
Sacramento. He had spent five months making the trip from Salt
Lake to his destination at the mines. In the fall of 1850 he returned
to Salt Lake by the Humboldt route, with C. C. Rich and others.]

B: DAVID SEELEY SKETCH

[In Ontario, Canada, David Seeley was born October 12, 1810.
After moving to Iowa he married Mary Pettit in 1846 and the next
year joined the Mormon hegira to Utah. After going to California
in 1849 he worked for some months in the mines and then returned
to Salt Lake City by the Humboldt route. He went to San Bernardino
with the Mormon colony in 1851 and engaged there in farming,
merchandising, and lumbering. He was elected Treasurer of San
Bernardino County in 1853. He made his home and reared his family
in San Bernardino.

The short account of his trip with the Pomeroy Train, which we
reproduce here is taken from the manuscript "Biographical Sketch
of David Seeley" in the Bancroft Library, University of California.]

On the third day of Nov. A.D. 1849 David Seeley and
his Bro. J. W. Seely and Brother-in-Law Edwin Pettit,
for the purpose of mining, embarked with Pomeroy's
Train of fifty Wagons two men to each wagon over
the South Route to California the trip was long and
many cattle died on the trip at Iron Springs in Cole
[Iron] county Utah we picked up nine men that had
at one time formed part of the Company that suffered
and perished in Death Valley, Nevada.[4] they was trying
to get back to Salt Lake they had experienced such
suffering for want of food and shoes we brought them
safe to California. D. seely and co and others left the

---

4 This apparently was part of the O. K. Smith party. Whether this is the
same party that Pettit says they picked up on the Muddy, or another, it is
difficult to determine.

Pomeroy train at Armagosa [5] and arrived some ten
days in advance. Camped at Jose Maria Lugos on the
Famous Ranch of San Bernardino and that year the
rains come early and by the middle of Feb. the Cattle
as they roamed at large made trails through the young
and verdant clover. the contrast from the ice bound
bays and lakes to our California climate produced in
us such exuberance of feelings that weary as we all
was we gave three cheers and our old worn hats went
up in the air, to the credit of the Lugos. we will here
mention that they killed a Beef and made a dance or
Fandango as they called it, which was enjoyed to the
utmost as a number of the Dark Eyed Senoritas favored
us with their presance. there was the first waltzing that
I ever experienced. we remained some two weeks to
give rest to our teams and take in the beauties of the
country. we finally broke camp for Los Angeles. we
halted one day at the ranch of John Roland at the
ranch of El pointy [Puente] 12 miles East of Los
Angeles. here the boys for the first time partook of
the pure California Wine which was taken in by the
gallon and we all drank to the health of our Wives
Sweethearts and country. on the following day we
started for Los Angeles. on the route we met a Bridal
party, the groom and Bride with best Man and Maid
rode in a low cart with a canopy over the top, with
two Indian outriders each with a long sharp goad
stick to excelerate the speed of one pair of Califor
Oxon yoked with a piece of wood lashed firmly to
each horn, but they enjoyed it hugely and so did we.
the next day we arrived in Los Angeles. it was on
Sunday. there was swarms of drunken Indians. the
Ranchers was in from the country on horse back. with

[5] Pettit, above, says he left the Pomeroy train at Muddy Creek.

their short saber at their sides. they would charge on the Indians with terrible results, the Indians in turn being drunk with bad Agua Dentay would fight back with stones and clubs like heroes but come out second best. we found that there was no scales in use at that time to weigh meat. for a dime one could get a large piece of Beef. American laws and customs was all in a transition state in this south country. at the time there was a Brig at San Pedro. . . we finally sold our teams and about sixty passengers engaged passage for nineteen dollars per head. As for myself I engaged a Cabin Passage.

C: EXTRACT FROM GOUDY HOGAN JOURNAL

[Goudy Hogan, who was born in Norway, September 16, 1829, came to America in 1837. He joined the Mormons in 1843 and migrated to Utah in 1848. He was Bishop at Leeds, in Washington County, Utah, 1876-77. He died January 30, 1898.[6]
The following sketch of his trip of 1849 is extracted from the "Goudy Hogan Journal" in the Brigham Young University Library. The copy was kindly supplied by Prof. Vasco M. Tanner.]

Bro. Browning from Farmington came and stayed all night and said his boys were going to start to California to dig gold. I had been counciled by President Young not to go to California but now after the crops were raised and gathered he gave his consent. Two of the Twelve [Apostles], Charles C. Rich and Amasa Lyman, were going to preside over the brethren and receive the tithing and when my father found that out he gave his consent for me to go and fitted me out being very destitute of clothing for the family and other things having been 3½ years since we left Nauvoo.

---

[6] Andrew Jenson, *Latter-Day Saint Biographical Encyclopedia*, IV, 593.

There were two brothers, Pomeroy, who were
Gentiles that came into Salt Lake City with 100
wagons loaded with merchandise with 3 or 4 pair of
oxen to each wagon. After they had sold out they
wished to get teamsters to drive through to California
the southern route. There were so many of our boys
that wished to go through to California as teamsters
that we had to board ourselves and received no wages.
The 3rd of November we started from Salt Lake City
south. There was a friend of mine that gave me some
very good council before I started. Said he, "Attend
to your secret prayers regularly. Do not associate with
bad company nor drink strong drinks nor play cards
and pay your tithing regularly and if you will remember and observe all these things and be a good boy, I
will promise to you, Goudy, that you will be blessed
on your gold mission and you will come back being
satisfied with your trip."

During the large emigration in the summer of 1849
I traded with one of the gold diggers for a new
Stubentwist No. 1 Shotgun and one new rifle. Before
starting on my journey to California I gave in for
tithing the shotgun and 25 dollars although I had but
very little property besides the rifle. When we started
we expected to go there in two months consequently
we run out of provisions since we were nearly 4
months on the road. We lived on rations and poor beef
that was given to us. We had to guard all the night
through after leaving Provo, there being no settlement
or fort until we reached lower California. Often the
beef given us was so poor and tough that the guard
would boil it all night and then in the morning it
would be as tough as shoe leather, but our appetites
were good for anything. The ox teams gave out and

died very fast having travelled through and across the plains in the summer. Very frequently when we would camp there would be a wagon or more that had to be left so we chopped it up for firewood. When we came to the Muddy the largest portion of the men left us and took a pack on their back. There was ten men of us that had run entirely out of flour and we asked Mr. Pomeroy and brother to let us have some. The only way we could get it was to sign a joint note of $1000. payable in California. I was one of that number that had to sign and I also paid on the note. If we had not been Mormon boys there would have been mutiny in camp. but having just lately been driven from our homes in the United States because of the Gospel of Christ we had learned to be patient in times of tribulation. After a long and tedious journey we arrived in lower California, Los Angeles or San Bernadina, Feb. 27. We found lower California the finest country that we had ever seen. Most of the boys went to upper California by land. Ten of us took ship at San Pedro and sailed up the coast on a barge, Freemont, to upper California, some 800 miles. Our fare was paid out of the $1000. joint note previously spoken of. We landed all right.

D: The Walter Van Dyke Account

[Walter Van Dyke, who later became a prominent citizen of southern California, set out for the far West from Cleveland, Ohio, in May, 1849. He did not reach Salt Lake City until October 8. This account of his trip to Los Angeles with the Pomeroy Train he gave in an address before the Historical Society of Southern California. It was published in the *Annual Publications of the Historical Society of Southern California* (Los Angeles, 1894), pp. 76-81. Being a reminiscent account, composed more than forty years after the trip was made, the story is inaccurate in places.]

Owing to the lateness of the season and from accounts of some Mormons returned from the gold mines on the American river, it was evident that before we could reach the foot of the Sierra Nevada it would be impossible to cross with any degree of safety. The fate of the Donner party was a warning against any such foolhardy attempt in the winter season. The great body of the overland emigrants by the South Pass route preceded us, going either by the Humboldt or Fort Hall, and most of them had already reached their destination in the Land of Gold. While we were thus delayed at Salt Lake, undetermined whether to remain over winter or attempt a southern route, some Missouri traders – Pomeroy Brothers – having sold out their merchandise, brought into the Valley early in the summer, were preparing to take their live stock and freight wagons to Southern California. We concluded to join them. A Mormon, Captain Jefferson Hunt, who had just returned from San Bernardino, where they had located a colony, was engaged as a guide.[7] We left Salt Lake the 3rd of November, 1849, pursuing a southerly and southwesterly direction along the foot of the Wasatch Mountains. The route is through a series of fertile valleys to the point where the road crosses the southern rim of the great Utah basin.

The first and largest valley south of Salt Lake is the Utah Valley. At the southern end of the Utah Lake we struck the old Spanish trail, the northern route traveled by the Spaniards between the pueblo of Los Angeles and Santa Fe.[8] A number of fine streams put down from

[7] The Judge is mistaken on this point, as the Hunt train had set out a month before.

[8] This was a northern extension, or variant, of the Spanish Trail. The main route of the Old Spanish Trail would not be encountered by Van Dyke until he reached the vicinity of present Parowan, Utah.

this range of mountains, flowing into the desert, timbered along their banks, the largest being the Spanish Fork and Sevier River. Where the range turns westerly there is a low depression called the Mountain Meadows. It was a famous camping place on the line of the old Spanish trail. The camp ground is near a spring at the foot of the mountain on the west side of the valley or meadow, with timber on the slope of the mountain. The night we camped there, it commenced snowing and we were obliged to corral the cattle and other stock and guard them; and build fires of the dry cedar hauled down from the side of the mountain to keep ourselves warm. The storm continued the next day with considerable violence and the stock were guarded to keep them from straying off. Owing to the snow there was no chance for feed here, so we were obliged to move on without delay. It was at this same camp ground, some years later, that a party of emigrants from Arkansas and Missouri were attacked by Indians and some Mormons as allies; and, after being given assurance of protection if they would surrender, were brutally massacred – men women and children.[9] Soon after we commenced descending the southern slope of the divide the weather became warmer, and from that on we had no difficulty as far as the climate was concerned.

We reached the Santa Clara, a tributary of the Rio Virgin, December the 11th. The Virgin River is a considerable stream, coming down from the Wasatch range of mountains that we had crossed, and flows southeasterly [southwesterly] into the Colorado. Along the Santa Clara and Rio Virgin we found considerable

[9] The Mountain Meadows Massacre of September, 1857, referred to earlier in this volume.

feed; but being without so long, already the stock were nearly starving; and many cattle gave out and were left along the road. I noticed along these river bottoms cornstalks and some squash or pumpkins still remaining on the ground, and also indications of irrigation, the work of Indians, of course, as no white people were then in this region of country. These Indians are the Piutes, described by Fremont in his report of explorations of 1843-4 as causing him considerable trouble on his return by this same route. They were a marauding and savage tribe of Indians and seek every opportunity to waylay and massacre small parties or stragglers from larger ones. Our company was so large, however, that we were not troubled with them except in the stealing and killing of stock that wandered from camp.

Las Vegas, further on this way, is another famous camping ground. It is a large meadow with several springs at the head which, uniting, form quite a stream flowing through it. One of these springs is so large as to make a good bathing pool, and the water is warm and boils up with such force as to buoy the swimmer like a cork.

We were at a point about where the state line crosses this trail at the close of the year 1849 and the beginning of that of 1850; as to which side there is some doubt. However, in after years, the Society of California Pioneers gave me the benefit of the doubt by admitting me as a member of its body; its constitution requires the applicant to have been within the state prior to January 1st, 1850.

So many of the cattle had died or been abandoned that the remainder were not able to move the trains except very slowly; and in consequence we had already exceeded the time anticipated in getting into the settlements, and our provisions were nearly exhausted. It was proposed therefore that some one should go ahead and send back some relief, and about a dozen of us volunteered for that purpose. We reached the Mojave River the second day after leaving the camp, at a point not far below Barstow, as near as I can judge. We continued along the same old Spanish trail that we had been following up that river and across to the northern end of the Cajon Pass, where we arrived quite late the last day of January. Our provisions being exhausted and there being a moon, we concluded to venture through the pass that night instead of remaining over till morning. From my notes I quote:

I never shall forget this night's adventure in this wild mountain pass. We issued from the pass into the valley about four o'clock the morning of February the 1st. We halted at the mouth of the canyon until daylight, and then renewed our walk. If we hadn't been in a famished and exhausted condition we might have appreciated with pleasure the agreeable change in the country. Even yesterday we were traveling in a dry and barren desert; today we are treading on beds of beautiful flowers and wild clover, and the morning breeze is laden with perfume.

We reached the Cucamonga Rancho about ten o'clock, February 1st. We found an American family here and were supplied with an abundance, including milk and butter – a rare treat, indeed, and a great change in the fare we had been accustomed to during the many months of our trip. A few days later we passed over to the Chino Ranch, better known among the immigrants of that period as Williams's Ranch. Colonel Williams, the owner, had, during that season, sent out many parties for the relief of the immigrants. The next morning Colonel Williams furnished me a

horse and a guide to come into Los Angeles, as I had
some letters and packages to deliver to parties here.
On the way we stopped at Rowlands on the Puente and
were treated in the same hospitable manner character-
istic of all the ranch owners here.

In a week or ten days the other members of our
Cleveland party came in with the train, and we had
thus crossed the continent. We had consumed eight
months on the trip – much longer than was anticipated
when starting – still all arrived well and no one had
been seriously sick on the way, though subjected to
many hardships. This could not be said in regard to
most of the overland companies of that year. The
numerous graves along the road up the Platte and
through the Black Hills were sad evidences that many
a poor fellow had dropped by the way.

The year 1849-50 is memorable as one of early and
heavy rains, as well as for deep snows in the Sierra
Nevada. At the time our large party came from Salt
Lake to this place, encumbered with ox teams and
heavy wagons, and without any further inconvenience
than the delay caused by the poor condition of the
stock, nothing but a bird or an expert on snow shoes
could have scaled the wall of ice and snow over the
Sierra Nevada range. This fact of itself shows that this
is the natural route for a railroad from Salt Lake to
the Pacific. The grades are much lighter and trains
could be run over it all seasons of the year without
the necessity of forty miles of expensive snow sheds.
[Nothing more on the 1849 trip.]

Part VIII

The Howard Egan Wagon Train

The last wagon train over the route in 1849 left Fort Utah (Provo) November 18, 1849. It started with ten persons, traveling with three wagons and fifteen head of animals. Enroute, the Egan party caught up with and passed the Pomeroy train.

A: HOWARD EGAN'S DIARY FROM FORT UTAH TO CALIFORNIA

[Howard Egan was born in King's County, Ireland, June 15, 1815. The family migrated to Canada and settled in Montreal. As a boy Howard went to sea. After several years spent as a sailor he settled in Salem, Massachusetts, and took up rope making. He married in 1838, became an American citizen three years later, and joined the Mormons the next year, settling in Nauvoo, Illinois.

When the Saints migrated to Utah, Howard Egan was a member of the pioneer band of 1847. He returned to the Missouri River that fall and brought out his family the next year. In 1849 he made the trip from Salt Lake City to California, as recounted in the diary printed below.

Subsequently, Egan continued his pioneering. In 1855 he opened, from Utah to northern California, a trail that ran a direct course south of the Humboldt River road. For years he carried mail across Nevada, and also engaged in the cattle business. He died in 1878.

Much of his career and that of his son Howard R. Egan, are recounted in *Pioneering the West, 1846 to 1878, . . .* (Richmond, Utah, 1917).

The diary of the trip to Los Angeles in 1849, reproduced below, is copied from the original manuscript now in the Coe Collection at Yale University library. This diary, which was graciously made available to us by ·the famous owner, differs considerably from the version printed in 1917 and cited in the preceding paragraph.]

SUNDAY, NOVEMBER 18th '49   Started from fort utah [Provo] in company with Bro. Granger & Bills. with three waggons and 15 head of animals & 10[1] souls for callifornia, it has stormed for three days previous to our starting which has made the road verry bad. 7½ miles came to a small spring branch. travled up a mile and camped at Hobble creek, a good camp ground feed & wood plenty.

MONDAY, NOVEMBER 19th 1849   morning warm & pleasant. Bro Olando Hovey started in company with us this morning with 1 waggon, 4 yoke of cattle and 4 men. our company numbers 14 men & boys. traveled 8 miles came to a creek about 10 feet wide, a good camp ground. wood plenty. came 9 miles & camped at a small spring branch. feed good. plenty of willows[2]

TUESDAY, NOVEMBER 20 '49   this morning had a severe storm of rain & sleet which made the roads very bad. this afternoon road much better. passed several good camp grounds. no 6 is a beutifull stream. there is two branches. wood plenty. all the streams and springs up to no. 10 are good camps. came 23 miles & camped on No. 10 [Salt Creek valley]. plenty of willows there is a branch of this creek a ¼ of a mile ahead.

WEDNESDAY, NOVEMBER 21 '49   this morning Bro

---

[1] The writing is a bit difficult, and this figure could be read as 10 or 40. The version of the diary printed in 1917 renders it "forty." But from information in the next paragraph it is clear that the figure is 10, for Egan is joined by four more men on the 19th and he says the party then numbers 14.

[2] Inasmuch as the creeks and usual camp grounds have been identified in connection with earlier journals, we shall not discuss them in connection with this diary.

Badger & Bro Burnet came to our camp with a letter from Salt lake, traveled 12 miles over a bad road & came to No. 11. a spring right of the road. a good camp ground pleanty of grass & sage plenty of wood 1 mile. came 5 miles to No 12. a spring branch and camped. feed good & wood plenty. this is the last camp in the utah valley.[3]

THURSDAY, NOVEMBER 22 '49   last night it commenced snowing and continued untill this morning. today we crossed the dividing ridge between the utah & seviere valleys. traveled 12 miles & camped at the severe river, No. 13. the river is about 4 rods wide & 3½ feet deep. south bank steep. feed good & plenty of wood & willows for camp use

FRIDAY, NOVEMBER 23 '49   morning pleasant. traveled 12 miles over a beutifull road to camp 14. feed & wood plenty. in the dry season you will have to go 2 miles east where there is a good spring. traveled 14 miles and camped at No. 15, a spring branch. feed good & plenty of cedar [Cedar Creek, Holden]. the road is good between the severe & this camp with the exception of about 4 miles

SATURDAY, NOVEMBER 24 '49   morning pleasant. traveled 3 miles & came to No. 16. a good camp plenty of willows. 5 miles further came to No. 17. a creek. wood plenty. traveled 10 miles & came to No. 18. a spring a good camp plenty of willows. came 6 miles & camped at No. 19. brackish spring a poor camp ground no wood & less sage. camped with a company of ox teams & hors teams.[4] feed is verry short.

---

[3] This is in Juab Valley, but the drainage is into Utah Lake.

[4] This important sentence, for some reason, is omitted from the 1917 printed verson of the diary. Apparently, the Egan party has overtaken a rear section of the Pomeroy train.

SUNDAY NOV 25 '49   this days travel has been over a crooked ruff stoney road. traveled 02 [5] miles & camped at No. 20 a spring branch. wood & feed plenty.

MONDAY NOVEMBER 26 '49   weather verry cold. traveled 6 miles & came to No. 21. a small creek a good camp ground plenty of wood & feed. traveled 19 miles & camped at No. 22 plenty of wood. feed short, we are now traveling in company with 6 Horse teams & 28 Men

TUESDAY, NOVEMBER 27, 1849   traveled 5 miles & came to a small creek, No. 23 a good camp ground. plenty of feed & willows, came a ¼ of a mile & crossed No. 24 a good camp ground. a ½ a mile further came to beaver creek No. 25. it commenced snowing & we camped. this stream is about one rod wide. wood and feed plenty. it is a beutifull camping place. our company is now organized. H Egan Captain. Bro Olando Hovey has joined our company. Bro Granger & Egan take his provisions

WEDNESDAY, NOVEMBER 28th '49   last night we had a severe snow storm. traveled about 7 miles down the beaver to the kannion & found the road was not possible. traveled 7 miles East close to the foot of the mountains where we struck a road that bore south through the mountains. traveled about 4 miles and found good feed & plenty of wood. no water. we traveled 18 miles & made 8 miles from where we camped last night [6]

THURSDAY, NOVEMBER 29 '49   morning pleasant. traveled about 13 miles & camped at a spring. feed good & plenty of sage. 10 miles of the road today was through a ruff mountain country & very rocky. Bro

---

[5] This figure is probably intended for 20. The camp appears to have been at present Cove Fort, as subsequent distances to Beaver Creek indicate.

[6] They had been misled down the Beaver Canyon by the tracks of the Jefferson Hunt wagon train.

John Bills broke his waggon tier in two places. Spring 26 [Buckhorn] where wee are camped is about 1 mile from the road & about 3 miles a south course from where you first enter the Little Salt Lake valley

FRIDAY, NOVEMBER 30 '49   traveled 10 miles & came to No 27, a creek, plenty of willows & feed. it is a good camp ground. came 6 miles & camped at No. 28 [Parowan] a creek about 1 rod wide. plenty of wood & feed. the road has been very good today. we are in sight of the little Salt lake. weather warm & pleasant

SATURDAY, DECEMBER 1, 1849   traveled 6¼ miles and came to creek 29. it is a good camp ground plenty of wood & feed. we catched up with Mr. Pomeroy's [7] company at this creek. he laid up to burn coal & do some blacksmith work. he has kindly oferd to have our wagon tier welded & anny other work done that we wanted

SUNDAY DEC 2 '49   traveled 4 miles & came to No. 30. a spring. a good camp ground. came 7 miles to the muddy creek No 31 [Coal creek, that runs through Cedar City]. a bad creek to cross. wood plenty, feed short. traveled 6 miles & came to a spring branch [Iron Spring] feed & wood plenty. met 4 men belonging to Capt Smiths company who had lost their road & had been living on Mule flesh for 16 days

MONDAY DEC 3 '49   traveled 16 miles & camped at 33 a spring branch [Antelope Spring]. wood plenty feed short

TUESDAY, DECEMBER 4 '49   last night it comenced snowing, morning cold & stormy. traveled 13 miles & came to No. 34 a spring branch [Pinto Creek, Newcastle] feed & willows plenty. traveled 9 miles and camped at 35 a spring branch feed & wood plenty

[7] In the 1917 printing of the diary this name is left blank, for the writing is difficult to decipher.

WEDNESDAY, DECEMBER 5 '49   this morning cold &
stormy. came 11 miles to No. 36 a spring branch. wood
plenty feed very short. came about 3 miles & camped
in a valley. feed & wood plenty no watter.[8] the storm
very severe. the last end of the road very bad

THURSDAY, DECEMBER 6 '49   last knight we experienced the hardest storm we have had since we started.
traveled about 8 miles over a ruff road to Sta clair
[Santa Clara creek] came about 2 miles further and
camped near the Sta clair. wood plenty. feed poor. it
has stormed all day

FRIDAY, DECEMB. 7th '49   morning very cold. traveled 3 miles down the Sta Clair when one of my wagon
tiers broke. Bro Granger unloaded his wagon & went
back with me to Mr. Pomeroy's camp about 30 miles.
we were gon 3 days. the weather very cold

SATURDAY, DECEMBER 8th   weather extremely cold.
12 degrees below zero

SUNDAY DECEMBER 9   this evening arived at our
camp 1 wagon had gon ahead. weather still very cold
and feed very poor

MONDAY, DECEMBER 10 '49   traveled 10 miles down
the Sta clair. road very bad. came a mile & a half and
camped at a spring. plenty of wood. feed very poor

TUESDAY, DECEMBER 11th '49   morning cold. traveled about 15 miles over a very ruff road. snow about
1 foot deep. stopped 2 howers & feed. the feed is very
good. up a ravine to the right of the road where we
stopped. traveled 15 miles further & camped at the
virgen.[9] plenty of wood. feed very poor. some little
bunch grass 1 mile up the hill

WEDNESDAY, DECEMBER 12 '49   traveled down the

---

8 They are in the famous Mountain Meadows.
9 They reached the Virgin River at the mouth of Beaver Dam Wash.

virgen over a heavy sandy road. through the most barren dessolate country I have ever seen. came about 8 miles and camped. plenty of willows and some salt grass. the virgen is about 02 rods wide here

THURSDAY, DECEMBER 13th '49 weather warm & pleasant. traveled about 18 miles down the virgen crosing it about 10 times. part of the road has been very sandy. the fords ar good. plenty of willows and some little feed. the first we have seen since we started this morning

FRIDAY, DECEMBER 14th '49 morning clowdy & some rain, traveled about 12 miles down the virgen road, sandy, crosed the river 4 or 5 times. then turned short to the right and traveled over a heavy sandy crooked road. came about 6 miles and found some feed to the left of the road on the side of the Mountain

SATURDAY, DECEMBER 15th '49 pleasant weather. Bro J. Bills's team gave out & he left his wagon & put his load on different wagons. traveled a ½ mile & came to a very steep mountain [10] which we had to cross. we took out part of loads & doubled teams. with a rope 250 feet long at the top of the mountain with a team and the assistance of 20 men we got up safe. came 5 miles & bated. then came to the muddy. feed good wood scarce. part of the road very sandy

SUNDAY 16th '49 weather pleasant. this day we remained in camp we seen a number of Indians this evening.

MONDAY DECEMBER 17, 1849 about noon today we moved camp up the [Muddy] creek about 3 miles. the road leaves the river here. it is called 55 miles to the next water after we leave hear. weather rainy roads bad

[10] This is the steep ascent of Virgin Hill, leading to the top of Mormon Mesa.

TUESDAY, DECEMBER 18th 1849 It has rained all night without anny cesation which makes the road very bad. we remain in camp today. it has continued raining nearly all day. last night the guard fired at what he supposed to be an Indian on the opisate side of the creek. it is with difficulty that we can get our animals to the feed. it is so mirey

WEDNESDAY, DECEMBER 19th '49 clear pleasant weather. traveled 10 miles & found some feed. stoped an hour & baited. for a ½ a mile this morning we had to help the teames with ropes made fast to the wagons. the road then was gravel & sandy. came about 8 miles. the roads very bad. the animals sunk to their knees every step. we found some watter in holes & some course bunch grass

THURSDAY, DECEMBER 20th 1849 traveled 10 miles & found some feed on the sand bluffs. the road much better. came 25 miles. the last 3 or 4 miles the road very bad, arived at the springs about 2 oc. in the morning. Mr. Foot & Parks left there wagons. Bro Granger left his wagon & took foots wagon it being lighter. feed scarce it being burned over. wood scarce. the spring water is milk warm. there has been 5 animals & 3 wagons left since we started

FRIDAY, DECEMBER 21 '49 this day we remained in camp Mr. Nagel left his wagon and packed we left our wagon and took his it being lighter. the weather is warm and pleasant

DECEMBER 22 '49 today we moved camp up the branch about 3 miles [to Las Vegas Springs]. the roads very bad. feed good. plenty of fuel.

SUNDAY DECEMBER 23 '49 traveled about 18 miles part of the road ruff and stoney. camped near a beutifull spring branch [Cottonwood]plenty of bunch grass on the mountain. wood plenty. 2 of our company were run by some Indians who were behind

MONDAY, DECEMBER 24 1849 about 2 o'clock this morning our animals were fired at by a party of Indians which caused them to scatter. they run off 4. 2 of our men persued them so close that they left 3. the other the[y] had killed & quartered belonging to Mr. Carr. one of the three was shot four times with arrows. here i left the wagon i had & took Mr. Carr's. traveled 4 miles & came to a spring branch. a poor camp. came 8 miles to a spring [Mountain Spring] poor feed. came 25 miles & camp at a spring. bad camp ground. water bad

TUESDAY, DECEMBER 25th 1849 started at day light this morning with the intention of stoping at a spring 5 miles ahead. traveled about 8 miles & stoped to bait. we then discovered that the road run 5 miles east of the spring. some of the company started without eating there breakfast or takeing in water. came about 23 miles over a ruff road and camped at a spring [Resting Spring] feed nearly all eat off. plenty of wood. water good. we arived here about ½ past 9 o'clock in the evening

WEDNESDAY, DECEMBER 26th 1849 we remained in camp today. Mr. Carrs hors that was shot by the Indians was left at this place he being unable to travel

THURSDAY, DECEMBER 27 '49 pleasant weather we found an ox here with an arrow stuck in his side. saw fresh Indian tracks. one of the gaurd seen an Indian in the brush just before daylight and fired at him. we started at 3 o'clo this afernoon and came 10 miles. part of the road sandy & part of it run over a low wet bottom. crossed a small stream [Amargosa River] several times. watter not good. at ½ past 7 o'c camped at a spring. feed & watter good. wood plenty

FRIDAY, DECEMBER 28th 1849   started at 3 oclo & came 13 miles over a bad road & camped at spring 48 [Salt Spring] left of the rode. watter brackish. poor feed. brush for fuel. arived in camp about 9 oclock. it rained for about 3 hours this evening

SATURDAY, DECEMBER 29th '49   started at 8 o'clok came 12 miles over a sandy road & stoped to rest. now feed. came about 12 miles more & stoped & got supper. came 25 miles & camped at spring 49 [Bitter Spring]. now feed. watter brackish. the latter part of the road good. arived here at 4 oclock in the morning. some of the company did not arive untill after daylight. passed a number of cattle today & some wagons that were left.

SUNDAY DEC 30th '49   remained in camp today. we found a little course bunch grass ½ mile west near the road. found 3 wagons with nearly all there loading in. left by some of the company ahead

MONDAY DECEMBER 31 1849   started this afternoon at 4 o'clock came 10 miles and stoped to rest. traveled all night. the first 16 miles of the road up hill & sandy. arived at the mahovy [Mojave River] about 8 ocl. in the morning. plenty of salt grass. watter good plenty of wood. came 40 miles

TUESDAY JANUARY 1, 1850   remained in camp today. part of the company came up about noon. their is some pretty good feed about a mile a cross the river. we have seen several wagons that were left & a number of dead cattle one of the company found a mule here in pretty good order. most of our company are short of provisions. we divided with them all we had to spare

WEDNESDAY, JANUARY 2nd 1850   started at 10 ocl. & came about 14 miles. feed good plenty of wood. the first 10 or 12 miles the road is sandy & runs from a ¼ of a mile to a mile from the river. crossed the river &

came 2 miles & camped. there was a company camped
here last night. there fires were burning when we
arived. some of our packers remained in camp. Parke
& Neagle & Fair

THURSDAY, JANUARY 3rd 1850   started at daylight
this morning & come about 7 miles where we found
capt Davis company. here the company lay up for the
day. i started for the settlements in comp. with Mr.
Foot. we traveled about 12 miles over a sandy road
and came to the river. traveled 4 miles further & stoped
for the night. feed good. plenty of wood

FRIDAY, JANUARY 4th 1850   started at daylight came
about 15 miles & stoped to feed. came 25 miles to the
cahoon [Cajon] pass. the latter part of the road very
ruff. camped at a spring. feed all eat out. plenty of
wood. this after noon it commenced raining without
anny cesation all night

SATURDAY, JANUARY 5 1850   started this morning
at 4 oclock the watter rushing through the pass about 3
feet deep. it was with the grate difficulty we could get
along. some places the watter would roll our horses
over. came 15 miles and found a wagon camped there.
stoped to feed. came 14 miles and stoped at a rancho
[Cucomonga]. it rained nearly all day

SUNDAY JANUARY 6 '50   came to Williams's rancho.
here I found Bro [Charles C.] Rich & [Jefferson]
Hunt & some 18 or 20 of the brethren. all well. this is
a beutifull valley. the hills look as green as the would
in the [Salt Lake] valley at may

MONDAY JANUARY 7th 1850   pleasant weather. the
brethren are all preparing to start

TUESDAY, JANUARY 8th 1850   pleasant weather. Bro
Rich is procuring wheat & corn & geting it ground for
our company. Bro [Sheldon] Stoderd came in this

evening and report the company 10 miles from here

WEDNESDAY, JANUARY 9th 1850   fine weather. our company arived today about noon all well

THURSDAY, JANUARY 10th 1850   pleasant weather the two ox teams belonging to Bro Rich's company started this afternoon. this day we spent in geting our grinding done. the distance to the settlement is about seven hundred and sixty-nine miles – 769 – from the utah lake

FRIDAY, JANUARY 11 1850   commenced our journey again today. came 10 miles & camped with the two ox teams belonging to Bro Rich's company. the feed is much better here than it is at Williams. it commenced raining this evening. we are camped near a stream. plenty of wood

SATURDAY, JAN. 12th 1850   remained in camp today. Brothers Rich & Hunt came up this evening. we organized. J. Hunt, Captain

SUNDAY JANUARY 13th   came 10 miles & camped near a stream. feed & wood plenty. the forenoon rainy which made the roads bad. the afternoon fair

MONDAY, JAN 14th 1850   pleasant weather. came about 7 miles & stoped to feed at the mission of S. Gabriel [11] which is a most beutifull location. we found plenty of oranges on the trees. the mission has been partially deserted since the [Mexican] warr. some of the fields are fenced in with prickly pairs that are planted in strait rows & grow from 5 to 25 feet high. traveled 3 miles & camped near a small stream. no wood

TUESDAY, JAN 15th   came about 4 miles and camped near a stream about 1½ miles from the city of peuble delos angles [Los Angeles].

---

[11] San Gabriel Mission. The 1917 printed version of the diary renders this "St. Gubrith."

WEDNESDAY, JAN 16th   remained in camp today to lay in our grociers. Bro Davis & some 2 or 3 others arived from Pomroy's train & report them in distress. they have sent in for assistance

THURSDAY, JAN. 17   came about 12 miles & camped near a small stream & a deserted ranch. feed good

FRIDAY, JAN 18th   pleasant weather this morning. killed a beeff. Bro Rich, Hunt & some others are preparing to pack and go a head of the wagons. the brethren were called together who were to remain with the wagons and Howard Egan elected captain by a unanimous vote of the company. traveled 12 miles & stoped near a spring. plenty of feed & wood [12]

[12] The diary continues its account of the trip until the company reaches the gold fields.

Appendix

MORMON WAY-BILL [1]

Route from Salt Lake City to Los Angeles

	[*miles*]
From Temple block, G.S.L. City to Willow Creek . .	20⅝
To summit of dividing ridge between Utah and Salt Lake valleys	4⅞
To American Creek	9¼
To Provo River and fort	11½
To Hobble creek, good feed	7¼
To Spanish Fork, good feed	6
To Peteetneet, good feed	5
To Salt Creek (several small streams between) good feed	25
To Toola creek ford, no wood, good feed from this to the Sevier, the road is sandy passing over a high ridge .	18⅝
To Sevier river, feed tolerable and willows for fuel .	6¼
To Cedar creek, the first stream south of the Sevier, good feed and wood, road rather mountainous and sandy .	25½
To 4th stream south of Sevier, crossing 2 streams, good feed, wood	17½
To Willow flats, the water sinks a little east of the road .	3⅝
To Spring, good feed and water	25
To Sage creek, wood, feed poor	22¼
To Beaver, good feed and plenty of wood . . .	5⅛
To North Kanyon creek, in the Little Salt Lake Valley, good feed, no wood, the road rough and steep for 6 miles	27¼

[1] Joseph Cain and A. C. Brower, *Mormon Way-Bill* (Salt Lake City, 1851). We reproduce here only that portion of the *Mormon Way-Bill* which is applicable to our present study. Joseph Cain was a member of the Flake-Rich Company of packers. The measurements are by the rodometer attached to Addison Pratt's wagon.

A copy of this very rare item is in the Coe Collection at Yale University, and the Daughters of the Utah Pioneers have a copy in Salt Lake City. The latter organization reprinted the *Way-bill* in the *Heart Throbs of the West* (Salt Lake City, Daughters of the Utah Pioneers, 1946), pp. 308-17.

[*miles*]

To 2nd stream, good feed and wood 5⅜

To 3rd stream, good feed and wood 6¾

To Cottonwood creek in Iron County, good feed and water 12⅞

To Cedar springs, good feed, &c 9

To Pynte Creek,[2] feed good about one mile up the Kanyon 23

To Road Creek, this is a small rivulet flowing down the
    Kanyon of the divide, road rough, feed good . . 9

To Santa Clara, road descending and rough, poor feed,
    from this point to Cahoon pass, look out for Indians 16

To Camp springs; 1½ miles before you come to this spring
    you leave the Santa Clara, feed good . . . 17⅛

To Rio Virgin, crossing over the summit of the mountain
    dividing the Santa Clara and the Virgin, road good,
    feed poor 22⅞

Thence down the Virgin, crossing it ten times, feed good
    down the river 39⅛

To Muddy, the road ½ a mile very steep and sandy, good
    feed 19⅝

To Los Vagus, good feed, &c, water is sometimes found at
    the distance of 23 miles from Muddy 2½ miles west
    of road in holes; also some grass about one mile from
    the road 52⅝

Thence up to Vagus, good feed 5

To Cottonwood springs, poor feed 17

To Cottonwood grove, no feed, feed and water can be
    found 4 miles west, by following the old Spanish trail
    to a ravine – thence travel to the left in the ravine
    one mile 29¾

To resting springs, good feed and water, lay by and rest
    your animals for the desert 21¾

To spring of pure water, left of the road which follows
    into the Amagoshe [Amargosa] or Saleratus creek;
    let no animals drink the saleratus water . . . 7

To Salt Springs, no fresh water, poor feed . . . 14⅛

To Bitter springs, good road, but poor feed . . . 38¾

To Mohave, good road, good feed 30¾

To Last ford of Mohave, good feed all the way up the
    Mohave 51½

---

[2] Now Pinto Creek; formerly called Piute Creek.

To the sumit of Cahoon pass 17
To Camp west of Cahoon pass, road bad down the Kanyon 10
To Coco Mongo ranche 11½
To Del Chino ranche (Williams) 10
To San Gabriel river 19⅜
To San Gabriel Mission 6
To Pueblo De Los Angelos 8¼

ADVICE TO EMIGRANTS

We would recommend emigrants who have cattle to shoe them, and we would advise, not to take them further on the route than Fort Hall, or Great Salt Lake, but exchange them there for others, or horses. It is useless for men to start from either of these places with worn out cattle, as they never will get them to their journey's end. Thousands of cattle and horses were sacrificed, because emigrants knew no better last year. The road from the States to Salt Lake or Fort Hall, is comparatively a railroad to the one from thence to California. We would recommend no man to overload his wagon with tools, &c., for spades, shovels, picks, &c., can be purchased cheap in California. Throw away your old yokes, chains, boxes, &c., for you will do so before you cross the desert, no wagon should have more than 800 lbs. with three yoke of cattle.

. . . Pack animals are the best all the time, and single men had by all means better pack. Hard bread is the best to take from either of these places; also dried beef.

Clothes can be bought in Sacramento and Stockton, as cheap as in the States, and it is useless for men to overload themselves with such articles, to retard their movements, . . . Men carrying ploughs, anvils, gold washers, stoves, or any other article of weight, may as well throw them away, or dispose of them; as it is perfectly useless to wear out their cattle, and at last leave the cattle, and goods between this [Salt Lake City] and California.

After the emigrant settles on his winter diggins, he had better secure provisions enough to last him until April; together with pickles, vinegar, etc. as a preventive to the scurvy.

Emigrants had better not dispose of their animals when they are poor, but place them in good hands on ranches; as a poor horse or ox will not fetch over $10 or $15, while a fat ox or horse is worth $100.

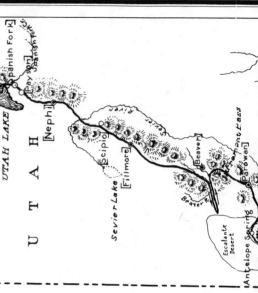

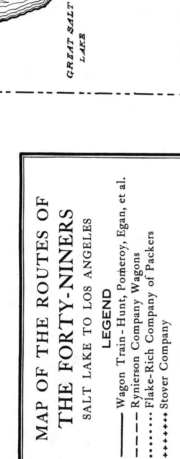

MAP OF THE ROUTES OF
THE FORTY-NINERS
SALT LAKE TO LOS ANGELES

LEGEND

—— Wagon Train – Hunt, Pomeroy, Egan, et al.

– – – Rynierson Company Wagons

.... Flake-Rich Company of Packers

+ + + + Stover Company

SCALE OF MILES

Prepared by Roscoe P. Conkling from material gathered by
LeRoy R. and Ann W. Hafen

Copyright, 1954, by The Arthur H. Clark Co.

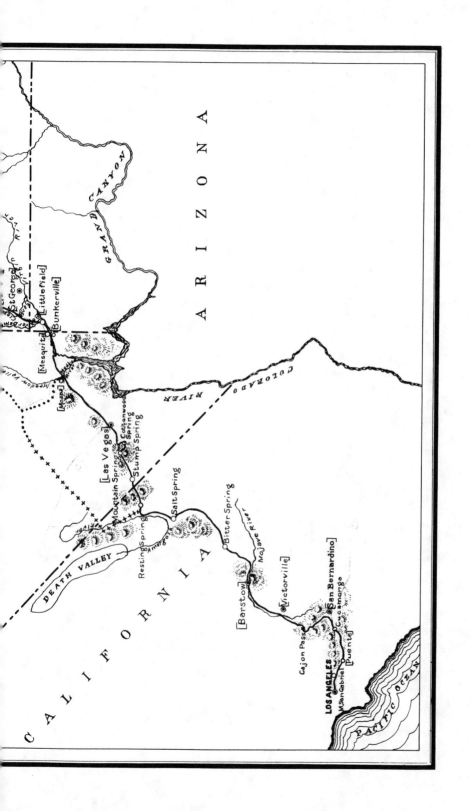

Index